Oliver Christian Bosbyshell

The 48th in the War

Being a Narrative of the Campaigns of the 48th Regiment, Infantry

Oliver Christian Bosbyshell

The 48th in the War
Being a Narrative of the Campaigns of the 48th Regiment, Infantry

ISBN/EAN: 9783337116453

Printed in Europe, USA, Canada, Australia, Japan

Cover: Foto ©ninafisch / pixelio.de

More available books at **www.hansebooks.com**

The 48th IN THE WAR.

BEING A NARRATIVE

OF THE

Campaigns of the 48th Regiment, Infantry,

PENNSYLVANIA VETERAN VOLUNTEERS,

DURING THE WAR OF THE REBELLION.

BY

OLIVER CHRISTIAN BOSBYSHELL,

Late Major.

PHILADELPHIA:
AVIL PRINTING COMPANY,
1895.

COPYRIGHT 1895,
BY
OLIVER CHRISTIAN BOSBYSHELL.

DEDICATED

TO THE

SONS AND DAUGHTERS

OF THE

MEN WHO FOUGHT FOR THE UNION

IN THE

FORTY-EIGHTH.

TABLE OF CONTENTS.

		PAGE
CHAPTER	I.—ORGANIZATION AND MUSTER-IN	17
CHAPTER	II.—HATTERAS	22
CHAPTER	III.—NEWBERN	38
CHAPTER	IV.—NEWPORT NEWS	52
CHAPTER	V.—WITH POPE	58
CHAPTER	VI.—MCCLELLAN'S LAST CAMPAIGN	73
CHAPTER	VII.—BURNSIDE IN COMMAND	91
CHAPTER	VIII.—LEXINGTON	104
CHAPTER	IX.—EAST TENNESSEE	117
CHAPTER	X.—VETERAN FURLOUGH	141
CHAPTER	XI.—WILDERNESS TO PETERSBURG	146
CHAPTER	XII.—THE PETERSBURG MINE	163
CHAPTER	XIII.—FINAL ASSAULT AND MUSTER-OUT	178
CHAPTER	XIV.—SECOND MARYLAND. SIXTH NEW HAMPSHIRE	190

PREFACE.

WHAT is more interesting to the old soldier than a rehash of former campaigns—a calling up of old camping grounds, and lingering along the trails made in the marchings and meanderings of the years of the war, with the scenes and incidents attendant thereon?

An attempt is made in this book to sketch the doings of the Forty-eighth Regiment, Pennsylvania Veteran Volunteers, Infantry, not with rule and compass, but as they happened under the notice of my own eyes. That it is not all it ought to be, I fully know; that it may seem somewhat tinged with partiality may likewise be so, but remember, it is the way in which it came under my own observation; it is not compiled from official data, or the say-so of others; it is simply as I saw it and as my ideas clothed it. Several comrades have helped in certain parts of the work, particularly in the campaign from the Wilderness to Petersburg. I am especially grateful to the lamented General Pleasants, who furnished invaluable data of the campaign named and the Petersburg Mine. Captain Francis D. Koch, of Company I, and Private Robert A. Reid, of Company G, have been particularly kind in aiding me.

A tender chord of comradeship resounds in my heart, whenever any who marched in the ranks of the Forty-eighth are named. For them, to keep alive some of their deeds, I have written what follows.

O. C. Bosbyshell

ERRATA.

Page 44.—For Thomas L. Reno read Jesse L. Reno.

Page 163.—For Fire Box in Sketch of Mine, read Air Box.

Flags of 48th Reg't Pa. Vols.

The 48th in the War.

CHAPTER I.

ORGANIZATION AND MUSTER-IN.

The Forty-eighth Regiment Pennsylvania **Veteran** Volunteers (**infantry**), was recruited in Schuylkill County during **the months of August** and September, 1861. **James** Nagle, a distinguished citizen and soldier of Pottsville, Pa., who served honorably and well **as** captain of Company A, First Pennsylvania Regiment, during the war with Mexico, and also as colonel of the Sixth Pennsylvania Regiment during the Three Months' Service, in the beginning of the War of the Rebellion, was authorized by Governor Andrew G. Curtin, on the fourteenth of August, 1861, to raise and organize **this regiment.** He was commissioned as colonel of the same, to **rank from the date named.** He at once empowered Daniel **B. Kauffman,** **James Wren,** Henry Pleasants, **Daniel Nagle,** William Winlack, Joseph H. Hoskings, Philip Nagle, Joseph **A. Gilmour, John R.** Porter and H. **A. M. Filbert** to **recruit companies** for the **regiment; each of these gentlemen being** subsequently commissioned **captain** of Companies A, B, C, D, E, F, G, **H, I and K,** respectively.

Company A was principally **recruited in** Tamaqua and Port Clinton; Company E in New Philadelphia and Silver Creek. Company F made Minersville its headquarters. Company **I found a** fruitful field **of** operations in Middleport and the Schuylkill Valley, whilst Company K **confined** its recruiting to Cressona and Schuylkill Haven. **The other companies, B, C, D, G** and H, made Pottsville their harvesting ground. As rapidly as men were secured they were forwarded to Camp Curtin, in Harrisburg, where the regiment rendezvoused. The medical examinations having been successfully passed the recruits **were equipped and** assigned to their respective companies. Drills were instituted by the squad and company, and twice **during** its stay at Camp Curtin regimental drills were had. **For** the majority **this** was their first taste of military duty; however, there **were many who** had served in the Three Months' Service, in the Sixth, **Fourteenth,** Sixteenth, **Twenty-fifth, and** other organizations. A number of those who first entered Washington City, and who are now known as the "First Defenders," re-entered the service in the Forty-eighth Regiment, nearly all attaining the rank of commissioned officers.

In a very short space of time the ranks were filled by Schuylkill Countians, it being Colonel Nagle's special desire to have a regiment composed of men exclusively from that county.

The field, staff, and non-commissioned staff were as follows: James Nagle, Colonel; David A. Smith, Lieutenant Colonel; Joshua K. Sigfried, Major; John D. Bertolette, Adjutant; James Ellis, Quartermaster; David Minis, Jr., M. D., Surgeon; Charles T. Reber, M. D., Assistant Surgeon; Rev. Samuel A. Holman, Chaplain; Charles Loeser, Jr., Sergeant Major; Alexander S. Bowen, Quartermaster Sergeant; Jacob F. Wagner, Commissary Sergeant; William H. Hardell, Hospital Steward, and Abraham Nagle, Principal Musician.

The companies were officered as follows:

Company A, Daniel B. Kauffman, Captain; Abiel H. Jackson, First Lieutenant, and Henry Boyer, Second Lieutenant.

Company B, James Wren, Captain; Ulysses A. Bast, First Lieutenant, and John L. Wood, Second Lieutenant.

Company C, Henry Pleasants, Captain; George W. Gowen, First Lieutenant, and Thomas J. Fitzsimmons, Second Lieutenant.

Company D, Daniel Nagle, Captain; William W. Potts, First Lieutenant, and Charles Kleckner, Second Lieutenant.

Company E, William Winlack, Captain; William Cullen, First Lieutenant, and Thomas Bohannan, Second Lieutenant.

Company F, Joseph H. Hoskings, Captain; Henry James, First Lieutenant, and John L. Williams, Second Lieutenant.

Company G, Philip Nagle, Captain; Cyrus Scheetz, First Lieutenant, and Oliver C. Bosbyshell, Second Lieutenant.

Company H, Joseph A. Gilmour, Captain; William J. Hinkle, First Lieutenant, and Edward C. Baird, Second Lieutenant.

Company I, John R. Porter, Captain; George H. Gressang, First Lieutenant, and Michael M. Kistler, Second Lieutenant.

Company K, H. A. M. Filbert, Captain; Isaac F. Brannan, First Lieutenant, and Jacob Douty, Second Lieutenant.

The regiment was the recipient of two stands of colors, one from the State and the other from John T. Werner, Esq., one of Pottsville's patriotic citizens, and the father of J. Frank Werner, who served so gallantly in the regiment. Inscribed upon the blue field of this flag were the words " In the cause of the Union we know no such word as fail." These colors were presented by Governor Curtin on the twentieth of September, and the glowing words of his speech made a deep impression upon the command. Through the war they were gallantly defended, and although shattered and torn by bullet and shell, were safely returned to the State, and now find sacred shelter in the flag room of the Capitol Building, in Harrisburg.

The regiment was ordered from Camp Curtin on the twenty-fourth of September, and left via the Northern Central Railway, presumably for Washington City; the destination was, however, changed en route upon the receipt of a telegram by Colonel Nagle, directing him to report to General Wool, at Fortress Monroe.

Within seven miles of Baltimore the train was detained over ten hours, by reason of a wreck ahead, so that the city was not reached until the morning of the twenty-fifth. A march of two miles through Baltimore brought the command to the wharf, where, embarking upon the steamer Georgia, the water life of the regiment began. The trip down the Chesapeake Bay was accomplished safely and really enjoyed by all, notwithstanding the fact that the Georgia was a precarious old craft, likely to fall to pieces. The captain wisely crept along close in to shore, not knowing what moment the timbers of the old hulk would separate. He was all anxiety, and his constant call admonishing to "trim ship" kept the boys moving. The night moved slowly away, the somnolent regiment unmindful of danger, although ever and anon through its weary hours the cry of "trim ship" caused a shifting of position. On the morning of the twenty-sixth the command disembarked at Fortress Monroe, just as the Twentieth Indiana was leaving for Hatteras, a region destined to be full of events for the Forty-eighth. Passing around the walls of the fortress over the long, narrow road and bridge connecting with Hampton, the command reached a camping ground within the confines of " Camp Hamilton," in charge of dear old General Mansfield. His mild disposition and benevolent heart, that caused him to be ever on the lookout for the welfare of his soldiers, combined, however, with a firm, just discipline, endeared him to all with whom he came in contact.

One dark, blustery night, and this camp was prolific of such kind of nights, Jake Haines let General Mansfield slip through the camp guard without challenge. Jake was as deaf as a post, and besides was walking away from him when the General entered. The General notified the officer of the guard to have the offender reprimanded the next morning at guard-mount, and then attempted to pass out of camp on the opposite side, but Rogers was there, and his "halt, or I'll prog ye" brought him up a-standing. Colonel Nagle reprimanded Haines next morning, but it was done in the low squeaking voice which the Colonel sometimes adopted, so that when it was over Haines inquired " What did he say?" Drills and inspections became the routine duty of the regiment, with an occasional detail for picket duty. Companies E, F, G and K were mustered into the United States Service by Colonel T. J. Cram, U. S. A., on the first of October, and the occasion was made quite enjoyable by Sergeant Stafford Johnson, of E, declining to be sworn as a sergeant. " Why, what did you come for, man ? " inquired Colonel Cram. "I kim fur a leu-tenant, sir," says Johnson. " Well, well," replied Cram, scarcely able to repress a smile, "stand up and be mustered as a sergeant; if you're not fit to be a sergeant, you are not fit to be a lieutenant."

General Wool, commanding at Fortress Monroe, frequently visited the camp. His venerable appearance, he being at the time the second eldest general in the army, won the respect of the boys, if Quinn did sometimes personate the shaky manner he displayed when lifting his hat at a review of the troops. On the third of October, the regiment, having been flooded out the previous night, moved to higher ground, occupying a camp vacated by one of the regiments that had been ordered away. The ninth of October was made memorable by the arrival of Sutler Isaac Lippman, with a great, unwieldy tent, which the boys pitched with infinite delight, although a heavy storm of wind and rain prevailed On the eleventh Shaw made himself famous by shooting in the leg a Massachusetts soldier, who attempted to pass his picket post—thought he was "secesh." On Sunday, the thirteenth, the first religious service was held, by the chaplain, Rev. Samuel J. Holman. These Sunday services became general, and at least a fourth of the regiment, many times a greater number, attended. Great interest was felt in the grand expedition fitting out here for the South Atlantic coast. Hampton Roads was crowded with vessels waiting to join the Armada, and a large force of troops was being gathered at this point. Daily the various organizations detailed as a part of this expedition would leave camp to embark on some one of the numerous vessels in waiting. On the fifteenth, Brigadier General Mansfield assumed command of all of the forces at Camp Hamilton, vice General Max Weber.

The passes required for visiting Fortress Monroe or other points of interest were prescribed by orders to be written on a quarter-sheet of foolscap paper, with an allowance of at least four lines for the assistant adjutant general's signature, and what a wonderful signature; "Drake DeKay," written with a paint brush!

How enjoyable the details for wood cutting, only a mile's march from camp, and one long day of jolly fun, with plenty of grapes, persimmons and crab-apples thrown in. On Sunday, the tenth of November, orders were received assigning the Forty-eighth to Hatteras Inlet to relieve the Twentieth Indiana, and it cannot be said that a very large degree of enthusiasm was manifested over this assignment. On the eleventh tents were struck, packed, and with baggage placed on steamer "S. R. Spaulding," the regiment marched to the wharf near Fortress Monroe, and embarked upon the same vessel. At dusk the steamer started, and in going out of Hampton Roads, passed between the ships of war, Roanoke and Minnesota, the former the better craft of the two. The "S. R. Spaulding" was a fine ship, only two years' old, delightfully fitted out with the best appliances and most comfortable conveniences. Very agreeable was her graceful motion as she steamed out of the Roads into the broad bosom of the Atlantic. The unexpectedly warm and balmy atmosphere, combined with the bright radiance of the silvery moon, made the journey down the coast delightful in the extreme; few of the members of the regiment sought repose until long after midnight. Many had their first glimpse of a sunrise at sea on the morning of the twelfth and enjoyed its glories to the full, out of a cloudless sky. By 8 o'clock, a. m., the steamer dropped anchor in Hatteras Inlet, and two hours later the regiment disembarked.

CHAPTER II.

HATTERAS.

Hatteras Island forms a part of the eastern boundary of North Carolina; it is some forty miles long and varies in width from a half mile to three miles. Its northern boundary is Loggerhead Inlet, and its southern Hatteras Inlet, and its sides are washed by the Atlantic Ocean and Pamlico Sound, respectively. Hatteras Inlet is the main entrance for vessels into Pamlico Sound. It is a narrow sheet of water, probably half a mile wide, connecting the ocean and sound. According to local testimony, it has not always been in its present location.

In August, 1846, so goes the story, a terrific storm, with wind blowing from the sound, broke through the island at this point and formed the inlet. A bar runs across the mouth nearest the sound, which at low water cannot be crossed by vessels of heavy draught. The local name of the bar is the "Swash," and many were the trials and tribulations of the Federal navy in battling with the "Swash."

Changes rapidly occur in the formation of Hatteras Island, thus confirming the story of the origin of the inlet.

The Twentieth Indiana Regiment was sent to garrison Forts Hatteras and Clarke—two earthworks near the inlet—during the early fall of 1861, and it had a peculiarly rough experience. During this regiment's sojourn there a terrible storm swept down on this coast. The ocean and the sound met across the narrow sand spit, submerging the camp, drowning a number of the Indiana boys, and leaving the rest in a most miserable plight—without camp or garrison equipage, clothing or provisions. The Forty-eighth boys remember how the men looked on their return to Fortress Monroe to recuperate—woe-begone, utterly fagged out—only paralleled by the returning prisoners from Dixie's land. This storm formed a new inlet across the island, between Fort Hatteras and Fort Clarke, which at high tide was five or six feet deep in the shallowest places. In going to and fro between the two forts this inlet had to be waded, and it became a source of great annoyance. To get over the difficulty Company B's boys erected a pathway, or bridge, by standing flour barrels filled with sand on end side by side, across the inlet. At low tide a dry walk was thus made, and a barrier was presented against which sand was washed by the action of the waves. In a few weeks the inlet was completely closed, and in three months no trace of its existence remained.

No one would choose Hatteras Island at the inlet as a cheerful place to live; not even for a sea-side resort.

The Schuylkill county boys, as they rattled down the 45° plank from the side of the "S. R. Spaulding" to the temporary wharf, missed the lovely wooded hills and grassy valleys of their charming mountain homes. No trees here, no bushes to relieve the dull monotony, not a spear of the sickliest looking shrub even, no green grass to gladden the eye, naught save sand and sea! Some jocose soldier suggested that it was the last spot made. The creation having been accomplished in a week, there had been no time to plant grass.

Some five miles north of the inlet, however, scrub oak and holly trees abound, adding greatly to an endurable life on Hatteras, relieving the wearisomeness of sand and sea. These groves are filled with mocking birds, whose brilliant song in the early morning make up a reveille of rich, joyous trills of music, thus adding poetry and pleasure to a life on the bare old island.

As stated, there were two large earthworks at Hatteras, named respectively Fort Hatteras and Fort Clarke. The first was built directly at the inlet, commanding the entrance from the ocean and from the sound, the latter fort, nearly half a mile north, commanding the approaches from the ocean. These forts were built by the rebels to aid the English blockade runners in getting through the inlet with supplies of arms, ammunition and clothing for the Confederates. Fort Hatteras was the most pretentious and mounted ten guns. Fort Clarke was a square redoubt and mounted seven guns. Negroes were used in the construction of these fortifications. Large pieces of swamp sod, brought from the mainland, laid one above the other, and pinned fast by long wooden pegs, served the purpose.

On the twenty-ninth of August, 1861, after two days of hard pounding, General B. F. Butler and Commodore Silas H. Stringham, with a combined force of land and naval troops, captured these forts. "No one of the fleet or army was in the least degree injured," said Butler in his report to General Wool. He added that the loss of the Confederates was "twelve or fifteen killed and thirty-five wounded."

The loss of these forts proved a great blow to the rebels. In the hands of the Federals the traffic they had been built to protect was prevented, and a way was opened up for very important results, which speedily followed.

Hatteras Island was, and possibly still is, inhabited by a hardy, raw-boned, tough-looking people, with rough, weather-beaten countenances, and possessed of a good stock of native shrewdness. There are few deaths among them, the chief disease is consumption. Avoid this fell destroyer and the native lives to a ripe old age. The women are pale, frail, attenuated creatures, who apparently never grow old. Tradition has it that they gradually shrink up, and at some remote period are blown away.

The men are ostensively pilots. Every house boasts its "lookout," an immense pole erected in the sand, upon which is nailed small pieces of wood, ladder-like. From these elevated perches observations are made for incoming vessels, in order to obtain work as pilots. Many are undoubtedly honest in this, but that there are men there who use their "lookouts" for an entirely different purpose, admits of no doubt. A free, uninterrupted view of the ocean is obtained. Approaching vessels can easily be observed. The coast is a treacherous one, the best possible for the work of wreckers, and in the use of decoy or false lights these worthies are well versed. Many of the stranded hulks with which this coast is strewn, owe their destruction to the action of bad men.

A kind word must be said for some of the Hatteras people. But for the assiduous attention and warm-hearted, motherly nursing given to a number of very sick soldiers, by old widow Whitby, for instance, there would have been more burials in the old churchyard. She and her son, Jackson, and old colored help, Aunt Hester, are deserving of especial mention. The remembrance of their kindness redeems much of the ills incident to a sojourn on Hatteras, and for their sake, and for the sake of some others like them, a warm spot remains in the heart for this sandy, wind-racked, desolate old island.

The dialect used by these people is difficult to describe. Once heard it is rarely forgotten and seldom successfully imitated. "Right smart," "aggravatin'," "reckon," and the like, make up the greater part of the conversations. "Right smart of sweet potatoes in the ground, but it is aggravatin' to have the soldiers yank 'em out. Reckon you can't stop it." A peculiar characteristic of the ladies of Hatteras is the dreadful habit of snuff-dipping, to which they are all, married and single, addicted. There's a grace about this habit that almost amounts to an art. A novice could not work the improvised brush with the skill of a native; one must be born to it. The brush is a stick, cut at one end into fine splinters about an inch in length. This is dipped into the snuff, then rubbed on the teeth, after the manner of cleaning the teeth with a tooth powder, but differing in that whilst the latter purifies and sweetens the mouth, the former befouls and blackens it most disgustingly. The female islander smokes also, and spits "just like a man."

Every house on the island seems to have been built after the same model, by the same builder, and many hundred years ago. They are all old, nothing modern at all in their appearance, square in shape, one story high, with a porch sliced into one corner, without cellars; not a house on the island enjoys this luxury, they cannot dig them; there are no foundation walls, because there are no stones to make them. Piles or large props are driven into the sand, and upon these the houses are erected. Fine white sand is sprinkled over the board floor, and constant wear and friction produce white smooth floors. There are no plastered walls, although many of the houses have a lining of paper—newspapers of various colors and shapes, illustrated and otherwise. One old lady seemed especially struck with the chaste character of a highly colored picture she had adorning her walls, representing a spirited contest between Heenan and Sayres. Quite a number of houses have a "grandfather's clock" ticking in the corner, or back of the door. The display of furniture is not extensive—indeed, it is generally scarce; pieces of wrecks and ship stock have to answer the purpose. The staple articles of food are fish and sweet potatoes. Corn, pigs and poultry are raised by some. Garden cultivation is very primitive and exceedingly careless. Some miserable oysters can be obtained, and an occasional opossum. All the sugar, coffee, tea and molasses used by the natives come from wrecks. They are a religious people, in their own peculiar way, vigorous in attendance at divine service, and any infringement of the local laws is tried and punished in the church. If their stock of provisions be short, they think it right and proper to pray that the coast may be strewn with wrecks laden with the kind of provisions most needed. So the ill fortune of the hapless bark becomes the good fortune of the devout islanders—another exemplification of the old Dutchman's saying: "Vat's one man's loss is annunderer man's gain."

Some six miles up the island from the inlet is an old Methodist meeting house, a plain frame building, built without special architectural features, no display of taste or beauty, but simple, homely, and for use.

The windows are irregular in size—placed here and there in the side of the building without the least regard to symmetry or order; plain wooden benches on the inside, a single rail for a back, which rail is so nicely adjusted that it catches the sitter just back of the neck. Directly opposite the meeting house is an old graveyard, wherein reposes the dust (if it is dust) of the ancient Hatterasins; a lonely old place, with some curious inscriptions on its tombstones. Here's one as a sample.

> In memory of
> Thos. Austin. Died 1845. Aged 70 years.
> Thos. Austin. Was. His. Name.
> Heaven. I. Hope. His. Station.
> Hatteras. Was. His. Dwelling.
> Place. And. Christ. Was. His. Salvation. Now. He. Is. Dead. And.
> Buried. All. His. Bones. Are. Rotten. Remember. Him. When. This.
> You. See. Least. He. Should. Be.
> Forgotten.

The author of that epitaph was not familiar with the peculiar virtues of that old burying ground. Thomas, rest in peace; your bones are not all rotten, old boy—oh, no; listen!

Diehl, of Company G, was buried in this graveyard. The authorities refused permission to send his body home. It is not the mere burying that makes the soldier's funeral so inexpressibly solemn, it is the thought that there is no one near to mourn for him; none but the moaning wind and the ever roaring surf. It was a doleful funeral, tramping through the sand, up the island to this old graveyard. Digging the grave was not difficult. It was tedious to make it as deep as it should be. Two feet below the surface developed water, and the balance of the depth attained was through a constantly increasing volume of water. The coffin was lowered into the grave, and by the aid of sticks was pushed down under the water and held there until a sufficient quantity of the wet, sandy soil had been thrown upon it to prevent it from floating. Diehl was buried in December. The following May his body was disinterred, placed in a lead coffin, and sent North. But what a metamorphosis had taken place in the short time it had lain in this old graveyard. Through some chemical action the work of petrifaction had begun, the forehead had already turned to stone. A longer stay in the grave would have undoubtedly completed the change. This incident causes doubt as to the "dust" of the old Hatteras folks reposing in this out-of-the-way graveyard, probably they are all stone statues, as it were. Had it been supposed that this was the case with the bodies silently resting here it would not have been remarkable, judging from the known tendency of some of the sojourners on Hatteras for practical jokes, to have discovered, on most any bright morning, all the old worthies unearthed from their salt, sandy, wet bed, and standing up as guardians over the places so long occupied by them.

It may not be generally known, but it is nevertheless a fact, that the people of Hatteras, Hyde County, North Carolina, set up a state government of their own during the war, utterly repudiating the Confederacy and avowing their firm devotion to and entire faith in the United States of America.

They met in convention at Hatteras and formally prepared and issued a "Declaration against the Confederate Government."

This high-sounding and pretentious document was nicely printed by a New York firm, on a large sheet of paper, enclosed in a colored border consisting of folded Union flags, and was sold to the patriotic and curious for the small sum of twenty-five cents, a sort of taxation imposed by the new State Government for the purpose of revenue. One of these papers is now in the possession of the Pennsylvania Historical Society. It was originally presented to the writer by Governor Taylor, personally.

Under this "Declaration" an election was held for governor, and the Rev. Marble Nash Taylor was elected to this high and responsible position. Governor Taylor resided on Hatteras. He was the minister in charge of the religious instruction for the entire community, and regularly expounded the gospel to them in the old frame church heretofore alluded to.

He was a gentlemanly looking man, very affable in manners, quite an interesting conversationalist, an avowed Unionist, and strongly in favor of cutting Hatteras loose from the government of the mainland. In this particular he was in favor of secession. His wife was a pleasant, agreeable lady, who enjoyed the enviable (in the eyes of the island belles) distinction of being the only lady in that region who could boast of a genuine hooped skirt. This article of female apparel, by the way, met with much opposition from the other of the frail sex of this section of the country. Some of the younger ones also cried out against the innovation, but by far the greater number of the girls envied the possessor, and went so far as to manufacture them out of green briars; all of which information is not gathered from personal observation, but is based entirely upon hearsay evidence.

Hatteras remains comparatively unknown, at least uncared for. An occasional wreck brings up the name. The ocean trade of Albemarle Sound cannot be had without passing over the "Swash" in the inlet, but who gives a thought to the rugged people living a lifetime on this barren spot?

What does the world know of them, or what does it care? The accident of war introduced their mode of living, their characteristics and their oddities. In the days of peace they will live on in the old routine, unthought of in their dreary, out-of-the-way nook.

Yet, with all its ills of winds, sands, barrenness and utter desolate loneliness, the several months spent upon its lone, bleak shores are treasured up in memory's storehouse as a pleasant page in life's history. Many and many a time subsequently, the barrack life of Hatteras was longed for in preference to Virginia mud or Tennessee itch.

The morning of November 12, 1861, saw the members of the Forty-eighth Regiment Pennsylvania Volunteers descending, one at a time, a plank at an angle of 45°, reaching from the old steamer "S. R. Spaulding's" side, to a floating wharf, within a few yards of Fort Hatteras, and taking up the line of march for Fort Clarke. The wading of the temporary inlet between the two forts added to the discomforts of the trip.

At Fort Clarke some of the companies occupied tents, others preferring the old wooden barracks erected by former occupants, vulgarly but suggestively named "Camp Louse."

Here the regiment settled, literally away from the rest of the world; left exposed to all the ills incident to such an inhospitable coast, and what was thought to be worse, the tender mercies of General Thomas Williams, with whom the boys felt disposed to quarrel the second day on Hatteras.

Generally it was not a difficult matter for a soldier to pitch a tent. It would not have been difficult at Hatteras if the wind could have been subdued. Wind! Speaking of wind, do you remember how the wind blew at Hatteras? What a dreadful draft it was! Hark! its snapping the tent-fly now. It is a mighty, rushing torrent of air, sweeping continuously in furious blasts, with irresistible force—keen, sharp, penetrating, unrelenting in its terrific power, unabating in its fury—driving the sand into mouth, nose, eyes, ears and hair. 'Twas such a wind greeted the pitching of the tents around Fort Clarke. The more the boys tugged and pulled to keep the tents upright, the more the wind seemed to howl, "You can't! you shan't!" then it would come along with such a whack that every muscle had to be strained to keep the tent in place. Under these circumstances the ordinary Yankee got his blood up, and wind or no wind the tents had to go up, and at last, at last, they were secured. It was night, however, and an early retirement after the day's hard labor was deemed advisable. To the sound of the flip, flap, flopping of the tent-flys, and ever roaring of the breakers, forgetfulness crept over the camp as each tent lodger snoozed calmly as a summer morn, when flop, whiz-z-z the corner of the tent blew up! Misplaced confidence in a sweetheart teaches the lover to sigh at the fickleness of woman, but, oh! to have a tent prove false upon "a lone, barren isle," and, in the midst of a terrific rain storm, be obliged to face a Hatteras wind, with scant protection against its fury, frantically holding fast to the frail canvas house, waiting for a lull in the blast (vain hope) to afford an opportunity to repeg, is so overpoweringly harrowing to the feelings, and so indescribably uncomfortable, that it is only those who actually experienced it who fully understand its supreme misery.

"Misery loves company," so the feelings were somewhat soothed by hearing all about in the darkness, fellow soldiers engaged in the same delightful occupation, growling, grumbling, and—yes, they went the whole figure—swearing at the blasts of Hatteras; whilst a comfortable barrack lodger, with his mouth at a convenient crack between the boards of his hut, propounded the never-to-be-forgotten, "who wouldn't be a soldier."

The writer's old tent-mate, good-natured "Cy," now of the *Exchange*, Pottsville, comfortably rolled up in his blanket on a bunk, heard the writer's side of the tent fly up, and when called on for help, answered, "Every fellow fix his own side." The difficulty was conquered alone, and the next half hour or more was thoroughly enjoyed listening to "Cy" tugging, and pounding, and sweating to get his side of the tent to rights, it having broken loose far worse than the other. Captain Philip Nagle and the writer spent nearly all of one night on the inside of the tent, holding it down by bearing on spades, so placed as to force the canvas into the sand, to prevent it from taking a voyage on the Atlantic. It is very well to talk and laugh about it these many years after, but there wasn't any poetry in its realization.

An amusing pastime consisted of a trap for the unwary soldier. A hole dug into the sand soon developed water. This hole, covered over with light sticks, and the sticks in their turn covered over with dry sand, left no sign of the pitfall beneath. The victim was inveigled to the spot, and without the slightest warning, one foot would suddenly disappear below the surface and a wet foot and leg would be the result. Tableaux. These pitfalls were scattered all about, causing unexpected disasters continually, at the most inopportune times. An unfortunate corporal of a fatigue squad fell into one of these traps with both legs, knee high, causing much amusement to his squad.

It was here the Forty-eighth received its lessons in the school of the soldier, company and battalion.

The post was commanded by the veteran, Brigadier General Thomas Williams, U. S. A., and those who had the experience of serving under him, well remember his severe discipline. There probably was no one man ever more heartily hated than this same General Williams by the members of the Forty-eighth. He was abused roundly every day for his tyrannical orders, rigid discipline, frequent calls for duty, severe guard regulations, excessive drills, thorough inspections, and the like. He issued an order depriving the regiment of the every day use of its flags. This seemed so harsh and uncalled for that all the denunciatory terms in the dictionary were poured upon his head. When least expected he would turn up, and woe betide the soldier found derelict. It is easy to remember the constant vigilance of the old General as he paced the front of his quarters, one hand supporting his coat-tail, the other twirling his stiff, wiry moustache, whilst his watchful eyes would detect a slouchy sentinel, and then, "Orderly, send the officer of the guard to me."

The senior captain of the Forty-eighth, making his report as officer of the day, with his arms folded majestically across his breast, broke down in the middle of his narration by General Williams' peremptory order, "Put down your hands, sir!" Down they dropped, little fingers on the seam of the trousers. Seven days after arriving at Hatteras, whilst enjoying the ills of the island to its full extent, at Fort Clarke, a review of the regiment was ordered. As the manœuvring had to be made in sand ankle deep, it was a rather laborious undertaking, especially as the General required the review to be in heavy marching order. The eighth corporal of "G" was a stout little fellow, noted for carrying the largest and fullest knapsack in the regiment. He bore the marching in review at common time, and then at quick time with some equanimity, but when the order came to "Pass in review, *double quick* time," his patience was exhausted, and as he trotted with gun at a "right shoulder shift," his left arm supporting his great knapsack, he gave vent to his feelings at every step, by hissing through his closed teeth, "White-livered —— — — ——," " white-livered —— — ——."

The General had few friends those early days on Hatteras, but as the weeks went by each day developed the fact that beneath the rough exterior and austere demeanor, beat a heart of true devotion to the old flag, a heart overflowing with love and regard for his soldiers. His strict discipline made the regiment a body of well-trained soldiers. Revering the flag with a feeling akin to holy awe, he sought to inculcate the same reverential feeling in the men, and whenever the standard was brought out the ceremonies attending its reception were of the most dignified and lofty character.

When he received his orders to proceed to Ship Island, the writer happened to be standing beside him on the ramparts of Fort Hatteras. "What," he exclaimed, "am I to go there and leave all these noble boys? What shall I do without them?" He was a true man and thorough soldier, and died where such a veteran would wish to die—on the field—at the battle of Baton Rouge, Miss. As the colonel of the Twenty-first Indiana was being borne severely wounded, from the front, General Williams rode up to that regiment and said: "Boys, your field officers are all gone; I will lead you." Almost immediately afterward a rifle bullet pierced his chest, and he fell a corpse.

The War of the Rebellion brought so many men into prominence through great deeds, grandly accomplished, that there is danger of forgetting the patient, earnest, loyal soldiery of the regular army, whose trained officers did so much as schoolmasters in bringing the raw material, gathered from all over the North, into shape for such stern work as war.

General Williams was one of these, and he deserves a place upon the same plane with the most honored heroes of the great struggle.

The life of the Forty-eighth on Hatteras is so suggestive of scene and incident, that it is difficult to know just what reminiscences to relate, and what had best be left unrecorded. The inhabitants we became more or less intimate with—the Fulchers, the Austins, the Fosters, the Tolstons, the Whitbys, etc., much could be written of each. Do you recall the sight of two buggies, drawn by the runtiest of Hatteras horses, with rope harness, driven by two of the Forty-eighth officers, the charming Fulcher girls their companions?

Who forgets old Caleb Stowe, that shrewd old customer, who Devine, of "F," sold a barrel of whiskey to? Salt water, every bit of it, with the bung liberally sprinkled with "commissary," obtained from a can of Isaac Lipmann's oysters. Harry Jackson, on Hatteras, orderly sergeant of "G," afterward second lieutenant, now sleeping in the National cemetery, at Fredericksburg, having been killed at Spottsylvania, made a number of sketches on Hatteras life, and this is what he wrote of old Stowe:

"'Old Stowe' is an institution on Hatteras. He owns several schooners, canoes, and all sorts of shallow water craft. His schooners trade in peace times, even as far as New York, taking naval stores and bringing back dry goods, groceries, etc. The old man is a Unionist, nominally, like all the islanders, though it is not at all improbable that the 'almighty dollar' is of more importance in his eyes than the Union. In other words, while professing loyalty, he would not be willing to make any *sacrifices* for the cause. Such a loyal man is as mean as a rebel. Old Stowe is hard of hearing, and it is a treat to hear him in conversation with some of the boys. Sometimes they may be seen actually holding fast to the fence while they strained their vocal organs to their utmost tension to make him even dimly comprehend what they were saying.

" 'Can we have your canoe to go up to Trent?' asks one of the Forty-eighth who wants to attend a molasses-boiling at that famous settlement. 'Don't hear,' says the old man. If your voice was as loud and sonorous as that of heaven's artillery, he would say 'don't hear' to your first remark. You raise your voice to a much higher pitch; he advances, elevates his eyebrows, opens his mouth and pricks up his ears. You repeat the question, elevating your voice to a pitch absolutely deafening. He approaches a little nearer to you, throws out his chin, opens his mouth a little wider, brings his right hand up to his right ear, and ejaculates, 'How?'

" With the energy of despair you summon all your physical and mental powers for a final effort; you grasp the door post, and bringing the whole reserve force of your lungs into action, yell out your question in a voice that shakes the very windows, and would be sufficient to wake the seven sleepers. He smiles, his features resume their wonted appearance, he hears. If he is in a good humor he lends you a boat. You thank him by pantomime and retire. The boys say that if you have some money to give him his auricular organs are much more acute in their perception."

The town of Trent is mentioned in this sketch and in the one following. This is rather an illusionary settlement, supposed to be some nine miles above the inlet. Any one going up the island went to Trent, whether they traveled nine or twenty miles, its exact location has never been satisfactorily ascertained.

The lamented Jackson so aptly describes a famous Hatteras institution, frequently indulged in at Trent, that it is introduced:

" Confidentially, now, wasn't that a 'gay' visit of Jim Chadwick's and mine to Trent in search of a molasses-boiling party? The evening was moonlight; it was 10 p. m., an hour or two after the usual bed-time—but we couldn't sleep—and there was to be a pulling party at Trent. So we got past the guard, cabbaged a canoe, and with a couple of poles, 'poled' ourselves to where we thought we were opposite that famous locality.

"On landing, we found ourselves in a swamp, a Hatteras swamp; but nothing daunted we waded through it, found the road, and also discovered the interesting fact that we were about a mile and a half from Trent. Still in the best of spirits we made our way to Trent on foot. 'Hush!' said Chadwick, after we had passed two or three houses, and the sweet, cracked music of half a dozen frail female voices was borne upon the gentle wind. Of course we struck for the music. We were not much surprised to find two other members of Company G there, besides us, to say nothing of other soldiers, particularly of Company K, who were great favorites at Trent.

"Had we an invitation, did you say? Not a bit of it, for you must remember that it is not according to the etiquette of Hatteras to give, or at least to require, invitations. Everybody is expected to know whether he or she is welcome or not and to act accordingly. But we wanted to see a molasses-boiling, and 'went in'—considering ourselves welcome, of course, and there, sure enough, were the girls, done up in their prettiest, and there were a couple of old women and several children, and the 'old man of the house,' all gathered up in the two corners, on either side of the chimney, and there was an industrious young lady stirring a kettle of 'mozy.' One or two of the boldest of the young islanders were inside making themselves agreeable to the ladies, whilst a greater number loitered about the door or lounged on the porch. I was graciously permitted to dry my feet at the fire, sitting next to the young lady stirring the 'mozy.' The rest of the boys were arranged artistically in various positions, inside and outside of the house, and things were going on in an astonishingly gratifying way.

"The molasses was discovered to be boiled enough and taken out to cool. It did not return immediately, it did not return for some time, in fact, it did not return at all, and there was a bustling and whispering among the ladies and the islanders. All up! The molasses had been taken to some other house, and the islander portion of the party, which means the whole party, had 'skedaddled.' The reason of their 'taking-off' was that there were too many soldiers present.

"I won't stop to analyze my feelings, it would be too great a task; nor to tell the very interesting story of how we got back to camp again. Suffice it that we got there in time to creep into our bunks before reveille, so that scarcely anyone knew we had been absent, and we ourselves would willingly have banished the memory of our inglorious retreat from our minds. Disgusted! did you say? Not a bit of it, for has not this incident afforded opportunity for jotting down a Hatteras oddity."

Cape Hatteras sticks its nose out into the Atlantic Ocean with such pertinacity and viciousness that mariners dread being in its proximity, and give it a wide berth at the least approach of rough weather.

This is the most easterly point of the United States, south of the Delaware Capes. Upon this uninviting spot stands one of the most necessary lighthouses the government has ever erected. It is furnished with the best light science has yet conceived for the purpose. The nearness of the warm gulf stream, about twenty miles, and cooling effects of the land, cause frequent commotions in the atmosphere occasioning violent storms.

With the wind blowing only a moderately stiff breeze, the writer started with Lieutenant Sheetz and Sergeant Dick Jones, on the twenty-fifth of February, 1862, to visit this lighthouse, an effort requiring ten miles tramping in heavy sand to and ten miles back again.

We left camp at 7.30 in the morning and reached the summit of the lighthouse at 11 o'clock, just three and one-half hours. The lighthouse was plainly visible from the start. It seemed to recede as we advanced, all efforts to get nearer were apparently unavailing. Trudge, trudge, trudge ; no use. Not an inch gained. This was unaccountable. On and on, when hope almost failed, and suddenly it seemed to stop out of pure good nature, and we reached it.

The walk was really very interesting, notwithstanding its disadvantages. Fragments of noble vessels stranded on these uncertain shores lie scattered everywhere. Could each wreck its tale of sorrow unfold, what a volume of horrors would be thus disclosed. Could the beach at Hatteras speak, how self-condemning the confession.

Thousands of beautiful shells, from the tiniest mussel to the largest conch, are showered over the beach, seemingly never ending in variety, both as to colors and shape. Curious to watch the sagacity of the little sand snipes as they search for mussels along the water's edge. When a great wave would break in upon the shore, these little creatures would run back, or if the wave came too strong would take to the wing and fly, but the moment it receded they would dart back after it, in a long row, keeping along the edge of the wave, bobbing down their beaks for the coveted treasures, that sank into the sand as rapidly as the wave disappeared. Thus, for miles, they follow up the waves, always in single file and always on the run, eluding the advancing waters with the most astonishing dexterity, and immediately as the wave again receded, hovering around its edge.

Some distance out, sporting amidst the waves, are immense schools of porpoises, rolling about, at times close into shore, all going in the same direction, either north or south, they look for all the world, with their sharp fins shooting up out of the water, like so many knotted logs bobbing up and down.

At several points along the shore are rude structures, very much dilapidated during the war times, where, before the conflict, the islanders manufactured oil—porpoise oil—and all around the sheds lie the bleaching skeletons of these ungainly animals. The remains of sharks, whales, cuttle-fish, and almost every species of oceanic inhabitants can be seen at nearly every step, and in great enough variety to give fresh interest to the curiosity seeker, and to while away the weary monotony of sand tramping.

At last the lighthouse was reached. There! cold, silent and alone, stood the home that held the beacon signal to warn the mariner of the treacherous coast—a monument of the bitterness of civil war. The spirit that raised its hand against the "Star Spangled Banner," obliterated the light from Hatteras lighthouse, and left the storm-tossed vessel to the awful mercy of the most dangerous coast of America.

Entering the large door at the base of the column and ascending one hundred and thirty steps, the summit is reached, when a scene of great grandeur bursts upon the sight. An uninterrupted view is obtained for miles—north, south, east and west. The shipping at Hatteras Inlet, fifteen miles to the south, could be distinctly seen. Lieutenant Jackson, heretofore quoted, was moved to write of this view, thus : "Standing there upon the summit floor of the immense tower, and looking through the cylinder of heavy glass plate that forms the upper portion of the lighthouse, through which the lights were to shine that guided the storm-tossed mariner, we beheld with bated breath a scene which for dreary, solemn grandeur can scarcely be equaled—the strong, fierce, howling wind, the drifting sheets of sand, the long line of gray, bald, desolate beach, stinted trees and wind-racked houses, and beyond these the magnificent breakers, frothing and white, rolling, plunging and roaring with a deep, continuous and indescribable solemn roar, that even the wild howlings of the hurricane could not down—all these, as the trembling lighthouse *shook* before the terrible force of the wind, filled us with a feeling of *awe!*"

Innumerable the thoughts that crowd upon the mind as one stands gazing from the lofty height. Imagination depicts the strained and doomed vessel, buffeted about upon the waves and vainly striving to avoid the remorseless breakers, cautioned by the light that used to here revolve. Now, alas, blotted out by the spirit of hate. A mighty stretch of the Atlantic Ocean spreads to the dim horizon, ever rolling and heaving in unwearied restlessness.

Then is pictured the old lightkeeper wending his way up the winding steps, to light the lamp whose rays glanced afar o'er the "weary waste of water," the solitary nature of his vocation, occupy the thoughts, and turning, gazing downward, the eye rests upon his old homestead, so far below, so cheerless in its abandonment, on the barren sands, deserted.

The lighthouse is built of brick and stone, and is about one hundred and fifty feet high. The light had been a revolving one, manufactured in Paris. The maker's name was found on a part of the machinery that remained: "Henry Lepaute-Rue St. Honore' N247 A Paris."

A door leads from the summit floor out onto a platform running around the top. Notwithstanding a protecting iron railing it is rather venturesome for one unaccustomed to so dizzy a height and such terrific winds to promenade on this platform, the rolling waves below, and uneasy shaking of the lighthouse, render it far from an easy task.

At this lofty elevation the lunch prepared before starting was eaten and writing our names at as high a point as could be reached, descended the one hundred and thirty steps, and began the journey back to camp. On the way we fell in with one of the islanders, who had been having an unsuccessful hunt for wild geese. Traveling on and on, growing more and more tired at every step, we contemplated bunking out for the night and resuming the tramp the next day, but our island friend buoyed us up with the hope of securing a boatman to take us back down the sound. With this in view we left the shore and turned into the woods and soon met the very man we wanted, but alas, his canoe (or " kennew," as he called it) was three miles away. We were assured that if we could find Ben Tolston he'd surely " carry us down." "The first white house was Ben's." The first house we reached was far from white. No one home there. The next was Foster's; he was away. An old lady said it was a "mighty little distance to Ben Tolston, to turn off at the first potato patch." We followed directions to the letter and found our man. He was at dinner and agreed to take us down in his " yawl," provided we waited until he had finished his dinner and the women folks had got some dinner for us. Flitch, fried eggs, corn bread and coffee (burnt beans), was soon set before us, to which we did full justice. We offered to pay for our meal, but no, anything we wanted, anything to eat, just give them a call and we were welcome to the best they had. Contributions to the children followed, and at 4 o'clock we set sail for camp, where we arrived in time for dress parade, a thoroughly played out party. A quarter apiece paid Ben, and we turned in to recuperate.

Hatteras has its beauties. The grand old Atlantic dashes its waves on the dreary, lonely beach—the long line of frothing, roaring breakers, as far as the eye can reach, so beautifully snow white, yet so fearful in their grandeur. Here they come, rolling, rolling smoothly along until the rising ground retards them, when they ripple as though irritated; then, at being further impeded in their progress, foam with increasing wrath, with the roar of a thousand Niagaras; then, with one last grand effort dash upon the shore with bitter, terrible fury, seeming bent on spending their wasting strength in overcoming the resistance offered to their advancement.

Who tires of gazing on the glassy waves as they shape themselves in myriad forms of beauty? When old Ocean rouses in his anger before the howling blast, how fearfully sublime they then become, rising higher, and higher, and higher, madly foaming on the beach, till lost in wonder at the grandeur of the same, the head bows in reverence before the mighty architect, who holds them in the hollow of His hand.

Such are the everyday sights at Hatteras, still there is no sameness. Endless the variety of ocean scenery, each day developing some new and heretofore unseen beauty.

More could be said of the Forty-eighth's sojourn on this island, the comrades' adventures thereon, the various dwellers, the Fulchers, the Austins, the Fosters, the Tolstons, the Whitbys, the mention of whose names will undoubtedly recall incidents forgotten.

Lippman's sutler establishment became quite an institution, and he secured a lively trade with the islanders. His canned oysters were remarkable bivalves; their sale was spirited to a degree, the effect upon the purchaser decidedly exhilarating. Devine, of "F," used a can of Isaac's oysters over the bung of the barrel of salt water he sold to Old Stowe.

Roanoke Island had been captured, an expedition against Newbern was in progress, the time had arrived for the departure of the Forty-eighth Regiment from Hatteras.

The regiment's sojourn there was a fortunate circumstance; it became its school-house. Little versed in war, here, under the able command of that veteran disciplinarian, General Thomas Williams, it became well drilled and well disciplined, fitted for the stern career it was destined to pursue.

CHAPTER III.

NEWBERN.

Upon the eleventh of March, 1862, Colonel Nagle received an order from General Burnside to have six companies of the Forty-eighth leave Hatteras at once, to accompany the fleet upon its expedition against Newbern.

Companies A, B, C, D, H and I were detailed for the purpose; the other four companies, E, F, G and K, were directed to remain at Hatteras, on garrison duty, and placed under command of Captain William Winlack, of Company E, until the return of Major Daniel Nagle, who was home on a leave of absence. The feeling amongst the men of the four companies left behind was one of chagrin. Knowing that an engagement was pending, they desired to take part in it with the rest of the regiment, but only six could go, so four had to remain.

Quartermaster Ellis was also detained at Hatteras; he was the Post Quartermaster, and could not be relieved. This necessitated the appointment of a temporary quartermaster for the regiment, and in order to retain all the officers of the line accompanying the expedition with their companies, Colonel Nagle selected Lieutenant Bosbyshell, of Company G, as the "Acting Quartermaster for the detachment about joining the expedition," his company being one of the four remaining at Hatteras.

At 6 o'clock on the morning of the twelfth the regiment was formed upon the parade ground at Camp Winfield, when the detachment moved out of the line, and amid the shouts of E, F, G and K, took up its march to Hatteras Inlet. The large side wheel steamboat, "George Peabody," had been selected to transport the regiment. When the command reached the wharf that vessel was discovered hard aground on the "swash." A bivouac on the shore was ordered. Here was an excellent opportunity for the whiskey dealers, abounding on the water craft crowding the inlet; so during the day many small boats containing the vendors made frequent trips to the shore and a brisk business was opened along the coast. The result of this occasioned the only serious disturbance of the kind ever happening the regiment. The orgies almost created a riot. The horrible scenes enacted in the "Hotel d'Afrique," in the midst of which poor, inoffensive old Galloway, the Colonel's servant, lost his life, is a sad page of the regiment's history.

The morning of the thirteenth found the "Peabody" afloat and the preparations for embarking immediately began. Tugs, surf boats, and the schooner, "Henry W. Johnson," were put into requisition to carry the regiment over the "swash." Being thus quickly placed aboard the steamboat, she, with the schooner and surf boats in tow, was soon moving nicely through the waters of Pamlico Sound, heading for Newbern.

Toward evening rain commenced falling and the fog thickened so rapidly that it was decided unsafe to proceed further, so the anchor was dropped in the Neuse River, some seventeen miles below Newbern, and half a mile in rear of the rest of the fleet.

General Burnside's plan for the reduction of Newbern, was similar in many respects to his attack on Roanoke Island. By a simultaneous movement upon the enemy by land and water, he hoped to carry their strong defensive works.

In furtherance of this plan his fleet of gunboats and transports left Roanoke Island, the former in the lead, and by the thirteenth of March his transports came to anchor in the Neuse River, near the mouth of Slocum's Creek, the point determined upon to land the troops, about fifteen miles from Newbern. The gunboats were some distance in the advance, shelling the woods along the river banks. At 8 o'clock in the morning, thirteenth of March, 1862, the signal being given by a sergeant and file of men of the Fifty-first Pennsylvania Volunteers, planting a flag on the shore, the troops commenced disembarking. The water was so shallow that the boats ran aground before reaching the land, and the men were obliged to wade some distance. Wet and muddy they finally all got ashore, and the muddy march towards Newbern began, the Twenty-fourth Massachusetts acting as skirmishers. The enemy abandoned all their outer defensive works, and concentrated their entire strength within their strongest line of entrenchments, five miles from Newbern. This line was reached by the Union troops on the night of the thirteenth; the attack was postponed until the following morning.

As defensive works this line was probably one of the best of its kind erected during the war. The Neuse River on the left was blockaded with sunken ships, iron pikes, chains and torpedoes, to prevent the approach of gunboats. The gunboats were also covered by the heavy guns of Fort Thompson, a fort erected on the river bank mounting thirteen large guns, and forming the extreme left of the rebels' line. Running back perpendicularly from the river to the embankment of the railroad from Morehead City to Goldsboro, were breastworks sufficiently strong to resist heavy artillery, and high enough amply to protect the rebel troops from rifle firing. From the railroad bank, in continuation of the line, a series of connected rifle pits and earth works for field pieces, ran to an impenetrable swamp, which was parallel with the river. Stretching then from the river to the swamp was a continuous line, a mile and a half in length, of heavy entrenchment, rifle pits and redans, the whole front swept by enfilading guns of heavy calibre from Fort Thompson, the thirteen-gun fort on the river.

Along the entire front of this line, for probably half a mile, the trees were felled and every possible obstruction placed to prevent the troops getting through, whilst in front of the rifle pits beyond the railroad, besides the felled timber, an ugly swamp hindered the approaches. Behind this strongly fortified position the rebels confidently awaited the attack.

Early on the morning of the fourteenth, Burnside fiercely assailed the entire line, with three brigades, commanded respectively by Generals Foster, Reno and Parke. Foster had the right with his centre on the wagon road, Parke the centre, taking in the railroad, and Reno that portion opposite the rifle pits on the left. It was success or capture with Burnside's forces. Every man he had was in the fight. He had no reserves. His troops felt the enthusiasm of their leader, and never dreamed of anything but victory. None doubted the result. The fleet of gunboats opened promptly upon the shore batteries, and threw shells over the heads of the attacking troops into the rebel lines, aiding most valiantly in the final defeat. The confidence of the troops never faltered. The impetuosity of the attack, and the dread of Burnside's prestige by the enemy, were also powerful adjuncts to success. The rain and the fog aided in making uncertain the numbers of the assaulting party. The fight become terrible along the whole line. Suddenly Lieutenant-Colonel Clark, with a few men of the Twenty-first Massachusetts, found themselves within the enemy's lines at the railroad, much to their own and the rebel's astonishment. Before they had time to recover from this startling apparition, and capture Clark and his party, he and his men returned safely to their regiment. The weak point had, however, been thus accidentally developed, and Colonel Rodman, of the Fourth Rhode Island, immediately ordered his regiment to charge, sending word to General Parke his action. Subsequent events justified this responsibility; a defeat at Newbern would have cost Rodman his sword!

The brave Fourth Rhode Island gallantly charged, and pierced the enemy's line at the railroad. Seeing the charge, Foster and Reno ordered their troops forward, and the men bore down with lively cheers, putting the rebel forces completely to rout, capturing all their camp, quartermaster, commissary and ordnance stores, the latter including three batteries of splendid field artillery, and all their shore batteries, making in all some sixty-nine guns. The enemy held out longer on the right of their line, in their strongly entrenched positions in the rifle pits and redoubts, but Reno's forces, with Parke charging them persistently, compelled them to fly, leaving about five hundred prisoners in the hands of the Union troops. A convenient railroad train conveyed away most of the fleeing rebels.

Burnside immediately pursued the retreating enemy, pressing them so closely that the capture of all of them was only prevented by their flight over the Trent River, and destruction of the two bridges crossing that stream. As it was, Foster's brigade was thrown across the river before night, and the occupation of Newbern was complete.

The battle of Newbern was one of the pluckiest fights of the war. It was a two-and-a-half hours' desperate conflict, principally fought by the musket and bayonet. The gunboats were powerful auxiliaries, but the brunt of the fight was borne by the land troops. No field artillery was used. A few guns brought ashore from the boats, were, it is true, gallantly handled, and brave old Captain Bennett, of the "Cossack," pushed his brass howitzer directly to the front and fought it nobly—still it can hardly be said that light artillery entered in any way effectively into the fight. To the infantry peculiarly belongs the praise. Hard, downright pluck and courage carried the day. It was a bold attack, and its boldness made it strong. From their own accounts, the rebels could not have had less than eight thousand men opposed to Burnside, principally North Carolinians, defending their own State. He was fully aware of their strength and of the preparations made to meet him, although not expecting the rifle pits and redans beyond the railroad, and yet attacked with seventy-five hundred men, whose ammunition had been damaged by the rain, and in some cases more than half destroyed. He was a commander, however, who thoroughly depended on the powers of his men. He had faith in them, and having overcome difficulties at the outset of his expedition at Hatteras, which would have deterred a less resolute man, felt that the justice of the cause, backed by the willing hands and stout hearts of his troops, must win. He never failed his troops and they never failed him. Upon hearing of the Fourth Rhode Island's charge, he exclaimed: "I knew it; the day is ours." He always acknowledged the great courage and endurance of his soldiers. In his testimony before the Committee on the Conduct of War, he says: "As at Roanoke, the troops in this action (Newbern) behaved as gallantly as any men could."

Let us now return to the Forty-eighth, who were left in the fog on the Neuse River on the evening of the thirteenth of March.

Early the next morning, the "Peabody" moved further up the river and joined the fleet of transports. All of the gunboats, with one or two exceptions, were up the river engaging the rebel batteries, the roaring of their guns being the music to which the Forty-eighth landed. The point of disembarkation was four miles further up the river than the mouth of Slocum's Creek, where the other troops were landed. Small boats conveyed the command from the steamboat to within fifty yards of the shore, where they ran aground, and the balance of the trip was made by wading. The regiment was formed on the beach, and about to follow up after the other troops, when an aid of General Foster's arrived from the battlefield for the purpose of hurrying forward ammunition, and directed the command to get ammunition ashore and carry it to the front as speedily as possible. The landing of the ammunition was a difficult task, occasioning great delay. It was accomplished with as much dispatch as possible. Forty thousand rounds were placed upon the only wagon ashore, and Company B detailed to guard it. An additional forty thousand rounds were carried by the five other companies. To accomplish this task the men took off their musket straps, and with them tied, or rather swung, the boxes on fence-rails, two men to one box. This was no light load. A heavy knapsack, old Harper's Ferry musket, cartridge box containing sixty rounds, and the box containing one thousand rounds of ball cartridges swung on the rail, made many of the fellows groan. By 3 o'clock in the afternoon the regiment moved forward, expecting to reach the main body of troops within three or four miles.

Constant reports from the front were brought by wounded men on their way to the transports. "We've got 'em, boys," and "The 'rebs' have been driven from their strongest batteries and are running towards Newbern!" This was cheering, and the men moved forward in good spirits through the ankle-deep North Carolina mud. The first part of the journey was on the Goldsboro and Macon Railroad, the latter portion of the way over the country road, rendered almost impassable by the heavy rains of the preceding night.

When near the battlefield intelligence reached the regiment of the entire rout of the rebels, our forces driving them before them, of their firing the railroad bridge over the Trent, and also setting fire to the city. Such news inspired all with renewed vigor. The heavy load was almost forgotten. On pressed the men, and just as the gathering shades of night were deepening into darkness the battlefield was reached. The regiment bivouacked immediately inside of the long line of breastworks, where the enemy had made a most desperate stand, a short distance from Fort Thompson.

In company with Colonel Sigfried, Adjutant Bertolette and Captains Gilmour and Potts, the writer walked over the battlefield the morning after the fight. The dreadful appearance indicated the terrible conflict.

The party had never seen any field of carnage that resembled in the least degree the pictures representing battles, where men, horses, cannon and drums are promiscuously heaped together, except this field at Newbern. Here literally, were horses, men, cannon, wagons, drums, and all the paraphernalia of war indiscriminately mingled in one mass. Horses lay dead upon every side, some hitched to the guns, half dragged out of their positions, showing an attempt to save them; wounded horses standing on three legs; here and there the form of a rebel fast locked in the arms of death; clothing, provisions, tents and ammunition scattered around; everything indicated a hasty retreat.

Trees barked and scratched by shot and shell, branches lopped off; some torn asunder, others cut completely off. Evidences of the fierce struggle met the eye at every point. It was a sad scene, and although the Union army had been victorious, the onlooker could not repress a feeling of horror. It mattered little to the stiff, stark bodies lying here, who gained the day. At Fort Thompson, all but three of the thirteen fine guns were spiked, but there were 40,000 pounds of powder in the magazine, safe and sound.

Nine splendid guns were mounted along the line of entrenchments and it was a matter of wonder how eight thousand men so strongly entrenched, permitted seventy-five hundred men to force them away. It did not look as if one Southerner was equal to two Yankees.

Colonel Nagle directed the writer to go on to Newbern, hunt up some one in authority and ascertain what disposition was to be made of the regiment, as no instructions had yet been given him, and he did not know to which brigade he would be assigned.

He took with him Quartermaster Sergeant Jacob Wagner. The way was by the wagon road, principally. However, when the railroad crossed it, the latter was taken, and after a good solid tramp the Trent River was reached, only to find further progress barred, the bridge having been destroyed. An effort made by the rebels to destroy our fleet by floating down the river vessels filled with cotton, soaked in turpentine, proved a boomerang; the tide and wind carried them up against the railroad bridge and set it on fire, so the story ran. However this may be, the way was temporarily stopped, until, fortunately, a small row-boat put in an appearance which was used to reach Newbern. General Foster's headquarters were at the Gaston House, but he had no authority to take the regiment under his care, and he advised that General Burnside be seen at once; he could be found on his boat, the "Alice Price." Going to the wharf a small boat was chartered and the General's craft boarded, but he was on shore. Again stranded, the boatman having left, a half hour elapsed before another boat was captured, and on reaching the shore it was discovered to be the opposite side of the river, again from Newbern.

Passing through the camp of the Ninth New Jersey, all haste was made to the railroad to intercept the regiment and report the ill luck. Fortunately, as the railroad was reached General Burnside was seen riding along, attended by an orderly. Leaving Wagner to wait for the Forty-eighth the writer hastened to him and reported the presence of the regiment, desiring instructions. He at once assigned the command to the Second Brigade, under Brigadier General Thomas L. Reno, and directed the writer to follow him to that General's headquarters. What follows is a fair sample of General Burnside's kindness of heart, and explains the warm attachment his troops had for him. The writer was a young officer—in appearance younger than he was—and only a second lieutenant, so when he approached the old frame house into which General Burnside entered, he felt a diffidence about entering, and loitered around the door. Soon an officer rattled down the stairs, and looking out, addressed him. "Are you the officer from the Forty-eighth Regiment?" He was. "General Burnside desires you to come upstairs." He was ushered into the presence of Generals Reno and Parke, and a lot of quartermasters and commissaries. General Burnside immediately approached him and shook hands, asked his name and severally introduced all in the room to him. General Reno was in bed, having had his ankle badly sprained in the fight the day before. The Forty-eighth became the general subject of conversation, and the writer was thoroughly posted as to the arrangements to make for its welfare. Whilst arranging about quarters, Commodore Rowan, the naval commander of the fleet at Newbern, came in, and the writer was the first person presented to him. [This kind-hearted greeting by General Burnside, and evident desire to free a young officer from all embarrassment, made a great impression upon that officer, and he cannot help comparing his manner of

GEN. AMBROSE E. BURNSIDE.

treatment with that of other officers of high rank in our army during the war, very much to these other officers' discredit. All this while it rained tremendously. When the regiment was found it was stretched along the railroad at the destroyed bridge over the Trent River, and Colonel Nagle and Lieutenant Colonel Sigfried both away—over in Newbern—to find out what there was to tell. Captain Kauffman, senior captain, marched the regiment back to the vicinity of General Reno's headquarters in rear of the rebel Fort Lane.

Late in the afternoon, by General Reno's orders, the steamer "Peabody" was placed at the entire disposal of Colonel Nagle, and he sent his acting quartermaster aboard to get ashore what baggage was needed for the night. During the whole afternoon it rained incessantly, and it is recorded that Dr. Reber, Captains Potts and Pleasants, Lieutenants Fitzsimmons and Bowen, Hospital Steward Hardell, Quartermaster Sergeant Wagner and the acting quartermaster spent the night very comfortably on board of the "Peabody," enjoying the best of quarters and meals.

The next morning, sixteenth of March, the sojourn of the regiment at Newbern may be said to have begun, and it ended on the sixteenth of July following, nearly four months.

The first regular camp was pitched on the east side of the Trent River, opposite the town, and was called "Camp Nagle." Here the old routine of camp life commenced again. Blacked shoes, white gloves and paper collars assumed their sway. Light blue trousers for the first time encased the regimental legs, and the old Harper's Ferry muskets gave way to the English Enfield rifle. The old county bridge was picketed by Company C for a while and then Company D had a share of it. In that same duty

> How the turkeys gobbled, which these two companies found;
> How the sweet potatoes started even out the ground.

One of Company C's men met by Captain Pleasants, with a pig under his arm.

"Where did you get that pig?" demanded the strict officer. "Sure Captain, it followed me!" said the ever-ready soldier. Company B was detailed as an artillery company, and its haps and mishaps with the fine four field pieces placed at its disposal, afforded great interest not only to the company, but the whole regiment. This battery was near Fort Totten, to which neighborhood the regiment moved on the third of April, encamping on the outskirts of Newbern, in a pleasant field, between the Neuse and Trent Rivers. Fort Totten, a large earthwork, was built by many hundreds of contrabands, all adorned with a broad white band around their hats, labeled "United States Service." This fort commanded the approaches to Newbern, down either river or from the land. Just here let it be said for the benefit of the "First Defenders," that the first anniversary meeting of members of that body was held in a house adjacent to the camp, on the evening of April 18, 1862. A series of appropriate resolutions were adopted. Refreshments were partaken of, with lots of songs, speeches and band music thrown in. It was a right royal jollification.

An expedition to demolish a lock in the Dismal Swamp Canal had peculiar interest for the Forty-eighth, inasmuch as it was at first selected to accompany it, but subsequent orders directed the regiment to remain in camp. There was, however, good material amongst the troops composing that expedition. The Fifty-first Pennsylvania was there and the stuff it was made of was well known. Led by that model soldier, the brave, modest Hartranft, it could not fail. How the Forty-eighth learned to love the Fifty-first! Their fortunes were identical, dangers and hardships mutual. Subsequently, at Antietam, who of the Forty-eighth can ever forget the Fifty-first's gallant determination to stand by it in holding the hill against an anticipated assault? Without a cartridge this big-hearted command proposed to defend with cold steel to the bitter end. All honor to the brave leader and men of the Fifty-first!

On the twenty-third of April the forces in the department were reorganized. Foster, Reno and Parke became commanders of the First, Second and Third Divisions. Colonel James Nagle was assigned to the command of the First Brigade, Second Division, and the brigade consisted of the Forty-eighth Pennsylvania, Ninth New Jersey, Second Maryland and One Hundred and Third New York.

How excited the boys of the regiment were at the news of the fall of Fort Macon, Lieutenant George W. Gowen, of Company C, being in that engagement in the capacity of an acting officer of Company C, First U. S. Artillery. The One Hundred and Third New York created a sensation by going on an independent scouting trip, led by its famous German commander, the brave and dashing Colonel Baron Frederick Von W. Egloffstein, who lost his leg through the rash adventure.

The Newbern portion of the regiment was made happy when the boys of E, F, G and K rejoined them on the twenty-third of May, 1862. There was a great hand-shaking at this reunion, and anxious inquiries respecting the health and happiness of all Hatteras friends and notorieties.

Constant were the visits of General Burnside through the camps of the various regiments, and frequent his interviews with the company cooks. He thus ascertained from this very essential "brigade," the character of the rations received by the men, and determined whether the commissary department was efficiently administered. Is it any wonder that the boys of the Ninth Army Corps loved their general? The nearest way to a soldier's heart lays right through his haversack.

The rations furnished the troops at Newbern were far superior to those furnished in any other department the regiment served, both as regards assortment and freshness, and many nice little delicacies were frequently found proceeding from the commissaries. The issue, too, was quite abundant.

On the twenty-ninth of May the regiment left the vicinity of Fort Totten, recrossed the Trent River, and went into camp on the banks of the river near the spot it first occupied. Upon its right the Second Maryland encamped, and immediately in front the One Hundred and Third New York was located. This camp was beautified with shade trees. Vigorous skirmish drills, with blank cartridge firing, were the order of the day. Great care was taken to make the "dress parade" faultless.

On the third of June the regiment went on guard in Newbern to give the Twenty-fifth Massachusetts a chance to participate in a review of the First Division. Captain Kauffman, of A, was officer of the day, and Lieutenants Hinkle, of H, Klecker, of D, Bohannan, of E, and Woods, of B, were officers of the guard. The occasion was a notable one, for there was great rivalry between the Forty-eighth Pennsylvania and Twenty-fifth Massachusetts. Reno bragged on the former, and Foster lauded the latter.

Reviews by brigade and division became frequent in the department. There was quite a surfeit of them. However, the result of one caused an inscription to be placed on the flag of the Forty-eighth. It happened in this wise: Immediately after the battle of Newbern a general order was issued directing all the regiments in the department to inscribe upon the flags the word "Newbern." Not having been in the actual conflict or even under fire, Colonel Nagle hesitated about complying with this order, from a modest notion that it was not deserved. On the seventh of June, General Burnside sent a special order directing the Forty-eighth to comply with his general order on the subject. This was neglected. On the twentieth of June a grand review of the entire force of the "Coast Department" was ordered, the occasion being the presentation of a sword to General Burnside, the gift of the State of Rhode Island. The troops were formed in a square, Foster's Division occupying two sides, and Reno's Division the other two sides, Nagle's Brigade being on the eastern side, the cavalry and artillery were formed outside the lines of the infantry. Adjutant General Mauran, of Rhode Island, made the presentation speech, and General Burnside replied briefly, and then the troops yelled. This was followed by a review of the forces, and the commanding general failed to discern "Newbern" on the flags of the Forty-eighth. This nettled the General, and he took Colonel Nagle to task about it, stating in substance that although not directly under fire, the Forty-eighth's hard work upon that eventful day made up a part of the general movement, and assisted so materially that it was clearly entitled to have "Newbern" emblazoned upon its standard, and there it is to-day, on the tattered old ensign in Harrisburg, the only battle inscribed thereon!

The hot weather of June was calculated to bring sickness, and care had to be exercised in guarding the health of the men. Too frequent bathing in the Trent was deemed imprudent, and Colonel Sigfried issued "Order No. 8," forbidding "all bathing except on Wednesdays and Saturdays," and no soldier was "allowed to bathe between the hours of 9 a. m. and 4 p. m., or remain in the water longer than ten minutes at one time."

A long, loud whistle on the Macon Railroad, one fine morning, roused the men in the various camps, and a rush was made over to the tracks, as the cry rang out, "Here comes an engine!" "Here comes an engine!"

It was greeted with rousing cheers, and its course watched as it crept slowly over the new bridge spanning the Trent River, as if feeling its way at every foot, until it safely reached the opposite shore and went howling through the streets of Newbern. This was "U. S. No. 1." No. 2 followed in a day or two. The regiment had not seen an engine for nine months.

The town of Newbern, when first occupied by the Union troops, appeared to be thoroughly deserted by the dwellers, but day after day store after store would reopen, home after home be reoccupied, as the people began to learn that the Yankees were not such terrible fellows after all. However, there was a general appearance of the place having become prematurely old; evidence of decay struck the eye at every turn; grass grew quite abundantly in the streets—this latter fact caused an old North Carolinian great joy, as he was glad to know the soil was rich enough to produce anything.

The "Gaston House" was the "swell" hotel; it was renamed by its new proprietor the "Union House."

Pollock, Middle and Broad are some of the streets the Forty-eighth boys will long remember.

Many of the adventures in and around Newbern belong to the unwritten history of the regiment. Every regiment has a history that will never be written. If handed down to posterity it will be "by word of mouth," as the traditions of ancient times. Much that was done needs to be forgotten, so this account will not rehearse the misdoings of the Forty-eighth at either Newbern or Lexington.

Early on the morning of July 2, 1862, the regiment was astir with three days' cooked rations in haversacks. At 5.30 a. m. the march into town was made. The steamer "Highland Light" was used as a lighter to convey the regiment aboard the "Cossack," which lay about a mile and a half from the landing, down the stream. Pardon a personal reference here, but the incident made a deep impression upon his mind, and furnished amusement to many. At this time the writer was captain of Company G, and after getting aboard of the "Cossack," discovered that through the negligence of some one, the company's coffee, sugar, and cooking utensils had been left behind. Finding that the steamer would probably be delayed some time, the writer procured a boat from Captain Bennett, and gathering a crew set off for the shore.

Not only G's missing articles were found, but also E's and K's. Securing the lot, the boat was pushed off to return to the "Cossack." The men pulled the oars gaily, as we neared the steamer, rejoicing at our good luck in recovering the lot of stores; to our horror, the vessel began to move slowly away, we knew not whither. Our feelings cannot be described—the expedition off, and we hopelessly striving to reach the steamer, a half mile in the rear! "Now, then, boys, a big pull, a strong pull, and a pull all together, or we will be left!" It was muscle against steam! A rain storm came on; it poured down in torrents, and soaked us to the skin. My, how we worked! Puff, puff, from the "Cossack's" smokestack! Pull, pull, went our oars! We waved our arms wildly, yelled ourselves hoarse, without effect—the vessel steamed on. No relaxation of effort, we worked with a will! For two miles the chase lasted; heaven alone knows how much longer it would have been if the "Cossack" had not stopped! But it did stop—we reached it, thoroughly wet, disgusted and exhausted, scrambling up on deck amidst the shouts of the fortunate ones, who laughed at our discomfort, and made game of our herculean efforts to outdo steam. It was an experience we shall never forget, and one the writer took care never to repeat.

Four o'clock in the afternoon the fleet started, anchoring some seventeen miles below Newbern, in the Neuse. Colonel Nagle was in command of the expedition, and he found upon opening his orders that it was to proceed to Hampton Roads and report to General Reno for further orders.

By 3 o'clock in the afternoon of the third, the "Cossack" reached Hatteras Inlet. Whilst preparing to cross the "Swash" the "Alice Price" steamed up alongside with the intelligence that "McClellan was in Richmond," and the command was directed to "remain where it was until further orders." Three rousing cheers for the news and three more for Little Mac shook the timbers of the old "Cossack" from fore to aft. The anchor was dropped, and in sight of the regiment's old Hatteras home the officers held a spirited meeting as to how best to celebrate the glorious fourth. A visit from Quartermaster Ellis, who still remained at this point as post quartermaster, convinced his friends that life agreed with him, for a healthier looking, jollier, more contented quartermaster never ran a tug.

When the fourth arrived, its celebration was greatly interfered with by the retrograde movement of the "Cossack," for by 4.30 in the morning that staid old vessel was plowing its way through the waters of Pamlico Sound, heading for Newbern. National salutes were being fired by the gunboats and shore batteries, bells were ringing and flags flying when the regiment arrived at the wharf at Newbern. By 5 o'clock in the afternoon the old camping ground was reached, and at eight the canvas houses were all in their places.

The fifth was spent at Newbern, but only to make preparations for a final departure, which began early on the morning of the sixth, when the "Cossack" was again taken possession of by the Forty-eighth. By 11 o'clock the vessel with several schooners in tow, steamed away from Newbern. McClellan was not in Richmond, he was very, very glad to be under cover of the navy's gunboats at Harrison's Landing, and wait promised reinforcements. So the regiment knew its destination. At 10 p. m. the "Swash" was reached, and the anchor dropped for the night.

The regiment had had much to do with Hatteras, and it is therefore not strange to find it hard for the old island to part with its favorite "boys in blue" without a tussle; so on the morning of the seventh, the command experienced the delightful sensation of sticking hard aground on the "Swash."

Notwithstanding the combined efforts of two tugs and the "Highland Light," with the shifting of the regiment to another boat, the "Cossack" did not get finally under way until two in the afternoon.

Steaming up the blue Atlantic on the evening of the seventh of July, 1862, the flashing waves dancing beneath a moon of unrivaled splendor, the command caught its last glimpse of Hatteras. There, restored by the merciful hand of a great government, to all its former glory, twinkled the light from Hatteras lighthouse. How merrily it shot forth its dazzling rays, as if gleefully dancing on the wave crests, rejoiced once more to be the beacon-watcher on this dangerous coast.

So has it been with this great and glorious Union. Once stripped of its bright, beautiful, sunny South, with the aid of the noble, self-sacrificing, heroic citizen soldiery, the light has been replaced, this jewel has been restored, and the glory and honor of the American Nation will shine brightly through all coming time.

CHAPTER IV.

NEWPORT NEWS.

Nine o'clock Tuesday morning, July 8, 1862, the steamer "Cossack," with the Forty-eighth Regiment on board, rounded Cape Henry, and entered the waters of Chesapeake Bay, heading for old Fortress Monroe. Crowds of schooners, brigs, frigates, and all manner of sailing craft, even to a Schuylkill Canal boat, were anchored in Hampton Roads. In comparison with some of the vessels to be seen the poor old "Cossack" looked like a conch shell. It was 2 o'clock in the afternoon before the vessel dropped anchor, within probably four hundred yards of the walls of the fortress, just above the lighthouse. The intense heat sent many ashore in the evening to get a good bath; the sensation was delicious. The trip to and from the beach was enlivened by the glare of the fires made by the company cooks, who were ashore cooking two days' rations.

The boys were made happy next day by the appearance of Dr. Charles H. Haeseler, who had been on a visit to the Army of the Potomac, and brought plenty of news from Schuylkill County; then a number of the men of the Ninety-sixth Regiment were also seen, and their accounts of the bravery of that regiment during the Peninsula campaign delighted all. Under orders the "Cossack" left the fortress at 6 o'clock in the evening, steamed up the James River and landed the regiment at Newport News about 8 o'clock, where its disembarkation was easily accomplished under the bright light of the moon. A convenient field overlooking the river made a fine place to bivouac. On the tenth, tents and baggage were taken off the steamer, and by evening all were comfortably quartered, ready to resume the old routine of camp life.

Newport News at this time was a village of barracks, fortifications and shanties. The "Lake House," a frame "shebang" of some pretension as to size, was kept by colored people. It was well provided with a variety of eatables and drinkables, thus affording an opportunity for refreshments, which many of the Forty-eighth were not slow in accepting; ice cream was one of the luxuries, brought all the way from Baltimore. Adjoining the Lake House was a rude looking barber shop, which fell in for a large share of patronage. The post was garrisoned by odd detachments. A company of the Eleventh Pennsylvania Cavalry formed a portion of it. Many of the officers had their wives with them, and it did the men of the Forty-eighth a power of good to see the bright faces of these Northern ladies—remember for a year no opportunity had been vouchsafed for gazing at more bewitching damsels than Hatteras belles; and from such as "sich" spare further infliction!

If there was one ceremony in which the Forty-eighth could excel more than another, it was dress parade. When the regiment made up its mind to do a dress parade with all its might, it could excel any other regiment in the field; and when the ladies graced the occasion with their presence, as they were sure to do if in the vicinity, the ceremony amounted to a poem! Thanks to the sojourn at Hatteras, the regiment was thoroughly well drilled and most proficient in handling the musket. The grand old woods in rear of the camp became a favorite resort for several reasons. The cool air found beneath the trees therein, shielding the rays of a fiery sun, was one, but the most potent was probably the fact that herein resided old Pringle. All remember old Pringle and his wife, Mary, no doubt. Their ale was good, the old man was jolly; the officers, especially of the Forty-eighth, were often thirsty, and frequent visits were made in consequence. Many a merry evening was passed beneath their roof, and many the mishaps getting back to camp—poor Gilmour's, for instance. What a time Pringle had pronouncing his name for "Pinky's" benefit, who purposely miscalled him Perriwinkle. These were happy-go-lucky, free from care times.

Some difficulty was had in securing proper camping grounds to escape the frequent rains. On the sixteenth of July large reinforcements from South Carolina reached Newport News, amongst them our old friends the Fiftieth and One Hundredth Pennsylvania, and Seventy-ninth New York (Highlanders). On the twenty-second of July the troops were organized into a corps, which was numbered the Ninth, and with this glorious corps the Forty-eighth remained to the close of the war. Schools for officers and non-commissioned officers were resumed at Newport News—a board of examiners, of which Colonel Nagle was chief, was appointed to question such officers as might be sent them by commanders of divisions. Brigade, regimental and company drills became frequent. A recruiting party consisting of Lieutenant Kleckner, of D; Sergeant Huckey, of A; and Corporal Dengler, of K, was detailed to proceed to Pennsylvania to recruit for the regiment. They left on the twenty-second of July. Orders for one day's cooked rations were promulgated on the twenty-fourth, throwing all hands into a state of great excitement. Many supposed a dash at some impudent rebels, said to be lurking around, was intended. The purpose, however, had no such sanguinary meaning—it was merely a trial march, as frequent moves were considered beneficial. Warwick Court House was the objective point. The expedition was the suggestion of General Reno, and was really unimportant when compared to subsequent marches, but to men as unused to marching as the men of the regiment were, it was quite a tiresome trip. On the way much mud and water were encountered. The three hours' rest at Young's Mills was greatly enjoyed. The Court House was reached at 6 o'clock p. m., the march having occupied eleven hours. The grain shocks which filled the field bivouacked in, soon disappeared, being appropriated for beds by the fagged-out soldiers. The Court House, if the small building scarce the size of a 'squire's office, can be dignified by so grand a name, is, or was then, a diminutive brick edifice, with a couple of jury rooms on either side of the main room, each about 8 x 5 feet. Numerous curious sketches, probably made by McClellan's army during its march to Yorktown, adorned the interior walls. The struggle between the Monitor and the Merrimac, the ill-fated Cumberland, etc., were the subjects. "Twas here the judges of " Ole Virginny " dispensed the law to the surrounding inhabitants, from the earliest dates of the country's history. The records were strewn to the wind, some bore the date of 1760. The jail was a mean two-story brick building, exceedingly small, dirty and miserable looking, no doubt a terror to all evil-doers of Warwick County. The office used for storing the county records was a much smaller building than either of the others. These buildings, with two large frame ones, one used as a tavern, the other as a school-house, church, assembly room or some such purpose, and a stable, completed the built up portion of the town of Warwick Court House. The surrounding country is truly beautiful. Large trees abound in profusion immediately about the settlement, beneath which an elegant lawn spreads out inviting repose. There is shade enough here to accommodate the inhabitants of the entire county. No doubt it was the custom of these inhabitants to assemble here to listen to the speeches of their fellow-citizens upon the important issues of the hour,—here is where they voted, held their conventions, etc. The mosquitoes held high carnival that night—they were peculiarly troublesome, and it was wonderful how some of the boys could make such a mistake as to wish them in a very warm climate when just the contrary destination would have "settled their hash." The return march commenced at 5 o'clock in the morning of the twenty-sixth, and camp was reached at Newport News, by 11.30 a. m., a little more than six hours, without further adventure, save the effort to stop a tendency some of the men had to straggle ahead.

Whilst at Newport News an opportunity was afforded to see exemplified the policy of using the negroes of the South as contrabands of war. Squads of cavalry scoured the country bringing in all the negroes they could find. These were sent in bodies of three or four hundred to McClellan, to do the digging for the Army of the Potomac. Considerable discussion to settle the seniority of rank of the captains of the regiment took place in various meetings held at the colonel's tent. Some thought the date of muster into the United States service should decide it; others, that the different posts of honor occupied by the respective companies ought to settle it; others again claimed it from date of appointment into the regiment, and others wanted an examination to settle the point by merit. This last proposition occasioned an amusing debate, as all who were present will remember. The result was the referring of the whole matter to General Reno, who decided that the date of muster into the United States service was the standard of rank. The morning of Friday, August 1, 1862, found the regiment in quiet enjoyment of its camp at Newport News, with nothing to disturb the even tenor of its way, until just as the afternoon napping time came, the announcement was made that the paymaster had arrived, which caused great excitement. All were fearfully strapped, indeed, the pocketbooks were very light when Newbern was left, and no wonder the advent of so important a person was followed by a great stir. In the midst of this welcomed news came orders to cook "three days rations immediately." Then baggage to be ready for immediate removal to the schooner "Gilbert Green." On the morning of the second the regiment was aroused at 5 o'clock and by eight snugly aboard its old friend the "Cossack." It was sunset before the balance of the troops were embarked. The "Cossack" had three schooners in tow, and before getting off snapped two stout hawsers. The quiet beauty of the scene, during the trip down the James River to Fortress Monroe, made a most pleasing impression. The magnificent sunset in the rear painted the heavens with bright gorgeous tints and dazzled the eye with the sparkling waters of the James. The deepening shadows of the bluffs, and the noiseless motion of the steamer, made up a scene of delicious repose. Passing the ill-fated steamers "Cumberland" and "Congress," by 8 o'clock the vessel dropped anchor in the bay, above the Fortress. All settled themselves for a good night's rest. Some, however, were aroused by the peculiar noise accompanying the weighing anchor, and watched the operation to discover, if possible, where the vessel was bound. At 1 o'clock a. m. all was ready, and silently steaming away from the shadow of the Fortress, the "Cossack" headed for the ocean, and just as all hope of going up the Chesapeake was abandoned, the boat rounded nicely for the Bay. At 4 o'clock the regiment was aroused by the discovery that Mattis Sheaffer, of Company D, in a momentary crazy fit, had shot himself through the abdomen, from the effects of which he died, in great suffering, twenty-four hours afterward.

The destination of the expedition continued to excite comment all the morning of the third; as the mouth of the different rivers emptying into the Chesapeake was approached, the vessel's course was closely watched. By 3 p. m. the "Cossack" was steaming grandly up the old Potomac, with the lighthouse on Point Lookout in the rear an hour. The bad fare on the steamer caused a "fodder rebellion" amongst the officers, and the haversacks were drawn on in preference to the steward's rations. At 8 o'clock p. m. anchor was dropped some twelve miles below Mathias' Point, leaving the ultimate destination of the troops still a matter of doubt. This doubt was removed on the morning of the fourth when the vessel anchored off Acquia Creek.

There was much bustle at the mouth of Acquia Creek when the Forty-eighth was aroused from slumber on board the "Cossack" on the morning of August 4, 1862. Troops were being rapidly landed from the numerous transports, and convenient railroad trains conveyed them into the interior. The Forty-eighth's turn to land came at 12 o'clock noon, but the old "Cossack" found the water too shallow, and to plow through the mud, heavily loaded, besides towing a schooner on each side, was too much for the boat, so she "stuck." By dropping a portion of the tow and exerting strenuous labor, land was approached near enough to permit the regiment to get ashore, but it was 4 p. m. before it was accomplished.

The first eight companies filled a train—leaving G and B behind to take a second train, which came up directly after the first left. The country between Acquia Creek and Falmouth resembles the scenery of Pennsylvania very much, and the boys were delighted with the ride. The Ninety-fifth New York and Fifty-sixth Pennsylvania were stationed along the railroad as guards, and as the various encampments of the detachment were passed, rousing cheers welcomed the Forty-eighth.

Falmouth was reached by 6.30 and the camp pitched on the summit of a hill on the north side of the Rappahannock River, immediately opposite the town of Fredericksburg, where an extensive view was had of the surrounding country. During the evening several Schuylkill countians, belonging to the Fifty-sixth Pennsylvania, visited the Forty-eighth, amongst them Professor Pres. Rossiter and Jim Hetherington.

Fredericksburg is beautifully situated, encircled by picturesque hills, very pleasant and delightful in scenic effect, but not nearly so pleasant and delightful when the same hills bristle with artillery and infantry, as the Forty-eighth found out about four months afterward. At this time the town appeared finished. It seemed larger than Newbern; had better houses, rather more thrifty in appearance, with, however, an air of self-satisfaction at having reached the proportions gained, but with no desire for further increase. Many of the inhabitants remained in town; their sentiments were decidedly "secesh," and intercourse between them and the Yankees by no means hearty. There were no guards placed in the town. A cordon of sentinels surrounded it completely cutting off communication with outsiders. Citizens were not permitted to pass in or out; not a special pass was allowed. All officers and soldiers desiring to visit the town were required to have passes. These could only be obtained for business purposes—business requiring to be transacted there and that could not be attended to outside. Orders were very strict respecting this, and they were rigidly enforced. The writer made a visit to the town to make some necessary purchases, and meeting Lieutenants Blake and Niles, with two other officers of the One-hundred-and-third New York, journeyed to a boarding house on Commerce street for dinner. Whilst indulging in the chicken, roast beef, corn, tomatoes, potatoes, etc., provided, some young ladies in the parlor overhead were heard singing the rebel song, "Bonny Blue Flag." They sang it very well. The party went up into the parlor, secured an introduction, and besought a repetition of the song, but the blue coats and brass buttons besought in vain—the ladies stoutly declined. They did sing "The Star Spangled Banner," however, out of compliment to their visitors.

Just without the camp, probably a hundred yards, in a ravine, an elegant spout of water jutted out of the ground, conveniently situated for standing under. Here, when "taps" had sounded, a number of the officers would congregate and indulge in a shower bath, the deliciousness of which cannot be described, following, as it did, those hot, arid August days. This was a particularly favorite resort of Captain Filbert, who enjoyed its refreshing effects nightly.

This, added to the gorgeously beautiful moonlight nights and magnificent scenery surrounding the camp, rendered the regiment's stay at Fredericksburg very pleasant and agreeable.

CHAPTER V.

WITH POPE.

On the ninth of August orders were received to retrench baggage, and send everything home not absolutely necessary. Dress coats, trunks and many extras of a like nature were hurried into the express office at Fredericksburg and shipped North. Each company was allowed but one wagon. This cutting down took away the natty appearance of the dress parade and inspection—blouses did not set the men off as well as dress coats, but promised earnest work in the near future could well replace good looks.

It was the twelfth before the looked-for order to move was promulgated, and by 6 o'clock in the evening the march to join Pope's army began. Whilst preparing for this move rain commenced falling, which made the roads dreadfully muddy, and although it cleared, with a beautiful moon overhead, the tramping was not at all agreeable. The march lay along the north bank of the Rappahannock River, up hill and down dale, with frequent rests, until 3 o'clock a. m., when the command bivouacked for the balance of the night.

The march was resumed at 7 o'clock on the morning of the thirteenth and continued, with occasional halts, until 11 o'clock, when a rest of four hours was had. The condition of the road improved at every step and the scenery was perfectly charming. There were many farms along the route in an excellent state of cultivation, with only here and there a house deserted. Some of these estates were really magnificent, and the sight of several churches seemed to indicate a religious neighborhood. Apples were plenty and generous supplies were laid in. The road traversed lay through Hanover and Fauquier counties. At 4 o'clock p. m. the regiment moved on. When four miles had been covered the summit of a hill was reached, from which there burst upon the sight one of the grandest views occurring in the whole of the regiment's military life. The full beauty of a number of succeeding valleys, ending in the Shenandoah Valley, was spread before the delighted vision. The Blue Ridge away in the background with its sharp peaks, towering toward the clouds, clearly outlined against a most gorgeous sunset sky. Beneath the lofty point of observation, a magnificent valley, with its light and shade strongly in contrast with the crimson and golden beauties of the charming sunset. As the men reached this point an involuntary shout of admiration paid tribute to the transcendent beauty of the scene. It was a grand sight, a long time was spent in wondrous admiration, the command seeming loath to lose any of its thrilling loveliness. A neighboring field afforded a desirable spot for a bivouac, and into it the regiment filed for that purpose. During the night an alarm in camp occasioned the rapid formation of the brigade into line. The cause was the accidental discharge of a gun by one of the Sixth New Hampshire men; the bullet passed through the poor fellow's hand, and whizzed over the Forty-eighth's camp. All thought the Johnnies were surely about.

The march was resumed at 7 o'clock on the morning of the fourteenth. After covering four miles of tramping, Bealton Station, on the Orange and Alexandria Railroad, was reached. Whilst waiting at this station for further orders, visitors from the Twenty-eighth Regiment Pennsylvania Volunteers made their appearance in camp. Especially remembered is Captain James Silliman, who was accompanied by Major Pardee. Jim was always a great favorite,—the hearty welcome he received upon this occasion must have convinced him of that fact.

Company B's and G's wagon rejoined the regiment at this point. It had been missing since the twelfth, and during the time had upset two or three times, once in a pool of water. The officers' mess-chest was completely demolished; the contents in an exceedingly disagreeable condition. An empty train soon approached the station, and the Forty-eighth was put aboard. There being no more transportation, the balance of the brigade were obliged to walk. Lucky Forty-eighth! A ride of twelve miles brought the regiment to Culpeper Court House, a very pretty village, surrounded at the time by a large army, whose tents dotted the fields in all directions. The regiment left the cars some hundred rods below the station, and marching about a mile and a half toward the Rapidan River, encamped for the night. A long line of rebel prisoners were marched through the town just as the Forty-eighth's train arrived, presenting rather a scaly appearance.

More Schuylkill County boys, from other Pennsylvania regiments, dropped into camp, amongst them Frank Hodgson, of the Signal Corps, "Dee" Pott and Lew Cresland. The next morning found all trying to dry themselves, after a rainy night, and in order to more rapidly stimulate the flow of the blood through the veins, many indulged in an exciting chase after calves, sheep, pigs and the like. Corn and potatoes were plenty; the boys lived well—on the country—obeying Pope's order. At 9.15 on the morning of the sixteenth the march was again resumed, and after tramping some six miles on the wrong road out of the way, the command went into camp about seven miles from Culpeper, on the banks of Cedar Creek. This location was about two miles north of the Rapidan, in full view of Slaughter or Cedar Mountain, where the recent fight between Banks and Ewell had taken place. In all the regiment's campaigns the fences never walked away so rapidly as they did at this place. There were plenty of them on the regiment's arrival, but the command "halt" scarce died away ere they melted in an instant. The great havoc made in the fresh meat found in the neighborhood at this time, caused orders to cease "living on the country" in so indiscriminate a way, to be promptly issued. Sheep, hogs, calves and chickens, not alone suffered, but heifers and even steers were brought low. The camps were all slaughter pens—the number of impromptu butchers immense. General Pope's order to subsist the troops on the country was being literally carried out, but not as he intended.

Whilst here, on the seventeenth of August, the regimental band was mustered out of the service, in compliance with orders from the War Department. The instruments were the property of the regiment, having been purchased through contributions made by the various companies, during its occupancy of Hatteras; so, now, what to do with these instruments became a question. It was finally agreed to permit the band to take them home, and there to place them in the hands of three trustees, Messrs. Frank Pott, F. B. Kaercher and Joseph Derr, all of Pottsville, who were respectfully desired to have a care to the regiment's interest in them. These gentlemen are all dead, and one of the most difficult questions to be answered is, Where are these instruments now?

Upon the eighteenth of August a special muster of the entire army took place. It was directed to be made by President Lincoln, in order to determine the actual strength of the army upon a certain day. During this day Generals Pope and McDowell rode through the camp, returning from a visit to General Reno.

It should have been stated before that the division of the Ninth Army Corps, doing duty in this campaign, was commanded by General Jesse L. Reno, not only one of the bravest officers in the service, but one of the best. The regiment always had a high estimate of Reno's abilities as a military man and believe had he lived he would have received high honors at the hands of his countrymen.

The regiment retired to rest just after "Tattoo" with three days' cooked rations in haversacks—prepared for an immediate move.

Quietly, at 11 o'clock, all were aroused—large camp fires were left burning, as the command moved off silently and quickly. The march was in an eastwardly direction, and rapidly conducted toward Stevensburg, and Fredericksburg, south of the Rappahannock and north of the Rapidan. Two creeks were forded during the night. A short halt, only to load, was had, when off again, with a caution to move forward with as little noise as possible, to accomplish which tin cups, canteens, and all rattling objects were put into the haversacks. At this point Jackson's and Longstreet's entire forces were within less than two miles. They were crossing, or had crossed, the Rapidan, bent on gaining Kelly's Ford, on the Rappahannock, to prevent General Pope's contemplated retreat or to intercept portions of his army in that retreat. Away the boys traveled rapidly, many dropping by the wayside, until after passing through the town of Stevensburg, a halt was ordered about 10 o'clock on the morning of the nineteenth in a large field, the first rest of any consequence since the night before, eleven hours of rapid marching. The tramp was resumed at 1 o'clock, after first wading a very deep creek, still at a rapid rate; five miles brought Kelly's Ford in view. It was crossed waist deep, and camp was established on the north bank of the Rappahannock. The regiment was pretty well fagged out with its severe march, probably the most severe experienced, but the ford was secured and the rebels were thwarted. Here it was learned that Pope's entire army had retreated across the Rappahannock with the loss of only a linch pin. What it all meant was a mystery then— the mystery now is, how the regiment escaped capture.

At Kelly's Ford everything indicated a brush with the enemy. The rebels were not far. On the twentieth a Sixth New Hampshire man was brought in wounded by their cavalry scouts. Reno's batteries went into position on a hill to the left of the ford. Companies A, F, I, D and C, composing the right wing, under command of Lieutenant-Colonel Sigfried, were reconnoitering all day on the south side of the river. They returned to camp at sunset, having had a sight of the rebel cavalry, but no opportunity to exchange shots. As these companies returned Company K started to relieve Company B, which company had been on picket the previous night. The three remaining companies, H, E and G had a sort of dress parade, with Captain Gilmour in command. That night every man slept with his gun in his hand. Matters were assuming a squally appearance. The presence also of the commander of the army added to the importance of the position held by the Forty-eighth. Generals Pope and McDowell, who, by the way, seemed to stick pretty close to each other during the whole of the campaign, made frequent visits to General Reno, thus giving an opportunity for the boys to see them often.

The aspect of affairs looked still more threatening on the twenty-first. General Buford's Brigade of cavalry, accompanied by a section of artillery, passed over the river, and were soon engaged in skirmishing with the enemy. A lively exchange of shots took place. Stevens' Division of infantry also crossed, and the Forty-eighth was ordered over, but this was subsequently countermanded, and a position was occupied at the river's edge, covering the ford. A natural embankment afforded excellent protection. The "rebs," however, concluded to try some other point of crossing, and no further trouble occurred at Kelly's Ford, although the night was passed with every preparation in readiness for immediate action.

At "reveille" of the twenty-second, the regiment fell into line and moved off in a westwardly direction, following the north bank of the Rappahannock River. The weather was murky, rainy and clear, by fits and starts, and intensely warm, hence marching was far from agreeable. The distant discharges of cannon, becoming more and more distinct as the march continued, indicated that trouble was brewing. A long rest occurred at Rappahannock Station, on the Orange and Alexandria Railroad. The regiment occupied a hill a little west of the station and awaited further developments. Immediately in its front, resting, stretched at full length under the shade of a tree, was the Commanding General, the plucky little Pope. The constant coming and going of officers on horseback, marked the rapidity with which the various parts of his army was moving, and indicated the approaching struggle. At 4 o'clock in the afternoon, in the midst of a drenching rain, the regiment moved off, and marching a mile and a half further up the river, bivouacked. A battery was posted in front, behind it General Stevens' Division drawn up in line of battle, and back of this Reno's Division in line. Immediately in the rear of the line of stacked muskets, the Forty-eighth dropped asleep, with the certainty of a down-pour of rain. The drenching came—thoroughly soaked, the regiment moved off early the next morning (the twenty-third), still up the river, marching slowly, with frequent halts, only making five miles by 3 p. m.

Whilst resting in a large field a terrible shower of rain came on; the lightning intensely vivid, flash rapidly succeeding flash. Not a hundred yards away the negro driver of the ammunition train was struck and killed, the shock stunning several other parties near. By 6 o'clock the regiment started again, and soon discovered that the cause of the slow marching and frequent halts was a bad place in the road. It was 9 o'clock before this swamp was crossed, the mud and water of which appeared to be three or four feet deep. The road now commenced getting hilly. It was 12 o'clock at night before the bivouac was called. A muddier, wetter or more forlorn set of men never sank down to sleep. The next day was Sunday the twenty-fourth; 4 a. m. found the Forty-eighth slowly plodding along, the route becoming more and more mountainous. The roaring of artillery sounded nearer and nearer. Whilst resting in a field behind a hill upon which a Union battery was stationed, a rebel shell, the very first the Forty-eighth had heard near, passed overhead with a "where-is-ye, where-is-ye, where-is-ye, here!" "They're throwing railroad iron," some one ejaculated. Soon came a second, then a third, and shelter was sought in a neighboring woods, whilst the battery in the front banged away at the rebel battery, and soon silenced it. The tramp was resumed, the way winding around several hills, slowly, in rear of a number of batteries that were constantly engaged in firing into the rebels, who occupied the south side of the Rappahannock River. An occasional reply was all their batteries deigned to give.

By evening the once famous "White Sulphur, or Warrenton Springs," were reached, and the night was spent a short distance beyond them. An artillery duel had been going on all day, and part of the ground now occupied by the regiment had been wrested from the enemy, this same Sunday morning, with the capturing of forty "reb" prisoners.

The beautiful weather of the twenty-fifth made all feel more comfortable, and the Springs were left just after sunrise, in jolly spirits, with a rumor floating around that Kelly's Ford was to be revisited. The lively nimbleness of a camp rumor beats Paddy's flea all hollow. About noon the pretty little town of Warrenton came in sight, where a halt of several hours took place.

Here a former officer of the regiment, Captain Edward C. Baird, then serving as Assistant Adjutant General on the staff of General Meade, called to see the boys, and Hospital Steward John Johnson, of the Fifth Pennsylvania Reserves, also dropped in. Both met with a hearty reception, and tipped a cordial canteen.

The march was resumed at 3 o'clock p. m., passing around on the south and east of the town, until the Warrenton Junction Railroad was reached; the line of the railroad was followed until 9 o'clock at night. It was a difficult march, mud abounded, and it was so dark that it was difficult to discern objects at a greater distance than the length of a man's arm. After the halt an officers' mess debated the propriety of eating some chickens secured during the day, before retiring, or to wait until the next morning. The march had been so fatiguing, it was unanimously agreed to risk the poultry until morning. An hour's march the next day (twenty-sixth) brought the regiment into camp in a large field at Warrenton Junction, where it remained all day. Many enjoyed the luxury of a good wash in a contiguous brook—the first bath since leaving Fredericksburg, fourteen days before.

More Schuylkill County friends found out the regiment at this point, amongst them Captain Wils Hartz and Lieutenant Jay Washburn.+ The latter was in the Quartermaster's Department of Siegel's command, and kindly smuggled through to Washington some letters written home by the boys.

The wagons which left the regiment at Kelly's Ford, rejoined the command, but left it again the next morning. On the twenty-seventh at daylight, the tramp commenced again, returning by the railroad tracks toward Warrenton. Two miles had been traversed, when orders to countermarch were received, and back to the Junction trudged the regiment—thence along the Orange and Alexandria Railroad toward Manasses Junction, where the rebels under "Stonewall Jackson," by a skillful flank movement, had succeeded in destroying a train of supplies, and in capturing General Pope's personal baggage. The Forty-eighth proceeded smartly on its way, resting some time at Catlett's Station, and ending the day's march at 5.30 p. m., within a short distance of a place called Haymarket, where a large body of the enemy were supposed to be. Hooker's, Reno's and Siegel's Divisions were congregated in the neighborhood. Generals Daniel E. Sickels and Phil Kearney, besides a number of other officers of note, passed through the camp of the Forty-eighth, indicating the presence of a large army—evidently a battle was imminent. On the twenty-eighth, at an early hour, the march was continued at a rapid rate toward Manasses Junction, which point was reached at noon. Here was the smouldering remains of a long train of cars containing army supplies, a memento of Stonewall's recent visit. A field just south of the station afforded a resting place, and arms were stacked. Toward evening the regiment moved off again, encamping for the night near the banks of Bull Run—Company G having acted as rear guard all day.

The next morning, Friday, August 29, 1862, camp was broken very early, and the line of march following on the Centreville Road, until, when within a mile west of the town, the regiment turned to the left, and moved toward the Gap which leads to the Shenandoah Valley, and rested on the summit of a hill in full view of the coming battle-field, that of the Second Bull Run. This point was reached at 1 o'clock in the afternoon, and orders were awaited.

Reno's Division was a fine looking body of men, and were held in high esteem by General Pope. Reno anxiously awaited the order to advance, and the men of the Forty-eighth really longed for some movement that should be full of powder and shot. This was to be the really first engagement the regiment had experienced. Newbern was felt to be merely honorary. All were more or less a trifle nervous, whilst waiting on this hill. I believe that every one felt like doing the very best possible; kind of "spoiling" to become engaged. The regiment's first fight, as stated, so all were somewhat over-patriotic and zealous. "We'll show 'em, only give us a chance; now we've got 'em; we'll give it to 'em," and the like, were ejaculations heard from the ranks. It was provoking, too, to have to wait there looking on, for the firing was terrific, and the battle was raging furiously. The artillery, posted on all the surrounding hills, poured an incessant fire of shot and shell into the dense woods, where the rebel regiments were concealed, and the sharp rattle of infantry, like the pattering of rain, roared fiercely just below the Forty-eighth's position. For two hours the regiment watched the fierce encounter, more eager every moment to become engaged—anxious to have a hand in the fray—in this it was not disappointed.

At 3 o'clock in the afternoon Nagle's Brigade drew up in line of battle, the Second Maryland on the right, the Sixth New Hampshire on the left, and, the "noble Forty-eighth" (quoted from Chaplain Beckley) fifty paces in rear of the line. Off marched the command, over a cleared field, down a fine open slope toward the dense woods out of which the enemy was to be driven.

This wood was skirted by a fence, which had scarcely been crossed —in fact the Forty-eighth was just getting over it—when bang! bang! whiz! whiz! and the fight was on, the beginning being brisk, fiery and bloody. The regiment did well, marching with the steadiness of regulars, it never quailed before the first shower of leaden hail.

General Strothers, aide on the staff of General Pope, well known as "Porte Crayon," brought the order to General Reno sending Nagle's Brigade into action, and he witnessed the advance, and says of it, "the order was promptly and gallantly executed, the troops moving in beautiful order and with admirable spirit. I accompanied the advance until they passed the guns beyond the summit and remained there admiring." He further says that "the air was lively with singing bullets," and after the brigade became engaged that "the roar of musketry was unceasing." After clearing that memorable fence, no time was allowed to dwell upon what was left behind—attention was fully needed for what was going on before. The battalions in front obliquing to the right and left, permitted the Forty-eighth to advance, which it did promptly, occupying the intervening space, when it opened a destructive fire upon the enemy. The regiment advanced firing for about a quarter of a mile, when Lieutenant-Colonel Sigfried halted it, commanded " cease firing," ordered an advance with bayonets, which were fixed. The movement was executed in good style, the enemy being driven out of two ditches, one of them being an old railroad cut, a position the rebels had not been dislodged from by either the troops engaged at this point before the Forty-eighth reached it, or after the regiment retired. Receiving a volley of musketry from the rear, and supposing that some of the union troops were firing by mistake, the Forty-eighth was ordered to the nearest ditch, and the firing to the front was resumed. The fire now poured into the Sixth New Hampshire and Forty-eighth from front, left and rear, was most terrific. The more frequently the colors were raised and spread out to the supposed friends in the rear, the more rapid became the musket firing therefrom. At last the rebel regiments made their appearance, advancing on the left and rear of the Forty-eighth. As soon as discovered the left companies of the regiment faced about and opened a lively fire on them. This contest was too unequal to last, the raking cross fire poured into the command from front, left and rear, left but one course to pursue, a retreat by the right flank, an order Colonel Sigfried gave, and one the regiment promptly executed, returning fire for fire, retiring in the rear of the approaching New York Excelsior Brigade and General Phil Kearney's Brigade, which commands became immediately actively engaged with the enemy. It is not meant to say that the regiment got out of the woods in perfect order; the men were scattered some, in fact a good deal. Kearney was exceedingly anxious to promote those retiring near where he was. All engaged can remember the occasion well, Kearney riding in with his troops—the reins guiding his horse, in his teeth, and sword in one hand, hissed through his clenched teeth: " Fall in here, you ——— ——— ——— ——— ——— ———, and I'll make major-generals of every one of you!" Some of the men under the lamented Gilmour returned to the fight with a Michigan regiment, but the commissions promised by Kearney never were forthcoming. Although the men came out of second Bull Run feeling that the longing for "just one little fight" was considerably cured, still the impetuosity of the regiment's attack was tremendous. Properly supported, it could have gone clear through the woods without a halt. The galling fire on the left flank and rear, which could have been prevented by a supporting column on that flank, was too much to require any troops to withstand. The Forty-eighth need never be ashamed of its fight that Friday afternoon; it was a brilliant one, and although unsuccessful, there remains the proud satisfaction of a duty well performed and one fully appreciated at headquarters. Woodbury, in his "Burnside and the Ninth Corps" (page 112) says: "The First Brigade of General Reno's own Division, composed of the Forty-eighth Pennsylvania, Sixth New Hampshire, and Second Maryland, was conspicuous on this day for the persistence with which it held its ground when assailed, and the gallantry with which it advanced to the attack."

It is difficult to note all the incidents of personal bravery. Colonel Nagle was everywhere cheering on the men and barely escaped capture. He was ordered to halt by the rebels several times, pursued and fired at, but escaped unharmed. His Adjutant-General, John D. Bertolette, was wounded in the thigh while ably attending to his duties, and his aids, Lieutenants Blake and Hinkle, were actively engaged throughout the entire fight. Upon entering the woods, Colonel Nagle and his staff left their horses tied to the fence on the edge of the woods. These horses were all captured by the rebels in the flanking movement mentioned. The brigade lost in killed, wounded and missing some 530 men, quite one-fifth of these going into action. Lieutenant-Colonel Sigfried was in the thickest of the fray, encouraging the men by actions, as well as words. The regiment lost some 152 in killed, wounded and missing.

One of the most melancholy features of the day was the roll-call at twilight that evening, and the noticing of the absentees. To lay bare this page of the Forty-eighth's record book would be a painful task. It cannot be forgotten who were left motionless in the dire wood, nor the unfortunate armless and legless ones. Whatever the past differences with them, all was forgotten in the one stern fact, that from henceforth they would no longer share the lot of their companions in the regiment, and the good God alone knew which of the survivors would soon be called to share theirs. Fervent prayers of thankfulness ascended to the Great White Throne that direful Friday night.

Although not personally engaged with the enemy until late in the afternoon of Saturday, the thirtieth of August, the Forty-eighth was under fire all day, and the men showed many excellent soldierly qualifications. The early morning found the regiment occupying the ground covered by it immediately after coming out of the fight of the afternoon before. A lull in the storm of leaden hail settled over the fiercely contested ground until noon, when the cannonading recommenced with all its fierceness, and roared incessantly until night. Soon the rattle of infantry added its ceaseless din to the uproar, and the work of carnage was fully at its height, extending along the entire line from left to right. The position of the brigade was changed somewhat further to the left, in rear of two other brigades. "Lie down," came the order, and down sprawled the men. The shells literally plowed up the ground all about. They sh-shssh shou'ed and banged upon all sides. The whole battlefield was visible, and presented a lively scene. An order to support the centre reached the command. Away toward the left marched the brigade, quite a distance, the shells and rifle balls filling the air with their shrieking, whistling horror. Halting in the rear of a battery that was being fearfully pressed, the regiment witnessed to the full the terrors of the battle. The battery was doing frightful execution to the rebel charging columns—opening great gaps in their ranks, and filling the ground with dead and dying men. Pope, with his staff, occupied a prominent spot immediately to the left and front of the Forty-eighth, on a knoll close up to the battery that was playing such sad havoc with the enemy. McDowell was immediately at the right of the regiment, offering words of encouragement to the fearfully slaughtered Fourteenth Brooklyn, filing back from the hot front line. Let General Strothers speak again—his account of Pope's campaign is so faithful, according so closely, as it does with the experience of the Forty-eighth, he knows whereof he writes. Of the position now occupied by Reno's Division, he says: "A division under Reno had been withdrawn from the centre and lay in reserve behind us. The fine appearance and firm attitude of these troops, with the smiling countenance of their splendid leader, served to dispel all remaining apprehension of a disgraceful rout, which for a time seemed imminent. The staff was again grouped around the commander, and we took a position with Reno's Division still under a biting fire of artillery, the air shuddering with all the varied pandemoniac notes of shell, round shot, grape, rusty spikes, and segments of railroad bars. This continued until about sunset, when the signal was given for Reno to advance. His troops, which had been massed in squares, now deployed, and advanced beautifully in two lines of battle. When they reached the edge of the woods in front, the roll of musketry commenced swelling higher and higher, until it resembled the stunning roar of Niagara. Our line, with the smoke of its fire, covered the enemy from view, but his advance could be understood by the musket balls which struck upon the open ground in front, throwing up little clouds of dust, first striking just behind our men and then advancing toward us like the big rain drops pattering on a dusty street, until we perceived ourselves enveloped in the shower, the leaden drops striking among and beyond us. As the enemy's infantry would fall back repulsed these insidiously fatal showers would cease, and the more appalling, but really less dangerous, storm of artillery would recommence, while Reno took advantage of the lull to change the position of his lines, the first line retiring and the second advancing by right of companies, threading through and reforming each on the ground just occupied by the other. This pretty manœuvre was repeated a number of times with a coolness and accuracy that would have been applauded on a parade ground, and as often as the enemy hurled his columns upon our position he met a bloody repulse from the steady fire of these veterans. I do not remember how many of these attacks were thus repulsed, but I am under the impression that there were four or five, and perhaps more. The enemy must have suffered severely here. Our loss was trifling, as I saw very few men fall, and very few wounded carried to the rear."

If "Porte Crayon" had been a member of the Forty-eighth, he could not have given a truer description of its position. How faithfully he has noted the movement through the small pines, and indeed he seems to have left no single point untouched. The regiment was the last to leave the bloody battlefield, and covered the retreat of the entire army to Centreville. It was 4 o'clock in the morning of the thirty-first, when the Forty-eighth reached this latter point, soaked to the skin, a heavy rain having closed over the scenes of the day. This was Sunday, and a damp, murky day it was, the endeavor to secure some rest proved futile for back over a portion of the last night's road trudged the regiment, in support of a battery posted on the Bull Run Road. On the way the Ninety-sixth Pennsylvania was encountered, and such a handshaking as took place between the two Schuylkill County regiments—it was their first meeting, and the boys of both commands were delighted with the occasion.

By evening the Forty-eighth returned to Centreville and a pretty fair night's rest was had, preparatory to the hard work of September 1.

How unprepared the command was for the battle of Chantilly. An engagement was expected to be sure, for the troops were hunting around for one, but the opening shots found many of the men of the regiment up the apple trees of some poor unfortunate's orchard, gathering all the luscious fruit within reach. The first shower of rebel bullets brought these chaps scampering out of the trees to their places in line, their pockets, shirts and mouths filled with apples. Many, from the appearance of their shirts, looked as though they had suddenly grown immensely corpulent, and so excited or scared was one of the fellows of G, that when Lieutenant Pollock desired a portion of his find, eagerly raised his arms and shoulders up, pulling his shirt out of his trousers, and as the fruit rolled down over his legs and feet to the ground, exclaimed: "Here, take 'em all!" The constitutional cowards, of which the Forty-eighth had but a few, were caught fast this time, and were put to the most desperate shifts to get to the rear. The first volley was succeeded by a lull, permitting the command to get into a good position in the woods, on the right of the line, whilst immediately on the left, the Roundheads (One Hundredth Pennsylvania) went charging into the woods, led by their former Colonel, the gallant General Isaac I. Stevens. He fell with the regimental colors in his hand. It was here, too, the brave Kearney lost his life.

Lieutenant-Colonel W. S. Clark, of the Twenty-first Massachusetts Regiment, told the writer that he witnessed the shooting of General Kearney. Having become detached from his regiment during the fight, Clark found himself within the enemy's lines, and to conceal himself lay close to the ground behind bushes. In an opening beyond was Kearney on horseback, with a cordon of rebel rifles leveled at and surrounding him. The enemy evidently wished to capture him, not kill him, but Kearney, when called upon to surrender, drove the spurs into his horse's flanks and with an oath dashed over the men before him—out blazed the murderous rifles and the typical American soldier dropped a corpse.

The Forty-eighth, although exposed to the rebel fire, held the position assigned it until long after dark. The bivouac was on the hill behind the apple orchard alluded to, until 3 o'clock a. m. of the second of September, when it took up the line of march for Alexandria.

What a grand spectacle the Chantilly fight presented! A terrible rain storm with terrific thunder and lightning prevailed during its continuance—this, combined with the booming of cannon and rattle of musketry, made up a most indescribable scene, outrivaling pandemonium itself. It was a terrific, horrible, phantasmagoria.

How eventful are the memories clustering around this campaign—a campaign, by-the-by, but little appreciated except by those actively engaged therein. The politicians and the press are responsible for robbing General Pope of the glory and honor essentially due him, for one of the most brilliant campaigns of the war. These great powers were educated into their belief of Pope as a great failure, through the influence wielded by the Army of the Potomac. This army at the time was so bound up in General McClellan, that any movement not directly under his supervision was deemed of slight importance, and its character belittled. Despite the action of later years, Fitz John Porter had it in his power to give the enemy a crushing blow at Second Bull Run, and thus have made General Pope the American people's hero of the hour, but this would have cast a shadow over the bright fame of McClellan.

His inaction that fated Friday afternoon nipped Pope's already increasing popularity in the bud, and kept the fame of McClellan in the ascendancy.

However, the Forty-eighth has no regrets, save the loss of brave fellows sacrificed, for its part in the campaign, and it has no cause for shame—its record will bear the most searching inquiry. Woodbury, in his book on page 107, says, "But whatever may be said of other parts of General Pope's command, that portion of the Ninth Corps, which came under his direction, did its whole duty in the most gallant and praiseworthy manner."

The Forty-eighth left the scene of the Chantilly fight at 3 o'clock a. m., of September 2, 1862, as stated. The rain had rendered the roads almost impassable—the mud was ankle deep. By sunrise Fairfax was reached, and a half hour's rest vouchsafed, after which a mile's further journey on the Alexandria road found the entire brigade stretched across the fields on either side of the road, stopping stragglers and "skedaddlers" from getting away. This was amusing work. The Forty-eighth occupied the road, and in a little while had halted nearly a regiment of these demoralized fellows.

By 9 o'clock the same morning the march was resumed. Alexandria was reached at 6 o'clock p. m., without a single rest, and camp pitched some two miles west of the town. The One Hundred-and-twenty-ninth Pennsylvania was encamped within a mile and a half, and the next day, the third, many of the Forty-eighth found their way to its camp, and many of the One Hundred-and-twenty-ninth visited the Forty-eighth. Among whom were Adjutant Green, Quartermaster Patterson, Lieutenants Clemens and Coho, and Captain William Wren.

A much delayed mail reached the regiment on the fourth, and whilst busy reading the numerous letters received, orders to "fall in" sounded, and by 9 p. m. the line of march was once more resumed. The route lay through Alexandria toward Washington. With but two rests the Long Bridge was reached by 2 o'clock a. m. Crossing the bridge into Washington City, the Forty-eighth trudged the streets without a single rest, and bivouacked in a grove on the east side of Seventh street, at its northern limit. Excessive marching, exposure to all kinds of weather, with the Bull Run and Chantilly fights thrown in, left the regiment in a pretty well used up condition, and it was hoped when this point in

Washington was reached after this last most severe march, time would be allowed for some recuperation. Early on the morning of the fifth, the command moved across Seventh street, and went into a sort of regular camp as well as it could without tents, knapsacks, or other baggage. A visit into Washington City exhibited wonderful improvements in the place within a year, the war had infused an enterprise unheard of before. Burnside, the ever popular and loved Commander of the Ninth Corps, visited the camps, and as usual the "boys" gave him rousing cheers. The pie and cake venders, who infested the camps, suffered greatly on and after the sixth, by reason of General Reno's order forbidding the sale to the troops of these articles of diet. The men consoled themselves with watermelons, peaches and ripe fruit generally. New clothing, blankets, knapsacks, etc., were issued to the command to replace those lost at Second Bull Run.

Bv't Brig. Gen'l Joshua K. Sigfried.

Bv't Brig. Gen'l Henry Pleasants.

Brig. Gen'l James Nagle.

Colonel Geo. W. Gowen.

Lieut. Col. Richard M. Jones.

CHAPTER VI.

McCLELLAN'S LAST CAMPAIGN.

Bright and early Sunday morning, September 7, the regiment was astir ready to leave at 8 o'clock, but the line did not move until eleven. A dusty, dirty march of some ten miles brought the command to a small place called Leesboro. At this point information was received of the reorganization of the Army of the Potomac, placing Burnside in command of the right wing of that army. Reno succeeded him in command of the Ninth Corps, Sturgis got the Second Division and Nagle remained in charge of the First Brigade.

The muster of the troops on the thirty-first of August having been impracticable owing to the Bull Run fight, it took place by orders, at Leesboro, on the eighth of September, and here also a further reduction in baggage was required, by which each regiment was only allowed four baggage wagons. This reduction brought about a proposition to consolidate the officers' mess. This proposition was agreed to and the consolidation was perfected, with Sergeant, subsequently Lieutenant, Edwards, of Company I, as caterer and general superintendent. Johnny Howell, of Company H, was made chief cook, with two colored men to assist in the heavy work.

Lieutenant, afterward Colonel, Gowen was selected as treasurer. The dining hall was to consist of five tent flies. The whole proposition was born, lived and died in just one day. It never materialized.

During the same day shelter tents were issued to the command, for the first time—an abode all soon became used to.

On the ninth at 4 o'clock a. m. the regiment was again on the move, in a northerly direction. The march covered from ten to fifteen miles, and the night's encampment was in a field adjoining the village of Brookville. The route lay through a pleasant country, abounding in handsome residences, and here and there were gathered in groups, ladies and gentlemen, to witness the passage of the troops.

An all day's rest on the tenth permitted the indulgence in the luxuries of the surrounding country—chickens, corn bread and the like. At 3 o'clock a. m. of the eleventh the regiment was routed out and left camp at daylight, bound, so Lieutenant-Colonel Sigfried informed the men, some two or possibly five miles—certainly not more than seven. The route was northwest. The little town of Unity, where a plentiful supply of apples was provided by one of its whole-souled Union men, was passed, and the night's camp was located some two miles north of Damascus, which village had been gone through, the Forty-eighth having made thirteen miles instead of the seven promised.

Seven o'clock the next morning found the regiment on the go. The march was slow and easy—enlivened here and there by the waving of handkerchiefs by the ladies, and cheers of the men living along the route. The Baltimore and Ohio Railroad was crossed near New Market, in which pretty little town a rest of two hours was had, where it was learned that the rebel forces had occupied the place the evening before. The march was resumed at 2 p. m., the little village of Kemptown was passed through, the bivouac made on the west side of the Monocacy, near the large stone bridge, and in sight of Frederick City. The Johnnies had attempted to blow up this bridge, but failed.

The start on the thirteenth was not made until 3.30 p. m., and the tramp through Frederick was a perfect ovation. The Stars and Stripes were visible upon all sides. Old and young, ladies, men and boys waving it at every house. Cheering greeted the troops at every step. Cool water stood before every house, and good things in abundance were given the men.

"We couldn't do this last Sunday, boys, so we'll do it now while we have a chance," shouted two young fellows, who were riding about on horseback, carrying an immense American flag. This outburst of enthusiasm was undoubtedly genuine, and cheered the troops up wonderfully. The way was through the main street, by the residence of Barbara Fritchie, who is remembered as a very old lady sitting at a window on the first story of her little home, with a very diminutive Union flag in her hand. Leaving the town by the pike, a march of eight miles brought Middletown in view, when at 9.30 p. m. camp was made. The writer has personally very vivid recollections of this night's camp, for 'twas here that prince of foragers, Adam Hendley, of Company K, presented him with a fine turkey. When Adam's haversack was empty, it was an indication of the country being campaigned in. If anything was to be had, he knew where and how to get it.

A bright full moon lighted the boys to bed that night—the last night some of the poor fellows were to have on earth.

Little did any one dream that the sun rose, this calm Sunday morning, September 14, for the last time to many a brave soul, and ere its setting yonder mountain would be ablaze with bursting shot and shell, and the air heavy-laden with quick whistling bullets.

"Fall in! Fall in!" sounded through the camp. The Forty-eighth promptly obeyed the command. Quietly marching through the peaceful village of Middletown, thoughts of home were awakened in seeing the children going to Sabbath school, and their gathering seemed holy and happy, as viewed through the open door of the neat little church. How great the contrast—without and within—the troops marching to the field of mortal strife, they gaining strength to battle for immortality.

Crossing the creek at the edge of the town, through the water—the fleeing rebels having destroyed the little bridge—pushing on up the hill, part of the way through rough fields, and again on the road, the cannonading growing louder, and coming nearer. Soon musketry commenced to rattle, and the Forty-eighth knew what that betokened. Turning off the road, to the left, into a corn field, the regiment deployed in line of battle, and pushing up the hill through the corn stalks, with showers of minie bullets whizzing through the air overhead, indicating the approaching conflict—reached a stone fence where a short halt was ordered. The knapsacks were unslung and packed behind this fence. Crack! crack! bang! whiz! bang! It was growing lively in front, the crowds of wounded pushing through the ranks of the Forty-eighth, on their way to the rear, showed that it was hot.

A group of dusty gray prisoners—amongst them a tall North Carolinian, who stretched his long neck out, as though peering into futurity, or adjusting it for a halter—convinced the regiment that the enemy was being shoved up the hill. "Forward, Forty-eighth!" On pushed the regiment until a little wooden knoll overlooking Fox's Pass was reached. On the opposite side of the ravine the enemy had a brass piece, from which they had the impudence to fire right into the command. Durrell's Battery soon put a stop to this nonsense—the first shot it fired landed right over the gun, and a great scampering took place. Nothing could induce those fellows to return for their gun—so the Union troops got it. Toward night the Forty-eighth retired from this wooded knoll into a cleared field immediately behind and the knapsacks were brought up. The firing, however, recommenced on the left, and the regiment was ordered to the front again. It advanced promptly over the wooded knoll to the front line along the fence which surrounded the little triangular field overlooking the house and garden, where the rebel dead were so thickly strewn around—Company B was thrown into the woods as skirmishers, covering and guarding the left flank of the regiment. Just as this position was assumed the firing slackened off—the foe seeming to have retired—but it was only a temporary lull. Two regiments were in reserve—behind the Forty-eighth—one to the left rear and the other to the right rear. The gathering shades of night were gradually shutting in surrounding objects, when the gallant Reno rode down the line of the regiment from left to right, and halting a short distance from the right, in a clear space, was observing the position of the rebel lines. A furious volley of musketry poured into the ranks, so suddenly and unexpectedly that the regiments in reserve replied equally as furiously, much to the great discomfiture of the Forty-eighth, as it brought the command between two fires. This onslaught ceased as suddenly as it began, and silence ensued, but how sad the consequences. During that fire Reno fell, mortally wounded, and who can say what bullets pierced him—friend's or foe's? Ah! the little General was well loved—his loss was a great blow to the Ninth Corps; the bitterness would have been lessened but for the lingering doubt of his having been killed by rebel shots.

As General Reno was being carried to the rear, on a stretcher, he hailed General Sturgis, in his characteristic cheerful manner. "Halloo, Sam, I'm dead!" His tone was so firm and natural that his friend could not believe him seriously hurt, and replied, "Oh, no, General, not so bad as that, I hope." "Yes, yes," he repeated, "I'm dead, good by," and died a few moments after.*

This disastrous volley was the first fire on the skirmishers, for soon after the sad occurrence related, the engagement again became general, and fast and furious came the leaden showers from rebel muskets. The regiment did as much in reply; shot was answered by shot, sixty rounds of ammunition per man was expended, and some of the boys were so excited that they forgot to withdraw their ramrods, in consequence of which the good fence, which kindly sheltered them from the deadly fire of the enemy, was tastefully decorated with several of these articles. The men of the regiment behaved admirably in this fight. The confusion occasioned by the regiments in reserve firing into the Forty-eighth was calculated to throw the best troops into disorder. The line, however, remained intact, and many of the officers and men assisted in arresting the disorder in the reserved regiments. The men were cool and collected, they fired deliberately, those of the rear rank rising to avoid the possibility of harming a front rank man. Hostilities ceased when it became too dark to distinguish objects ahead. The Second

---

* Strother's Personal Recollections of the War.

Maryland coming up relieved the Forty-eighth, which retired to replenish empty cartridge boxes and fill up nature's haversack. A first-rate night's sleep was had in the corn field immediately behind the stone fence, where the knapsacks had first been left, and the command awoke the next morning much refreshed.

During the night the "rebs" had decamped and South Mountain was in the undisputed possession of the Union troops. The result of the preceding day's work was curiously examined. Sergeant Robert Smith, of G, obtaining permission to go on a tour of observation, reported back in about an hour, that he had counted 105 bodies of dead rebels immediately around the little triangular field, one side of which the Forty-eighth occupied! Sickening horrors and dreadful sights surrounded the house and garden referred to before. A well in this garden became the grave of seventy-five dead Confederates. A rude board, marking the spot, had roughly carved upon it the letters "C. S. A." War makes brutes of human beings, these dead soldiers were men like those burying them, but no one stopped to think of that; haste to cover them out of sight was the principal thing, and the well afforded a convenient receptacle!

Procuring a fresh supply of ammunition, the Forty-eighth moved off at noon, of the fifteenth, going through Fox's Pass, westerly, noting at every step the sad havoc made in the ranks of the retreating foe. Many a stark dead body marked the ground they had been driven from; there were instances where they were piled on the side of the road, having been dragged out of the way of the wheels of the artillery. A number of straggling Johnnies were picked up on the way, rather glad at being made prisoners. A halt was called at 6 o'clock in the evening, and whilst preparing to bivouac in a large field, General Burnside came along, and directed a further move forward. An hour and a half additional marching was made before the command halted for the night.

The advance was continued on the sixteenth, the Forty-eighth moving at 3 p. m., but only making about a mile, taking up a position in a gully behind a corn field, to the left of a wagon road. At this point, and indeed all day, the command was exposed to the fire of the rebel batteries, stationed on the bluffs bordering on Antietam Creek. It was not a pleasant sensation to the men of the Forty-eighth, lying still, hiding in a gully behind a corn field, listening to the bursting of shells all about. The lack of provisions was a serious inconvenience at this time, so General Burnside was gladly welcomed as he came riding up with encouraging news respecting rations. He urged all to do the best they could for the time—that a few days would bring all the food needed—that the advanced position the regiment had constantly occupied placed the wagon trains far in the rear. This advice, or rather counsel, could well be relished, as some of the Forty-eighth had seen General Burnside, the same morning, breakfasting on one ear of corn, which he had roasted for himself. So long as the beloved commander shared the privations of his corps, his soldiers willingly endured empty haversacks. The regiment received a fine supply of rations the same night, however, about 12 o'clock.

Those were no unmeaning sounds that awakened the men of the Forty-eighth early on the morning of the seventeenth of September, 1862. How the hills and vales reverberated with the roar of many cannon, thundering along the banks of the meandering Antietam Creek, and hurling their death shots into the camps of the enemy, answered by the equally terrific shower of deadly missiles whirled into the ranks of the Union Army, from the mouths of rebel guns. 'Twas a fearful morning—fit harbinger of the bloody scenes to follow.

The regiment moved up to take part in the work allotted it most gloriously, and right well it maintained the proud record made at Second Bull Run, Chantilly and South Mountain.

Charles Carleton Coffin, under the *nom-de-plume* of "Carleton," gives, in a little book called "Following the Flag," one of the best descriptions of the battle of Antietam. His account of the portion of the line occupied by Sturgis' Division of the Ninth Corps, is so faithful that it is here given:

"General Burnside's task was the hardest of all. The banks of the river by the lower bridge are steep and high, and the land on both sides is broken. The road leading to the bridge winds down a narrow ravine. The bridge is of stone, with three arches. It is 12 feet wide and 150 feet long. The western bank is so steep that one can hardly climb it. Oak-trees shade it. Half way up the hill there is a limestone quarry,—excavations affording shelter to sharpshooters. At the top there is a stone-wall, a hundred feet above the water of the winding stream, and yet so near that a stone may be thrown by a strong armed man across the stream. A brigade of rebels, with four pieces of artillery, guarded the bridge. There were sharpshooters beneath the willows and in the thick underbrush along the bank of the stream. There were riflemen in the excavations on the hillside, and behind the trees. The four cannon were behind the wall, with the great body of infantry in support. The bridge, the hills and hollows on the eastern bank are raked and searched in every part by the infantry."

In getting into the position assigned, the Forty-eighth moved rapidly over the ground in the corn field overlooking Antietam Creek and did not linger long around the old log building, or behind the fence skirting the creek, but inclining to the right, across the wagon road, formed the first line of battle within the shelter of a wooded knoll just over and immediately in front of the stone bridge.

The regiment was placed here to support the charge of the Second Maryland and Sixth New Hampshire in an effort to secure the bridge. The four left companies, B, G, K and E, being the only ones advantageously posted for proper execution, did good work in directing the enemy's attention away from the operations at the bridge. It was here that a number of the officers of the regiment tried their hands at shooting. Especially active in this way was Lieutenant Douty, of K, and Captain Wren, of B. The writer confesses to a little of the same exercise himself, and he remembers a man of his own company being terribly frightened by what he supposed was a mortal wound. A minie ball passed between his legs, just cutting the skin on the inside of one of them, and going through the bottom of his canteen. The water poured down his legs, and having been warmed by the sun, he imagined it was blood. He was greatly relieved when he learned the truth. The rebels on the opposite bluff were fair targets, and the men of the regiment made it lively for them.

"The Second Maryland and Sixth New Hampshire charge upon the bridge. Instantly the hillside blazed anew with musketry. There were broad sheets of flame from the wall upon the crest, where the cannon, double shotted, poured streams of canister upon the narrow passage. The head of the column melted in an instant. Vain the effort. The troops fell back under cover of the ridge sheltering the road leading to Rohrback's." *

The slaughter was terrible, and many a poor fellow was left with his "toes turned up to the daisies."

Another effort must be made, and this time the Second Brigade (Ferrero's) was selected. As in the first attempt, two regiments were used, the Fifty-first Pennsylvania and the Fifty-first New York, under the command of the Colonel of the first, named John F. Hartranft. Like the wise, cool-headed, safe commander of troops he always proved himself to be, Hartranft first inspected the ground approaching the bridge, and finding that the shortest cut led directly down the slope immediately off of the bluff occupied by the Forty-eighth, he determined

---

* Following the Flag, p. 261.

to make the rush from there. Massing his own regiment and the Fifty-first New York behind the Forty-eighth, at a given signal they rushed down the open hillside, led by himself, and never once stopped until they had swept over the bridge, clearing a path for others to follow.

"Carleton" in his admirable account says: "The long, dark column is in motion. It emerges from the shelter of the ridge. Again the hillside and the wall above became a sheet of flame. Up to the bridge, upon it, dash the men in blue, their eyes glaring, their muscles iron, their nerves steel. The front rank goes down. Men pitch headlong from the parapet into the water. Stones fly from the arches. Shells, shrapnel, canister tear the ranks asunder, but on to the centre of the bridge and across it, with a yell louder than the battle, up the steep hillside, creeping, climbing, holding their breath, summoning all the heroism of life, all energy into one effort, charging with the gleaming bayonet, they drive the rebels from the bushes, the trees, the quarries, the wall!"

What an opportunity the Forty-eighth lost! Had it rushed from its sheltered knoll down the hillside, while the Second Maryland and Sixth New Hampshire were struggling up the road, nothing could have prevented the capture of the bridge by the first brigade. But this is an aftersight—the bridge was wrested from the enemy and almost immediately came the command, "Forward," and the Forty-eighth rushed down the hillside, over the bridge, up the steep declivity to the top of the bluffs, from which the enemy were fleeing at a rapid rate. Going up the steep road, the body of a rebel officer was seen propped up against a tree. "Captain," said Private Clem Evans, "may I get that officer's sword?" The desired permission was given. He returned to the ranks with the trophy in a few moments, saying that he did not secure the belt because the man was not quite dead! Later in the fight, Evans, too much burdened with his find, asked his Captain to accept it, otherwise he would throw it away. The Captain took it, and it is still among his treasures of the war.

On reaching the top of the bluff, the left companies were at once deployed as skirmishers, and this skirmish line reached to the top of the second hill in time to observe the Ninth New York (Hawkins' Zouaves) make their famous charge. The rebel artillery made it most wofully hot for the skirmishers, on this open hill top, and the line got under cover behind a large hay-rick, where the enemy's operations could be observed with more comfort and safety. The Second Brigade in the meantime forming line of battle, advanced and occupied the summit of the hill, thus allowing the Forty-eighth's skirmish line an opportunity of rejoining the regiment. Soon word came to move to the front line, and how well it was executed—beautifully the regiment in line of battle swept up the hill, scarce a waver discernible, passing the Ninth New Hampshire at the foot, just returned from an unsuccessful effort to climb the hill, and who cheered the Forty-eighth lustily as it swept on.

"The Division re-entered the fight with the greatest alacrity and enthusiasm, and, though they were already somewhat exhausted and short of ammunition, they presented a bold front and with great courage held the enemy at bay."*

The command did not walk all the way up that hill—it literally crawled a considerable distance. It wasn't healthy to exhibit much of one's person in that locality, and care was exercised in this respect.

The men of the Fifty-first Pennsylvania, lying flat on the ground, were blazing away, whilst the Forty-eighth crept as close behind them as possible. When the Fifty-first's ammunition gave out, the Forty-eighth relieved it—the men scratching forward into the places occupied by the men of the Fifty-first, whilst they crawled out and took the places left vacant by those of the Forty-eighth.

My! that was a hot place! Thermometer way up above the nineties. Whiz! whip! chung! the bullets came pelting into the ranks. With a bang and a splutter along came that destructive old shell, which filled Douty's eyes with dirt, and bruised his shoulder, tore off Sergeant Seward's leg and left Sergeant Trainer minus one arm, as it drove the ramrod he was just replacing into poor Cullen's breast. Cullen jumped to his feet, tore open his shirt to show his captain the wound, and then dropped dead at Winlack's feet. Ah! many a fine fellow met his death on the top of that hill and many another carries sad mementoes, gathered at its summit. The boys never faltered however—no; cheered on by Sigfried's encouraging cry, "Stand your ground, men—the Fifty-first are behind you as supports! the brave Hartranft and his good men, although without ammunition are determined to back up the Forty-eighth with cold steel!" the line held its ground. Thus the fight went on, the honor of Pennsylvania being maintained by two of her best regiments, either willing to sacrifice all sooner than have her fair fame tarnished.

Holding that hill was too big a task for two infantry regiments without ammunition—even the generals thought that—especially as the artillery could not get into position to offer support; so, having exhausted

---

* Woodbury's "Burnside and Ninth Corps," p. 148.

every cartridge, the Forty-eighth and Fifty-first retired obliquely toward the right to the bank of the creek, where, after replenishing the empty cartridge boxes, the Forty-eighth moved up to the front again, just as the day faded away. Company G was placed on the front line, deployed as skirmishers, to keep watch for the night.

Solemn thoughts crowd the mind during the silent watches of the night succeeding a hard fought battle. Men who arose that morning full of health and life had been called to their long account, and those left behind might well wonder what the coming day would bring forth—where the next twenty-four hours would find this night's survivors. These thoughts were quickly dissipated by the appearance of Quartermaster-Sergeant Wagner, with a fine lot of boiled beef and fresh coffee, which he had prepared by the cooks and all the men of the regiment he found in the rear. What a relish that midnight repast had. But, oh, my! the long pull Jake's soothing syrup canteen was subjected to! Ah! it was the most delicious draught mortal ever quaffed!

The morning of the eighteenth found the regiment occupying the front line, a little to the left of the spot defended so fiercely the day before. The fight of the eighteenth was nothing more than picket-firing—both sides seemed to be exhausted. "One crowd was afraid and the other darsen't," as the youngsters say. General Grant commanding at Antietam wouldn't have been so quiet on the eighteenth, and thus given Lee the opportunity he took advantage of to get back into Virginia. Picket, or rifle pit firing isn't pleasant any way, and the Forty-eighth suffered from it—a number were killed and wounded. Amongst the former brave Sergeant Prince, of Company B. Whilst humanely trying to give a wounded comrade just over the skirmish line some water for his parched lips, a minie ball pierced his heart. His death-cry as he leaped in the air, and fell to rise no more, is still heard in the ear of imagination.

The long hours of that weary day were passed in waiting and watching for the reinforcements promised by McClellan, away the afternoon before. Hour after hour passed, still no rest, no sign of the approaching troops; tired, exhausted, hungry, and weary, the position was tenaciously maintained. At 5 p. m. the anxiously awaited orders to retire to make way for other troops reached the command, and the regiment's arduous task was ended. The bridge over Antietam Creek, so fiercely wrested from the enemy some thirty hours before, was recrossed, and an encampment had in an adjacent field, where straw was plentiful, and the night's rest was a good one. The memories of the bloody work endured on those Antietam hills bound the remnant of the Forty-eighth asleep on the banks of the creek, as no other tie could, and each man felt drawn closer to his fellow, through the dangers shared together.

Early on the morning of the nineteenth intelligence was received of Lee's retreat across the Potomac, and orders were promulgated to be ready to move at a moment's notice, with two days' rations in haversacks. At 10.30 a. m. the regiment moved off, across the bridge so gallantly won from the foe, over the battle ground of two days before, and rested upon the Sharpsburg road, just on the edge of the town.

At this point Colonel James Nagle rode up, and inasmuch as he had just been made a Brigadier General of Volunteers, receiving his commission on the battlefield of Antietam, a speech was demanded. The speech was made, and as the General rode off the air resounded with the Forty-eighth's congratulatory cheers.

The march was resumed in a southwestwardly direction. Near the Antietam Iron Works the regiment went into camp, remaining here until the twenty-sixth of September, but not without incident. At 4 a. m. of the twenty-third the command was routed up rapidly and ordered under arms at once.

It appears intelligence reached General Burnside that the rebels intended to recross the Potomac between the point occupied by the Forty-eighth and Harper's Ferry. The alarm was temporary—the only loss sustained being a couple of hours sleep.

There were several unsuccessful attempts made to move and when the move finally came, on the twenty-sixth of September, it only resulted in a march of two or three miles. The regiment went into camp in a large field—with Clark's Battery, Fourth United States Artillery, bordering directly on it. Sturgis' entire Division (second) was congregated in close quarters. The fields of the whole neighborhood were occupied by troops.

The Forty-eighth remained here, undisturbed, until the seventh of October. During this sojourn frequent excursions (or incursions might be the better word) were made into the surrounding country for provisions other than hard tack and salt horse.

A soldier's taste becomes dainty after he's in camp a while, and your army fare must give way to more delicate food. Visits to Sharpsburg were indulged in to thoroughly inspect that battered old town. The close proximity of the Ninety-sixth, One Hundred-and-twenty-ninth and other Pennsylvania regiments, composed in part of Schuylkill County men, gave occasion for an interchange of friendly visits with the Forty-eighth, such as had not previously occurred. The curious had ample opportunity in such visits to examine the army balloons—as the ascensions were made from a neighboring field to Sharpsburg. Dress parades were held by brigades. Being very closely encamped, this manœuvre was perfectly convenient, and the effect eminently satisfactory—much enjoyed by the participants. Another interesting occurrence happening at this point was the presentation by the citizens of Norristown, of two new and exceedingly handsome flags, to their much-prized regiment, the Fifty-first Pennsylvania. The ceremonies were witnessed by the men of the Forty-eighth with almost as much pleasure as the recipients themselves. Drills, inspections, etc., were resumed—a regular daily routine of duty observed.

A rapid packing up took place on the thirtieth of September, owing to orders for a move being promulgated—which were discovered to have been a mistake, when an unpacking soon settled the regiment again.

Schuylkill County visitors began pouring in, and hearty receptions were accorded them. It might be noted here that this influx of visitors continued all along until the advance into Virginia, the twenty-seventh of October following. It was at this camp that the business of grating corn on home-made graters (a piece of tin jabbed full of holes) became an occupation of daily occurrence. Much fried mush was the consequence. It was here also that the entire army was reviewed by President Lincoln, Generals McClellan and Burnside. This was a review of more than usual significance. The greater part of the Ninth Corps was drawn up in line in a field adjoining the camp of the Forty-eighth. General Nagle's Brigade (first) was on the right—the second next, and so on. To the right were the batteries, and way in the rear the cavalry. Upon the approach of the President, a salute of twenty-one guns was fired and three rousing cheers given by the men. Then Mr. Lincoln, accompanied by Generals McClellan and Burnside, followed by an immense staff and cavalry escort, reviewed all the troops. The thin, care-worn appearance of the President is distinctly remembered—a marked change from a year before. He was dressed in a suit of black, with a heavy band of crape on his high black hat. At the conclusion of the review he passed through the camp of the Forty-eighth, riding between the line of tents and Clark's Battery. "Which is 'im?" said a sorrel-topped Irishman of the battery, as he rushed out of his tent to see the President. The lank, ungainly form, mounted on a small-sized horse, his feet almost touching the ground, was pointed out to him. With a disgusted look he gave vent to an exclamation more forcible than elegant, and immediately sank back into his tent. A notable incident of the review was the fact of General Burnside participating in it, without his sword on—an omission, he afterward explained, caused by sheer forgetfulness.

On Sunday, October 5, the entire brigade, with sidearms, marched to McClellan's headquarters—where a service was held, conducted by Chaplain Holman, of the Forty-eighth. General Burnside was present.

When the regiment disembarked at Acquia Creek Landing to join Pope's Army, a lot of boxes, bundles, etc., were left behind. This delayed baggage reached camp on the sixth of October, in charge of E. H. Silliman, of G, the "Little Corporal."

Here McClellan's stringent order, in regard to straggling whilst on the march, was promulgated.

Tuesday, October 7, following this strict order, saw the command astir before daylight, and off to Pleasant Valley by 6.30 a. m.

The march was over an abandoned road, leading across the South Mountain at one of its highest points. It was a difficult tramp—the road in places being almost perpendicular. When the summit of the mountain was reached, a glimpse of the valley just marched through, revealed a stretch of grand scenery. Farms spread out beneath and beyond as far as the eye could reach—whilst the winding Potomac was lost to sight amidst the hills far away to the northwest. It was but a glance vouchsafed as the regiment rapidly passed on, but the impression remains to this day.

Descending the mountain on the east side, Pleasant Valley was reached, and here was a lovely piece of country indeed. By 1.30 p. m. camp was pitched on the hill at the western side of the valley. It was most delightfully located, on a charming bit of ground, some two miles from Sandy Hook. The hills stretching up on either side of the valley were filled with camps. The scene was delightfully picturesque—especially at night, the camp fires dotting the landscape for miles.

The reveille and tattoo never sounded so beautifully, during the whole service, as in Pleasant Valley. The first clear notes of a solitary bugle sounding out the reveille, then bands and drum corps, from the innumerable camps spreading over the valley—swelling out in the air, and anon gradually fading away, made up a harmonious "concord of sweet sounds" seldom equaled, and, once heard, never forgotten.

The regiment remained in this delightful locality from the seventh to the twenty-seventh of October, 1862, which gave ample opportunity for friends from home to visit the command, and every day found plenty of these visitors in camp. The prisoners captured during Pope's campaign, who had been paroled, and subsequently exchanged, rejoined the regiment in Pleasant Valley. The mess was greatly improved by the ample supply of good things to be had from the farmers in the vicinity. Apple dumplings became a staple dish. To all of these comforts and delights, the blessing of most charming weather for the most of the stay, was vouchsafed. The brilliant moonlight nights, lovely sunrises and charming sunsets, were exceedingly enjoyable. Fine log-cabin huts, with canvas roof, were indulged in by the company officers, and quite a rivalry sprang up as to which quarters should be the grandest and snuggest. Regular drills and school for officers were resumed. On the fifteenth of October, an order to be in readiness to move at a moment's notice, caused considerable uneasiness, but not coming on the sixteenth, the regiment felt easier; but an order read on dress parade the same evening, to be constantly ready to move on short notice, kept the command continually stirred up. From this camp frequent visits were made to Harper's Ferry, where, owing to the destruction of the bridges, the Potomac had to be crossed on a pontoon bridge. The ruins of the United States Arsenal at Harper's Ferry, with its accompanying manufacturing shops, was evidence of the devastating hand of war. Leaving the pile of broken walls and ruined machinery, climbing the adjacent heights, an earthwork thrown up to resist an attack from Bolivar Heights, first met the view. The relic hunter could here satisfy his appetite in that line, for the ground was strewn with pieces of shell, shot, old belts, canteens, etc. This is the knoll of ground around and on which the village of Harper's Ferry lies. From its summit a magnificent view is had. Looking down the Potomac, the Loudon Heights rises in sublime grandeur to the right, whilst the Maryland Heights, equally grand, towers up upon the left, and the Bolivar Heights frowns over all in the rear. Away to the right flows the Shenandoah—pitching with great force over the rapids at the Ferry, while to the left the meandering Potomac comes as quickly along, and the two uniting immediately beneath, flow on in one grand river! Jutting out boldly from the sides of Loudon Heights—watching over the destinies of the Potomac, is the Old Man of the Mountain— a face and head formed of solid rock. Turning around, the Bolivar Heights, with its hundreds of camps, confronted the beholder, and here as far as the eye could reach, the ground was dotted with innumerable tents—an army of thousands occupied them! Descending, a view was had from "Jefferson's Rock," revealing the Shenandoah in a different light—perched as this rock is, directly over it, whilst straight down the precipitous side of the hill, lies the town. One turns from the dizzy eminence with a feeling of relief.

Thus, by frequent visits in the neighborhood, the Pleasant Valley Camp was relieved of the monotony of "awaiting orders" life.

On the twenty-second of October, the commissions for the officers promoted by reason of General Nagle's elevation to a Brigadier, reached camp in charge of Mr. Joseph W. Bowen.

These commissions promoted Lieutenant-Colonel Sigfried to colonel; Captain Pleasants, of C, to lieutenant-colonel; and Captain Wren, of B, to major. First Sergeant Daniel D. McGinnis, of H, was made adjutant, *vice* John D. Bertolette, appointed captain and assistant adjutant general, and assigned to duty with General Nagle.

Owing to the absence of Colonel Sigfried, Lieutenant-Colonel Pleasants being in command, entertained the officers of the regiment at his company's headquarters the same evening. The atmosphere thereabouts was heavy!

On the twenty-fifth, an order to move the next day turned everything topsy-turvy again—at 6 p. m. of the same day, it was countermanded. On the twenty-sixth, just before the regular Sunday inspection, an order to move by 10 o'clock a. m. was received. Ten came; twelve came; dinner was eaten; 5 p. m. came, and with it orders to remain for the night. The regiment retired in the midst of a heavy rain-storm.

Tents were struck early the next morning, October 27, and the regiment was in line ready to move at 12 m. By 1.30 it was off, marching steadily to Weaverton and Knoxville. Resting a while at the latter place, the march was resumed, and passing under the Chesapeake and Ohio Canal, through a culvert, proceeded down on the towpath of the same to Berlin, where the Potomac was crossed on a pontoon bridge, and the command was again on the "sacred soil" of Virginia.

The march was continued until about 7 o'clock in the evening, when camp was pitched in a fine large field in the neighborhood of Lovettsville.

The night proved a very cold one, and the next morning a heavy white frost covered the ground, whilst some canteens held ice water. The regiment remained here all day, and aided by lots of straw obtained in the vicinity, passed a more comfortable night. At 3 o'clock on the afternoon of the twenty-ninth, camp was struck, and the march resumed. Lovettsville was soon reached. Like all Virginia villages, it was composed of one-story frame houses, with large porches. The citizens appeared to be at home.

At one corner of the street a bevy of bright-eyed, rosy-cheeked girls, caused quite a sensation in the regiment; the men seemed terribly and suddenly afflicted with some bronchial affection, and just as they passed these girls, their throats troubled them a great deal, judging from the coughing.

The porches of a large house, no doubt at a former period a hotel, were crowded with officers, soldiers and citizens. The day's march covered about seven miles, and camp was had some four or five miles south of Lovettsville.

The command was in line and off by sunrise of the thirtieth, and by 9 a. m. six miles of ground had been traversed. Tents were then pitched in a field adjoining a grist mill, and the balance of the day was occupied in preparing the muster rolls for the morrow's muster.

The thirty-first was spent in camp. At ten Colonel Sigfried mustered the regiment for pay. Four months' pay was due, and "strapped!" was the exclamation from all quarters. The evening's dress parade was unusually fine, the entire brigade being in line, and the manœuvres gone through together. At this time there were five regiments in the brigade, and the display made is well worthy of record. The next day, November 1, General Nagle indulged his large command in a brigade drill—a diversion he knew only too well how to conduct, and of which he was exceedingly fond. Orders were received this day directing Captain Gilmour, of H; Sergeant Robert Smith, of G, and Sergeant M. Condon, of C, to proceed to Harrisburg, Pa., to bring on 500 drafted men to fill up the ranks of the Forty-eighth. This detail left during the night.

By 10 o'clock on the morning of Sunday, November 2, the march was resumed. The route was through Purcellville, a small one-story frame house Virginia village. The march covered twelve miles. Company G was placed on picket duty a mile from the regiment. Early the next morning, third, some of the "boys" of this company brought down a fine young shoat that had been endeavoring to pass the guard without giving the countersign. Foraging some potatoes and borrowing a pot from the farmer foraged from, a fine mess of pork and potatoes was indulged in. Several turkeys and chickens insisted in occupying the men's haversacks. The instinct these fowls seemed to have for a soldier's haversack was remarkable. All this, too, with McClellan's strict orders about foraging in existence. These soldiers, however, had had a taste of Pope's style of campaigning.

At 2 o'clock in the afternoon of this day, the regiment started off and marched about six miles—passing through the town of Bloomfield, where, the preceding day, a slight skirmish took place, between the advance of the Army of the Potomac and the Confederates. Twelve o'clock this night the command was aroused, with orders to load—an attack being anticipated, as the pickets had been fired on.

A march of four or five miles on the fourth brought the regiment near to and in view of Upperville. The enemy who had threatened the evening before had disappeared so entirely that the scouts failed to discover his whereabouts. Camp rumors stated that the main body of the rebel army was retreating southward. Astir at 4 o'clock of the fifth and off by 7 a. m. The weather was cold, cloudy and intensely disagreeable. Upperville was passed through shortly after starting, and a gloomy enough looking place it was. There were no signs of life in the town. It was voted horribly secesh. The town is beautifully located, and the outlook exceedingly fine. There were some pretty residences to be seen at this time, but the majority of the houses were poor wooden structures in a tottering condition. Its general appearance denoted desolation and decay. The pike leading out of the town, trudged by the Forty-eighth, ran a little east of south in a straight line for some miles. Piedmont was reached by 12 o'clock noon. This is a station on the Manassas Gap Railroad, the regimental encampment being in a field immediately across the railroad. Generals McClellan and Burnside rode by the camp during the afternoon. As usual, the cheering was immense. The bulk of the army was encamped in the immediate vicinity. Distant cannonading was heard during the greater part of the day.

On the sixth the regiment was off by 8 a. m., but after accomplishing a mile's march, was obliged to halt until 12 o'clock noon, to permit of a division of troops coming in on another road, to precede it. The rest of the march was disagreeable in the extreme, entirely at too rapid a gait, and with but two rests.

An ammunition wagon belonging to the First Division of the Ninth Corps exploded on the road, igniting from a camp-fire. A wide circuit had to be made around this wreck, to prevent accident resulting from the discharge of any unexploded material.

Encampment was made at the "Summit," at 7 p. m. The weather was quite cold. During the seventh of November, a heavy snow storm set in, lasting all day, and completely covering the ground. Large fires were built to keep all warm, and it was hoped that another night would be spent in this camp, but 4 p. m. saw the regiment on the move. Trudging along in wretchedly cold weather, with wind blowing, and snow falling rapidly is not the most pleasant occupation in the world. Whilst resting at a little place called Orleans, General Burnside passed—the cheering was lusty. Great concern was expressed for the General, lest the cold snow flakes beating down on his bald head, as he uncovered in acknowledgment of the cheers, might be injurious to his health.

Darkness overtook the command as it trotted on. A long halt was had on top of a bleak, barren hill, where the wind had full scope. Conjectures as to the cause of the halt were set at rest by the discovery that the "wrong road" had been taken.

Back tramped the regiment, the men cold and cross at finding themselves four miles out of the way. On reaching the right road a bivouac was ordered.

This march inspired the poetic mind of Captain Reno, of General Sturgis' staff. He is emphatic of language, but having been there, the Forty-eighth believe he only does justice to the occasion.

It must be remembered that it was the Second Brigade, not Nagle's, that lead the march on this occasion.

Reno gave vent as follows:

> The d—dst march that ever was made,
> Since the days of old King Pharaoh,
> Was that march made by the Second Brigade,
> Under Brigadier-General Ferrero.

The snow storm ceased during the night, and the weather moderated considerably by the morning of the eighth of November.

The march was resumed about 9 o'clock a. m., and lasted a couple of hours, when the Rappahannock River was reached at a place called Waterloo, where the regiment encamped in a fine large woods. This was the point intended to have been reached the evening before.

The camp was quite picturesque—the little white shelter tents dotted all through the woods, contrasted beautifully with the deep shade and sombre foliage of the evergreens. The next day an order was issued dated Washington, November 5, 1862, directing General Burnside to relieve General McClellan of the command of the Army of the Potomac. General Burnside reluctantly assumed command on the ninth so that this day ended McClellan's connection with the army. This change caused much comment.

CHAPTER VII.

BURNSIDE IN COMMAND.

On Sunday, the ninth of November, 1862, General Burnside assumed command of the Army of the Potomac. General Orlando B. Wilcox commanded the Ninth Corps; General Samuel Sturgis, the First Division, and General James Nagle, the First Brigade.

On this morning the regiment, snugly sheltered in the woods, listened to a discourse from Chaplain Holman, shortly after which came orders to move. The Rappahannock was crossed after an hour's march, at Glen Mills, when the turnpike running from Warrenton through Waterloo and Amissville toward Front Royal was reached. The march was about three miles on this pike, passing through the villages of Cockeysville and Amissville. Near the latter point, on the road toward the town of Little Washington, the Forty-eighth encamped for the night in a neighboring field. Shortly after being aroused on the morning of the tenth the booming of cannon close by betokened a fight. The command started back over the turnpike, the wagons and ambulances hurrying to the rear. "Looks like a skedaddle," say the boys, but no. After passing through Amissville the road was left for the field south of it, where the entire brigade, the only infantry present, was deployed as skirmishers, first platoons of company on line, whilst second platoons were held in reserve.

The whole day was employed in this duty. The calvary in the front was busy popping away, and the artillery was engaged all day. A rebel brigade of infantry, some batteries and a large body of Stuart's calvary had been sent from Culpeper to retard the forward movement of the Army of the Potomac. At sunset the Forty-eighth was recalled, and encamped for the night near the previous night's camping ground. Just about this time persimmons were plenty, and in that delicious condition when it is safe to eat them without whistling. The eleventh was spent in camp. At 4 a. m. of the twelfth the command was off, back over the Warrenton turnpike, through Amissville, traveling the road taken the previous Sunday, re-crossing the Rappahannock at Glen Mills, passing the camp of Sunday, through the camps of the First Division, and at noon settled some two miles southeast of Sunday's camp. Settled? Yes, until 3 p. m., when tents were struck and the march resumed in the direction of Warrenton. At 6 o'clock a road was reached recognized as having been tramped over by the regiment on the twenty-fifth of the preceding August, during Pope's campaign. So at this point was completed a circuit, bounded by Warrenton Junction, Manassas, Alexandria, Washington, Antietam, Lovettsville, Upperville and Sulphur Springs.

Two miles further down the pike brought the command to Warrenton White Sulphur Springs, where it encamped in close proximity to a camp occupied by the regiment during Pope's retreat.

The thirteenth was occupied by many of the men in an examination of the buildings at and about the Springs, and in tasting the excessively disagreeable water. The main hotel was a ruin. During the visit of the August previous, the smoke made by its burning was distinctly seen. The place had been a beautiful summer resort, but it was a sad wreck at this time. The camping ground was changed at noon to one more eligible, on a beautiful spot of ground, with wood and water handy. The supply of crackers had become exhausted and cries of "hard tack" assailed the ears from all sides. Remained quietly in camp all day of the fourteenth, preparatory to General Burnside's onward movement. On the fifteenth, at 6 a. m., the regiment was off, passing by the springs, taking the same old road traveled the August before. The baggage-train was shelled by the enemy—his batteries occupying precisely the same position held in August, and the Union guns were brought into position on the spot occupied then. Two or three wagons were damaged, and some men were wounded. It was at this time and place that Lieutenant McIlvaine, of Durell's Battery, was killed. The trains were moved in front of the troops and the regiment followed at a brisk pace, encamping for the night at Fyattsville. Companies G and H were detailed for picket, and were thrown about a half a mile in front of the regiment. On the sixteenth—Sunday—the Division (Second, Ninth, A. C.) got off early, and after a severe and rapid march of ten miles in a northeasterly direction, encamped on the Orange & Alexandria Railroad, midway between Warrenton Junction and Bealton Station. Here provisions were supplied in abundance. It was 1 o'clock on the afternoon of the seventeenth before the Forty-eighth got off, moving in a southeasterly direction toward Fredericksburg. Three divisions of the Ninth Corps marched side by side. The Second and the wagons occupied the road, whilst the First and Third marched through the woods and fields on either side. Ten miles were marched in this way, and the regiment bivouacked on the north side of the road. In a disagreeable, drizzly rain, camp was left at 6. a. m. on the eighteenth, and some twelve miles of road passed over before encamping. Many old landmarks, first seen in the march of the preceding summer from Fredericksburg to Bealton, were noted in passing along. The rain continued on the nineteenth, camp was left at 6.30 a. m., and eight miles' march brought the Rappahannock River in view. Passing on through Falmouth, which the Fifty-first Pennsylvania occupied, the Forty-eighth encamped back of the Lacy House directly opposite Fredericksburg. This place was now in possession of the rebels. The pickets on either bank of the river delighted to quiz each other. "How did you like Bull Run?" said the rebels. "Better bury your dead at South Mountain," replied the Union boys. "What do you think of the election in New York?" retorted secesh. "How do you fancy Lincoln's proclamation, what do you think of Butler?" added Yank. "Oh, the Louisiana Tigers will bring him to Richmond," rejoined Confed. "The Louisiana Tigers? Pooh! there's none of them left—the last died running," sang back the Unioner, and so it went on. Durell's Battery was posted in front of the regiment with its guns commanding the streets of Fredericksburg. A visit to the bluffs overlooking the town brought it in full view. The inhabitants were busy—apparently numbers were moving—wagons heavily ladened with household goods were visible, and people were seen hurrying here and there with bundles and packages. Rebel cavalry patrolled the streets, and a heavy line of pickets occupied the southern banks of the river. The regiment remained in this camp until the twenty-ninth of November, resuming drills and dress parades. The life was a monotonous one. "Supporting Durell's Battery," was the army way of denoting the duty in this camp. At 6 o'clock on the morning of the twenty-ninth, having been relieved by the Fourth Rhode Island, the regiment moved off and rejoined the brigade—encamping in a heavy pine woods, about a mile back of the river. Here comfortable log huts were built by the men, with genuine chimneys in them, and before this spot was vacated by the troops the handsome forests surrounding the camps were leveled to the ground. On the afternoon of December 1, General Nagle resumed brigade drills —much to the disgust of all hands interested. The most noteworthy event of the second of December was the arrival in camp of Isaac Lippman, the best sutler in the corps, with a full supply of "cheeses."

The third and fourth passed without special incident. The afternoon of the fifth brought a most disagreeable storm of snow, hail and rain, robing the earth in a fleecy garment. The weather was bitter cold, and the fire-places in the log huts were piled with fuel. Some of the enterprising spirits of the regiment arose at 1.30 at night to witness an announced total eclipse of the moon. It was found entirely too cold for much extended observation.

Nearly all of the regiment picketed the river bank on the sixth. The weather continued cold, the ground was hard frozen, and there was plenty of ice.

The inspection on the seventh was rather a matter of form—only about a hundred men in line—the picket detail not returning early enough to participate. The day was intensely cold and the ground was still covered with Friday's snow. On the eighth an order was received from Division Headquarters for the men to build log huts, and to make themselves as comfortable as possible. For this purpose no duty was imposed, other than guard duty, for two days. Then commenced a slaughter of the woods, and the erection of log huts of a more pretentious kind than the temporary efforts before essayed.

Whilst thus busily engaged, orders for a general inspection at 3 p. m. reached camp. This was countermanded about fifteen minutes before three, and the inspection was indefinitely postponed.

The hut building was renewed, although a general cleaning-up had taken place. On the tenth there was a regimental inspection. The pleasant countenance of General Burnside looking on at the regimental dress parade, is a notable event of the day. A meeting of the company commanders took place at Colonel Sigfried's tent the same evening, for the purpose of preparing for the anticipated movement against the rebel entrenchment at Fredericksburg. The part expected of the regiment was explained, and the company commanders directed to keep their own counsel.

The eleventh of December, 1862, was the eventful day. The men of the regiment were aroused at 4 a. m. by order of the Colonel. Blankets, with shelter tents enclosed, were rolled to be carried across the shoulder as a sash. Three days' rations were placed in haversacks and knapsacks, and all unnecessary baggage was left in camp, in charge of the sick. The regiment started at 8 o'clock, with the brigade, to participate in the assault on Fredericksburg. The artillery stationed on the many eminences overlooking the town, opened early and kept up an almost incessant cannonade all day long. The Forty-eighth was drawn up in line of battle on the summit of a hill, about a half mile east of the Lacy House—in the neighborhood of the Phillip's House—awaiting the completion of the pontoon bridge. The laying of this bridge was a very difficult task—the rebel infantry stationed along the edge of the south bank of the river, kept up a rattling fire upon the sappers and miners engaged therein. The latter gallantly returned the fire, and continued with their work. Some thus engaged were killed, and quite a number wounded. Then the rebel sharpshooters, with which the houses along the river abounded, turned their attention to our cannoniers, who were making it uncomfortable for the rebel infantry along the river bank.

As the artillerymen began to fall, Burnside ordered the town shelled. The batteries responded with a will, roar succeeded roar in rapid succession, pouring into the doomed town a terrible shower of deadly missiles. The cannonading at this time was terrific, rendered a thousand fold more deafening by the reverberations arising from the peculiar formation of the country. The deep bluffs overhanging the river giving back a hollow sound, like the rolling and crashing of thunder!

Noon came. The regiment still lay idly in line. The pontoon had not yet been laid. At 3 p. m. it was the writer's good fortune to accompany Lieutenant-Colonel Pleasants nearer the town, where opportunity was afforded for a better look at the condition of things. Adjutant McGinness kindly loaned his horse. Pausing in our route, at General Sumner's headquarters, there was spread below the once beautiful town of Fredericksburg, now in flames, and from all appearances doomed to soon become a mass of ruins. Whilst gazing on the destruction, Colonel Frick and Major Anthony, of the One Hundred-and-twenty-ninth Pennsylvania, came up, and proposed going to the river edge, which was lined with Union batteries, in order to obtain a still better view. Down we galloped, and very soon we became interested spectators of a most glorious scene. We were directly over the spot where, all day long, the sappers and miners had been endeavoring to build a pontoon bridge. This was almost immediately beneath the bluff on which the Lacy House stood. The engineers were supported by the Seventh Michigan Regiment, and just as we reached the scene, a part of this gallant regiment took two of the pontoon boats, and paddling them across the river, drove the rebels from the banks and sent them running through the town. This was done in the face of their sharpshooters. The Michigan boys were a determined set of men and not to be dismayed. Soon the entire regiment got across, using the boats for that purpose, and although the rebels rallied and far outnumbered them, the Seventh stood to the work, beating the foe back in grand style. The artillery came to their aid and poured into the town a destructive shower of grape and canister. This was enough, and when we rode away from the river the brave Michigan men held the town. Having both banks of the river the bridges were completed speedily.

Whilst on this inspecting tour with Lieutenant-Colonel Pleasants, the regiment had received orders to return to camp, which it did. As preparations were under way to occupy the old quarters for the night, orders to "fall in" were given. Back again it marched, expecting to cross the river. Another halt, and another order to return, took the regiment to the old camp, where it remained for the night, with orders to be ready to move in thirty minutes after notice. A sufficient number of troops had been sent across the river to hold the town during the night.

Early on the morning of the twelfth the regiment marched toward the river with the intention of crossing over into Fredericksburg. Two pontoon bridges, side by side, were thrown across the river, toward the upper part of the town. Couch's Corps, the Second, went over just before the Forty-eighth. Whilst passing over, the enemy's batteries threw shells into the river with the evident design of destroying the bridges. The range was accurate enough, but fortunately the missiles fell into the water on either side, or struck the opposite bank, not one striking the pontoons. Whilst the Forty-eighth was crossing, several shells fell uncomfortably close, but without damage.

The regiment formed in line on the second street from the river, and remained until the afternoon, when it was ordered further to the left, and into the street next to the river. A bivouac was had in this street—the men lying on fence boards laid on the pavement. Some occupied deserted houses. The rebels had kept up a lively shelling of the town all day—without doing much damage, however.

Saturday, December 13, was an exceedingly pleasant day, so far as the weather was concerned—warm and balmy—but anything but a pleasant one to the torn, shattered and maimed soldiers, who passed through the fiery ordeal of that day! The streets of the town were very muddy. Of course the command was aroused early, and all could guess the momentous events to come, by the unusual activity among the staff officers, who could be seen galloping here and there, conveying orders. The Forty-eighth was soon formed, and marching still further to the left, halted in line below the railroad. Whilst waiting at this point, General Thomas Francis Meagher rode by. Who can forget his magnificent appearance! Dressed in a faultlessly fitting suit of dark green cloth, black shoulder knots, in the centre of which were embroidered silver stars, and his yellow silk sash crossed over his breast, denoting a general field officer of the day—superbly mounted on a deep bay horse, he made up a picture of unusual grace and majesty. One can well understand how, later in the day, his Irish brigade fought with the tenacity of tigers, inspired by the magnificent presence of its intrepid leader.

It was not long before the work of carnage began—opened by battery after battery sending their terrible missiles hurtling through the air, until the vast amphitheatre reverberated with the sound of three hundred rebel cannon and as many Union guns. Above the din the sharp rattle of musketry soon arose, adding to the terrible work of death.

The regiment moved to the back of the town toward Marye's Heights, and for a time remained stretched out in a street running perpendicular to the river. Whilst lying here the grape, canister and shells of the enemy wounded several men in the ranks. Captain Gilmour, of H; Sergeant Nies, of G, and others were slightly wounded, one man of Company A was killed. At this point the novel experience of seeing a ball or shell coming from the rebel artillery was vouchsafed. The ball could be distinctly seen in the air, and the ground immediately on the left of the regiment was frequently struck; the shots would roll over and over, in the most awkward manner.

General Nagle and staff were standing under cover of a brick stable, not far from the right of the Forty-eighth. A solid shot struck the building penetrating both walls—coming out just above the heads of the General and staff—throwing the brick-bats amongst them, and covering the party with dust and dirt. It was a narrow call, but little time was permitted to ponder over it—the order to advance being given. This was about 2 o'clock in the afternoon. The Forty-eighth marched by the flank toward the right a short distance until some obstruction had been passed when the command, "Left face, double quick time," came, and running over the clear space down into a hollow, and up a slight rise in the ground, the regiment became hotly engaged with the enemy. This movement was made under a terrible storm of deadly missiles. The command was in full view of the rebels and within easy range. As one of the regiment puts it in his diary, "the advance to the front over a clean ground with death staring us in the face as grim as ever any troops met it." How different the experience of two persons apparently placed in similar circumstances. For instance, Lieutenant Jackson and the writer were side by side in that "double quick" advance to the front line. A shell exploded seemingly immediately in front of us, and just above our heads. He was unharmed, save dazed by the brilliant flash—whilst Jackson's neck was pitted and marked by the powder from that shell—looking as though he had the black small-pox. Poor fellow, he was unfortunate in every engagement he was in, and finally lost his life at the battle of Spottsylvania.

7

The regiment remained on the front line until 7 o'clock in the evening—expending sixty rounds of ammunition per man, to great purpose—for the batteries immediately in its front were at times completely silenced by the marksmanship of the men. Lieutenant-Colonel Pleasants passed along the line, directing that the ten best marksmen of each company should elevate the sights of their pieces and pick off the men manning the guns. The effect of this action was soon made apparent by the decreasing fire of the artillery.

"Sturgis is in the hollow, so near the hill that the rebel batteries on the crest cannot be depressed sufficiently to drive him out. He is within close musket-shot of Coll"s Brigade, lying behind the stone wall at the base of the hill. Sturgis' men lie down, load and fire deliberately, watching their opportunity to pick off the gunners on the hill. In vain are all the efforts of Longstreet to dislodge them. Solid shot, shells, canister, and shrapnel are thrown toward the hollow but without avail. A solitary oak tree near is torn and broken by the artillery fire, and pitted with musket balls, and the ground is furrowed with deadly missiles; but the men keep their position through the weary hours. The division is composed of two brigades—Nagle's containing the Sixth and Ninth New Hampshire, Seventh Rhode Island, Forty-eighth Pennsylvania and Second Maryland; and Ferrero's containing the Twenty-first and Thirty-fifth Massachusetts, Eleventh New Hampshire, Fifty-first Pennsylvania and Fifty-first New York." *

The regiment was relieved by the Twelfth Rhode Island, Colonel Brown. "At dusk the hill became crowded, and seeing other regiments still coming up, Colonel Clark (Twenty-first Massachusetts) and myself concluded best to return to the city for ammunition, and give room for fresh troops to get under the shelter of the hill."† The command passed off the hill by the left flank, and retired under cover of a deep railroad cut—returning to the same street and occupying the same places utilized the night before. Fresh ammunition was distributed and the men literally worn out soon fell asleep despite the angry tempest of lead still raining in the front. The loss was sixty killed, wounded and missing.

General Wilcox, commanding the Ninth Corps, said in his report of the Fredericksburg fight, referring to his command, "All these troops behaved well, and marched under a heavy fire across the broken plain, pressed up to the field at the foot of the enemy's sloping crest, and maintained every inch of their ground with great obstinacy, until after night fall. But the position could not be carried."

---
* "Four Years of Fighting,"—Coffin, p. 171.
† Letter of Colonel Sigfried, December 16, 1862.

Colonel Sigfried, commanding the Forty-eighth in this fight, in a letter to the *Miners' Journal*, dated December 16, 1862, said : "Too much praise cannot be given *all* the soldiers (and the following officers who were in the battle, viz., Colonel Pleasants, Major J. Wren, Adjutant D. D. McGinness, Captains U. A. Bast, G. W. Gowen, Winlack, Hoskins, O. C. Bosbyshell, J. A. Gilmour, John R. Porter, Isaac Brennan, and Lieutenants H. Boyer, Eveland, John Wood, Humes, Charles Loeser, Jr., Bohanon, Fisher, James, Williams, Jackson, Pollock, A. Bowen, Shuck, Douty, and Stitzer) for their gallantry during the entire engagement. Their line was steady and unbroken while advancing under the most murderous shelling of the enemy, and their fire deliberate, well aimed and effective."

Sunday the fourteenth was a beautiful day—the weather was delightful. There was a truce to the fighting—both sides remained inactive. If the troops were quietly resting, there was a great stir among the commanding officers. Up at the Phillips' House, Burnside was in consultation with his grand division commanders—not so much in consulting as in directing what he hoped would result in a great victory. This interchange of views was of mighty import to the Forty-eighth for if Burnside had carried out his intention, the probability is that but few of the command would have been left to tell of the fight. The regiment was the senior regiment of the corps, and would have been directly in front of the proposed assault on Marye's Heights.

" When the Commanding General left headquarters on the morning of the fourteenth, he had made every preparation to recommence the action by storming the heights. He knew in such an emergency the Ninth Corps would not fail him, and he had accordingly selected the troops whom he had before led to victory, to make the attack. He had decided even to direct the assault in person. A column of eighteen regiments was formed and everything was ready for the movement, when the three grand division commanders earnestly appealed to him to abandon the attempt. He could not refuse to listen to their persuasions and arguments."*

" General Burnside, eager to achieve victory, prepared to hurl his old corps (the Ninth) on the following morning against the fatal barrier which had withstood French, Hancock, Howard and Humphrey. He was dissuaded by the brave Sumner, who was supported in his opposition to the proposed movement by nearly every general officer." †

So the day passed quietly, the Forty-eighth remaining in the same street occupied the two preceding evenings.

---

* Woodbury's " Burnside and Ninth Corps," p. 227.
† Lossing's " Civil War," Vol. II, p. 494.

Monday the fifteenth found the same inactivity—the regiment staying without incident where it had been stationed during the occupation of the town. At 7 o'clock in the evening orders to "fall in" were given, and the command moved down the same street toward the lower pontoon bridge. A halt for some little time took place, when the regiment moved to the rear of the town, out on to the front line, and occupied houses and out-houses—in the walls of which holes were pierced large enough to push rifles through. Every preparation was made to hold this position against any attack the enemy might make. At midnight the men of the Forty-eighth were quietly aroused, and moved rapidly and noiselessly to the upper pontoon bridge, where the river was crossed and shortly thereafter the command entered its old camping ground, disgusted and worn out.

The writer remembers a rather singular circumstance connected with the fight on the crest of the hill, on Saturday. It was shortly after Pleasants had directed the picking off of the artillery gunners. He and Captain Koch were standing together talking, when a minie ball struck the latter in the breast, and came out of his back passing through the rolled blanket he had slung over his shoulder. The singular part of the matter was that the writer's eyes happened to rest upon the exact spot where the bullet made its egress from the blanket, as he distinctly saw the separation of the fibres as the bullet passed out before he knew Koch was shot. Fortunately the bullet did not end Koch's life, as he is still living in Manayunk and has furnished some details relative to the regiment, that have been of value. Lieutenant Jackson, of G, commanded a burial party from the First Brigade, which proceeded to the battlefield under a flag of truce, to bury the Union soldiers, still lying on the ground. Whilst performing this duty he conversed with a number of rebel officers. One said to him, "You Yankees don't know how to hate—you don't hate us near so much as we hate you. You've yet to learn how to hate," then, pointing to a number of the dead Union soldiers, whose bodies had been stripped of every vestige of clothing, he added, "Is that not very revolting to you?—don't you think it terrible!" Jackson replied that he did, and that no civilized people would be guilty of such desecration. The rebel officer replied, "Indeed, I could not be to any other save a *Yankee*."

After the Fredericksburg failure the army settled down into winter quarters. More substantial log huts were built with ample chimneys, and the cold weather found these preparations necessary for comfort. The regiment remained here quietly until the ninth of February, 1863, all the usual routine of camp life. Occasional duty along the river on picket added variety to the general monotony. The rigor with which old General Sumner exercised his authority was felt severely in some cases. Leaves of absence were positively refused. When Colonel Sigfried made a personal appeal to the General for some of the officers of the Forty-eighth, he replied, "Colonel, tell your command to consider themselves out at sea for the present." The expedient of resigning was tried by some who were obliged to go home, but General Sumner put a peremptory stop to this plan by endorsing on such resignation, "Having resigned in the face of the enemy (naming the officer) is dishonorably discharged from the service." Two valued officers of the Forty-eighth were unfortunately amongst those who were summarily dismissed. In the light of after years, General Sumner's action must be commended. He was every inch a soldier—just and fearless, and very much in earnest in the work he had to do. Whilst in temporary command of the Second Division, General Nagle ordered a division drill. This took place on the sixth of January, 1863, and was eminently successful. General Wilcox, commanding the corps, was an interested spectator of the drill, and commended in high terms all connected with it. The winter afforded great opportunities for interchanging visits between the various regiments. Officers and men of the Ninety-sixth, One Hundred-and-twenty-ninth and others were frequently in camp and many parties from Schuylkill County found their way to the army. On Tuesday, tenth of January, General Burnside reviewed the Ninth Army Corps—the Forty-eighth Regiment occupying the extreme right of the line—the post of honor. On Friday evening, January 20, orders from General Burnside were read at dress parade announcing a move "upon the enemy" the succeeding day. The left Grand Division had been going by the Forty-eighth's camp all day, up the river. The order stated that late victories in North Carolina and the West had evidently weakened the rebel army on the Rappahannock so that the auspicious moment to strike a blow had arrived.

Terrible rainy and muddy weather set in. The twenty-first came and the twenty-second came, with the Forty-eighth still in camp ready to move any moment. The roads were in a horrible condition—teams, cannon, etc., stuck fast in the mud at almost every step. Part of a pontoon train belonging to Franklin's Grand Division got stuck so securely in the mud on the evening of the twentieth, that all efforts to release it proved unavailing. It unfortunately happened to be on a part of the road exposed to the rebel's artillery fire. To prevent its falling into the hands of the rebels, it was burned.

This move of the army proved abortive—the elements were more powerful than the army, and the expedition was abandoned. The Forty-eighth did not leave its camping ground, and soon became comfortably fixed again—willing to banish the recollection of "Burnside's Mud March" from the memory.

On the twenty-sixth Burnside's farewell order to the army came to hand. It was a sad event to the command to lose one in whom every confidence was had. In this order, he says, in taking leave of the army, he hopes he may be pardoned for especially taking farewell of his "well-tried associates" of the Ninth Corps. The Forty-eighth regiment, during the rest of its stay in the Army of the Potomac, was occupied in routine duty—for Burnside's adieu to that army was quite speedily followed by an order severing the Ninth Corps' connection with it. Somewhere about the sixth of February, 1863, orders were received to proceed to Acquia Creek Landing, and there to embark on transports to be conveyed to Fortress Monroe to report to General Dix. At noon on the ninth, the regiment boarded a train and was soon speeding toward the Potomac thoroughly afflicted with "Surfeit Rappahannockus," as Commissary Sam Keys, of the First Brigade, put it. At Acquia Creek Landing, the Forty-eighth took the United States transport "North America," which, as soon as all were on board, shoved out in the stream and anchored for the night; this was about 5 o'clock p. m. The "North America" was somewhat crowded, having on board the Sixth New Hampshire, the Second Maryland and the Forty-eighth Pennsylvania, besides a provost guard of about sixty men and numerous hangers on. Early Tuesday (tenth) morning the vessel started, steaming down the Potomac, entering Chesapeake Bay about noon. The weather was most charming all day. Fortress Monroe was reached by 9 o'clock the same evening, and under its protecting walls the steamer dropped anchor for the night. Under orders the vessel steamed up to Newport News on the morning of the eleventh, the regiment disembarking at 1 o'clock, and encamping about three-quarters of a mile from the landing, in rear of the fortifications, on the magnificent plain stretching along the James River. The regiment remained here until the twenty-fifth of March without any startling incidents. On the twenty-sixth of February a grand review of the corps was had by General Dix, which passed off with great credit to all concerned. Of course the Forty-eighth made the finest display of any regiment in the corps. On the twenty-seventh, the one—only—Sutler Isaac Lippman arrived in camp; his welcome was tremendous. Many amusements were indulged in during the stay at Newport News—horse racing, cricket matches, base-ball and the like. Leaves of absence became frequent just at a time when the stringent order of General Dix looked as if they might not be granted. The Enfield Rifles, after a rigid inspection, were condemned, and before leaving the camp the regiment was armed with the improved "Springfield Rifled Muskets," as much behind the present magnificent breech-loading Springfield as those that replaced Enfield's are ahead of the old buck and ball muskets.

One o'clock p. m., of March 25, orders to pack and leave at once reached the regiment, and by 4.30 p. m. the command was on board the "John A. Warner," and by seven anchored off the wharf at Fortress Monroe. New and strange territory was before the Forty-eighth, but exactly where it would be sent was unknown. Whether the boat would pass out to sea between Capes Henry and Charles, or steam up the bay, was a matter of profound mystery.

CHAPTER VIII.

LEXINGTON.

The "John A. Warner" quietly cast loose from the wharf at Fortress Monroe at 3.30 o'clock a. m., of Thursday, March 26, and was soon heading up the Chesapeake Bay. The weather was delightful, the bay as smooth as a mill pond and the trip to Baltimore thoroughly enjoyed by all hands. This city was reached at 9.30 in the evening. The Ninth Corps at this time was commanded by Major-General John G. Parke, an officer much esteemed by the troops; the Second Division by Brigadier-General Samuel G. Sturgis; the First Brigade by Brigadier-General James Nagle, and the Forty-eighth by Colonel Joshua K. Sigfried, all officers of ability and merit, who had the confidence, respect and esteem of the men. Crowded on the same boat, companions in the same trip, was the regiment's firm friends, the gallant Sixth New Hampshire, with which the Forty-eighth was brigaded during its entire service.

Early Friday morning (twenty-seventh of March) the regiment disembarked, and took a train of cars on the Northern Central Railroad. The good people of Baltimore vied with each other in showering kindnesses on the men; all sorts of eatables and drinkables were provided by them, and the really demoralized condition of a vast number of the men of the regiment before that city was departed from, is entirely "too numerous to mention." The trip, began so auspiciously, proved an exceedingly delightful one. It was much in the nature of an ovation, as crowds greeted the "boys" at every station, and a plentiful supply of good things was constantly distributed by friends. At the towns of York, Mifflin, Altoona and Pittsburg, in Pennsylvania, Caddy's Junction, Newark, Columbus and Cincinnati, Ohio, bread and coffee were also provided. At Pittsburg the regiment was escorted to the City Hall, where a fine repast was prepared, and greatly enjoyed — especially in having present many of the Smoky City's fine ladies, who, although the hour was 2 o'clock in the morning, lent the charm of their presence to enliven the "soldier laddies'" hearts.

At Cincinnati the men of the command were entertained in the Market House with a most appetizing feast, whilst the officers enjoyed the hospitality of the proprietor of the Gibson House, at a breakfast all too delightful to dwell upon. The ride through Ohio was made on Sunday, March 29. The enthusiastic crowds of girls, boys, women and men that greeted the regiment at every stop, was an experience so charming to the men who had been so long campaigning in a country hostile to them, that it made the trip satisfactory in the extreme. At Harrisburg, the Northern Central road was left, and the Pennsylvania Central conveyed the regiment to Pittsburg. Here a change of cars was had, and the route lay over the Ft. Wayne & Chicago, then by the Columbus & Cincinnati road. The Ohio was crossed in a ferry-boat to Covington, Ky., where cars were taken on the Kentucky Central road, and the city of Lexington was reached about 3 o'clock Tuesday morning, March 31.

The regiment encamped in the old fair grounds, about a mile from the business part of the city, and prepared itself to enjoy to the utmost what old soldiers termed a "soft snap," in their being assigned to provost duty in so charming a spot. In chronicling the regiment's sojourn in Lexington, no attempt is made to jot down daily happenings—a whole book, indeed several volumes could be written of what occurred there during the Forty-eighth's over five months' stay. It was one long happy holiday. General Edward Ferrero was made military commandant of the post of Lexington by General Burnside. Upon assuming command, he issued General Orders No. 1, appointing Colonel J. K. Sigfried provost marshal of the city, and detailing the Forty-eighth Regiment as provost guard thereof. Colonel Sigfried entered upon his duties on the morning of April 3, with Captain Edward Hurlburd, of the Eighteenth Michigan Regiment, as assistant provost marshal, and a detail of the regiment relieved the previous guard. The ceremony of guard mounting took place in the open space beside the Court House, and was witnessed by a large crowd of the citizens. Captain O. C. Bosbyshell, of Company G, was the officer of the day, and Lieutenants Jacob Douty, of Company K, Thomas Bohannen and Joseph H. Fisher, of Company E, were the officers of the guard. The guard looked well—boots were nicely blackened, belts, trappings, buttons and brass plates glittered, and white gloves adorned the hands. That first day's provost guard duty won the hearts of the girls, and the boys were ever after satisfied to stay in Lexington. The command moved into town on the fourth of April, occupying various vacant houses, and the Broadway Hotel and Phœnix Hotel became the eating places of many of the officers. On the same day General Nagle relieved General Ferrero of the command of the post. Dress parade was begun in the town on April 6, and was witnessed by a large crowd, of which a number of ladies were conspicuous. Praises most lavish were bestowed upon the regiment, and by its good conduct, it soon won its way into the kind hearts of the citizens.

General Orlando B. Wilcox was placed in command of the Central District of Kentucky, with headquarters in Lexington, relieving General Q. A. Gilmore, who went to the front. By General Wilcox's orders the Forty-eighth was to be reported as on detached service at Lexington. Colonel Sigfried was relieved as provost marshal and appointed commandant of the post. Captain Hurlburd was made provost marshal. Lieutenant Henry C. Jackson was appointed on General Wilcox's staff as acting assistant provost marshal of the district. On the tenth of April the regiment was ordered out of the houses occupied by the companies to encamp near the edge of the town. A dusty tramp out Limestone street, resulted in an order to re-occupy the deserted houses—so back the command marched. This was again disturbed on the eleventh, and the very spot out Limestone street, reached the Friday before, was occupied by the regiment, and became its permanent camping ground during the entire term of duty as provost guard. This ground was enclosed by a high board fence, with an excellent green sward. A large hemp warehouse occupied the centre, and made comfortable barracks for the companies—amply spacious for all needs. Two large hospital tents, two sibleys, and three wall tents, erected on the green lawn, served as quarters for the officers; except those of C, H and K, who quartered in a building inside the same enclosure. Lieutenant-Colonel Pleasants' wall tent was erected in the centre of the line of tents, but in advance of them—to his right and left respectively the adjutant and major had each a wall tent. On the adjutant's right was a sibley occupied by F's officers, and on its right, a hospital tent for Company B and G's officers. On the major's left was A's officers' sibley, and on its left the hospital tent of the officers of D, E and I. The surgeon's and regimental hospital used one of the buildings in the enclosure. Orders became stricter; passes were required of all officers or enlisted men who desired to be in town, and the patrols had many adventures in enforcing these provisions. Theatre-goers, especially the officers, were loath to show their authority for being outside of the camp limits. The regiment was blessed with doctors in this camp: Surgeon Blackwood and Assistant Surgeons Morrison and Huston, and they found very little to do, for the boys were distressingly healthy. Can Morrison be forgotten, as he dashed out Limestone street on his little sorrel mare, with "go in,

Fourth Cavalry," bursting from his lips, and darting into camp with a wild war-whoop, rushed clear through the hospital tent occupied by the officers of B and G, nearly wrecking that canvas home? He was a gay one, but who did not love him? On the twenty-ninth of April, Captain Bosbyshell, with Corporal Edward Silliman, of G, and three privates, escorted a large number of rebel prisoners from Lexington to Louisville, and turned them over to the military authorities there. During this absence, orders were received directing the Forty-eighth Regiment to rejoin the brigade. Colonel Sigfried was relieved as post commandant by Colonel Byrd, of the First Tennessee Regiment, and the same regiment took the place of the Forty-eighth on provost duty. However, in less than twenty-four hours, these orders were all countermanded. Colonel Sigfried and the regiment resumed the duties they had been relieved from. It appears that the citizens of Lexington petitioned the commanding officer to permit the Forty-eighth to remain on duty in their city. The entire Ninth Corps was on the go, concentrating near Columbia, Ky., with the intention of advancing into East Tennessee. About the thirteenth of May, Captain Joseph A. Gilmore, of Company H, was appointed provost marshal of the city, relieving Captain Edward M. Hurlburd, a popular and much respected officer, who, desiring to rejoin his command, had sent in a request to be relieved. The officers of the Forty-eighth found detail for guard quite frequent—not more than two days intervening between the time of duty. Much of the hardships of war were brought to notice in Lexington. Loyal Kentuckians and Tennesseans were daily driven from their homes by the rebellious element, and scores of refugees flocked into the city. It was an every day sight at the provost marshal's office to have refugees come in with the most pitiable tales of suffering. On Sunday, May 10, a poor woman, with six children, entered the office. She had walked over the mountains from East Tennessee, with her children, the eldest but fourteen years, a distance of over 150 miles. Her sufferings can be imagined. Dependent for food and shelter upon the inhabitants by the way, with a dread of bodily injury to herself or her wee ones, not knowing where to go, who were friends or who were foes! Good people of the North, what do you know of war? Especially the Civil War of '61 in the border States. Instances were numerous where the same family furnished men for both armies, and the daughters of Union men were wives of rebel soldiers. Whilst commander of the Department of the Ohio General Burnside determined to prevent, so far as his jurisdiction extended, the giving of aid and comfort to the enemy by persons living in the North and border States.

Parties were constantly engaged in furnishing information of the plans of the government by means of secret mails, which they established and carried on as regularly as the United States mail—in some parts of the border States more regularly. He therefore issued, on the thirteenth of April, 1863, his "General Order No. 38," which became so famous through the notoriety given to the arrest and banishment, under its provisions, of Clement L. Vallandigham, the celebrated Ohioan, who so frequently declaimed with great vehemence against the government and boldly defied its power. The effect of this order was soon felt in Kentucky. The concluding portions of it show the force with which it applied there, and the peculiar duties imposed on the Union troops stationed therein.

"It must be distinctly understood (the order read) that treason, expressed or implied, will not be tolerated in this department.

"All officers and soldiers are strictly charged with the execution of this order."

The order was very sweeping in its designations of those who fell under its provisions, and it became the daily duty of the "officers and soldiers" stationed in that State, to serve notices on the "suspects" to move into the rebel lines. This duty was a painful one. In many cases it seemed to work especial hardship. It had a most tranquilizing effect, however, and was of the greatest importance in encouraging the civil authorities in their efforts to keep the citizens true to their allegiance to the government, and in upholding the hands of those who remained staunch all through the war.

The writer was commissioned to serve a notice, under this famous order, on the wife of a rebel colonel, and it brought him in contact with one of Kentucky's large-headed, brainy men.

One bright summer afternoon, riding out from Lexington, on the Limestone street pike, a ride of three or four miles—it may have been further—led to a large estate; it could hardly be called a farm; it rather answered to the country seats of English lords. A neat porter's lodge on the road marked the entrance to the grounds. The drive then wound around through a beautiful wood, for—well, it seemed half a mile before the great mansion was reached. Here, surrounded by all the marks of comfort and plenty, lived the well-known Rev. Robert Jefferson Breckenridge, D. D., a firm friend of the Union.

He was at this time about sixty-three years of age, and somewhat stooped in figure. Evidently greatly addicted to snuff-taking, as on his upper lip and down over his beard were the marks of recent indulgence in the habit. Bareheaded, with his hair pushed about as though plowed through by his fingers, he was pacing up and down the broad piazza in front of his home. It is needless to say that the bearer of the order felt the great delicacy of his mission. Dr. Breckenridge was so prominent a man, so strong in his justice of the Union cause, and, above all, so good and wise, that it seemed an unusually harsh measure to put a relative of his under the ban. The leader of the old school Presbyterian Church; a former president of Jefferson College, in Philadelphia; the principal author of the common school system of Kentucky; in favor of the manumission of slaves, and an avowed Unionist, was scarcely the man to " give aid and comfort to the enemy." Unfortunately, he had a daughter who was the wife of a man who, at that time, served in the rebel army as a colonel. This lady was then living at her father's, and the " powers that be " decided that to harbor the wife of a rebel officer was an offence under Order No. 38, and so the daughter must go. The venerable doctor read over the notice carefully, after politely requesting its bearer to be seated, and as its import impressed itself upon him, the lines about his mouth hardened, and his countenance became grim and stern, as he said: " This order shall be obeyed." And it was.

The people of the North scarcely understand the meaning of loyalty. They were not surrounded by an element thoroughly antagonistic to any sentiment upholding the Union. To be a loyal man in the South, during the War of the Rebellion, required sacrifices and trials the like of which no dweller in the Northern States was called upon to endure. To be a loyal man in the interior of Kentucky during that struggle was as difficult a test devotion to country was ever put to. Where such an one was found he inspired the utmost confidence. There were some there—steadfast as a rock and true as steel. The Forty-eighth found them and can never forget their unceasing kindness, attention and helpfulness.

A grand review of the troops about Lexington took place on the fifteenth of May, the Forty-eighth carrying off the honors.

The "boys" were delighted on Sunday the seventeenth to have the good chaplain of the Sixty-fifth Illinois Regiment expound the Gospel to them, in a vigorous and soul-stirring way. Not having a chaplain of their own at the time, it was quite refreshing to borrow one. Private William P. Atkinson, of Company G, an experienced printer, was placed in charge of a confiscated printing office, to do army work, and whilst thus employed edited and published the *Kentucky Loyalist*, making it a bright, newsy paper, filled with good local matter.

General Wilcox made his headquarters in a large mansion, which had been vacated by its rebellious owner. Having been the recipient of much attention by the good people of Lexington, he, with his staff and other officers stationed in the city, gave a grand hop in this spacious house, to the ladies and gentlemen of Lexington on the evening of the twenty-first of May. The house and grounds were handsomely decorated —flags, swords, guns, drums, etc., being artistically used for the purpose—the music came from Cincinnati, which city likewise furnished a famous caterer who served the banquet. This was spread in a large tent or series of tents opening into each other, erected on the lawn, and entered from the porch, upon which the windows of the parlor opened. It was a grand affair—thoroughly enjoyed—indeed, the dancing was kept up until the next morning, it being full daylight when the guests took their departure.

With much regret the Forty-eighth learned of the serious condition of General Nagle's health, which occasioned that greatly respected officer to resign from the service on the ninth of May. He was highly esteemed by the command, and all were pained to part with him. He left Lexington for home on the twenty-second of May with the earnest wishes of his soldiers for a safe journey and speedy restoration to health.

On Monday morning, May 18, the men and officers arose at 4 o'clock a. m. for the purpose of bidding good-bye to their major, James Wren, who, having resigned his commission, started homeward. Major Wren was much liked by the command. He was a good soldier, careful officer and genial companion. When he found all the "boys" up so early, at the station, to show their respect and esteem for him, he was greatly affected. He departed amidst the lusty cheers of the command.

On June 3, General Wilcox was relieved of the command of the district of Kentucky, by General Hobson. At this time, General Hartsuff commanded the Twenty-third Army Corps, and he made his headquarters at Lexington.

Who can forget the unceasing kindness, not only to the sick, but to the well also, of good Mrs. Eliza H. Macalester. Many times her servants left, at the camp out Limestone street, reminders of her good-will in the shape of the best of provender. She was one of many, but her attentions were unremitting. The men of the regiment procured a handsome and tasty memento, to attest their regard for this good lady, and presented it to her with a note of explanation. This elicited the following reply:

To the Rank and File of the Forty-eighth Regiment P. V.

Gentlemen: Allow me to make my most grateful acknowledgments for the very elegant present and flattering note received from you this evening, and at the same time to return my warmest thanks for the marked compliment you ave paid me. Be assured, I shall ever hold in high appreciation this testimonial f your regard, not alone for its beauty, nor as having deserved it, but as the fering of true and noble hearts and from sons of our great Keystone State, here devotion to their country, in their country's need, has been fairly tested. hat a kind Providence may surround you, guide, guard and protect you and estore you in happiness to your families, is the earnest wish of

Your Friend,
Respectfully,

Lexington, Ky., June 6, 1863.   ELIZA H. MACALESTER.

    Captain Bosbyshell, early in June, secured a leave of absence to o home to join the ranks of the benedicts. He was married on the wenty-fourth of the same month, returning to Lexington, with his ride, on the eighth of July.

    The following order is published as an interesting episode in the ife at Lexington:

OFFICE POST COMMANDANT.

GENERAL ORDERS, NO. 7.   Lexington, Ky., July 3, 1863.

    At the present time, when the United States is making gigantic exertions o crush out a rebellion which threatens to destroy its nationality, it is especially appropriate that the anniversary of the day when the liberty of its people vas achieved, and their rights secured, should be held sacred and suitably elebrated.

    It is therefore ordered, by the Lieutenant-Colonel commanding this post, hat in honor of the eighty-seventh anniversary of the Independence of the nited States of America (July 4, A. D. 1863), two National Salutes, of thirtyive guns each, be fired from Ft. Clay—one at dawn, and the other at mid-day.

    It is also ordered that the Forty-eighth Regiment P. V. have a street arade at 7 o'clock a. m., to be ended by a Battalion drill.

    By order of   LIEUTENANT-COLONEL H. PLEASANTS,
Commanding Post.
D. D. M'GINNES,
Post Adjutant.

    Quite an excitement was occasioned during the first week in July by the threatened approach of John Morgan and his command. The Forty-eighth were stationed near the fortifications, in line of battle, for bree days, awaiting his appearance; but Woolford's Cavalry and thers of General Hobson's forces got after them, soon ridding the ountry of their presence.

    Captain Gilmour, having been promoted major of the Forty-eighth, vas relieved from the position of provost marshal, by Captain Bosbyhell, on the eleventh of July. About the eighteenth of July, Lieutennt-Colonel Pleasants was appointed provost marshal general of the Twenty-third Army Corps, and his administration of the duties of that position reflects great credit upon his judgment and good sense. Many citizens, who had been arrested and confined in prison upon the most trivial testimony, for disloyalty, he, after thorough investigation, released and sent home happy. On the first and second of August, a large consignment of prisoners, captured by Sanders from Scott's rebel forces, reached Lexington—mostly Louisianians—there were 360 of them, and their presence caused considerable excitement amongst the rebellious portion of Lexington's people. They were sent under guard to Louisville early on the third, and seemed greatly pleased with their treatment whilst in Lexington. The hanging of a murderer, at the junction of two streets, in the suburbs of the city on August 1, by the civil authorities, gathered a crowd of the most disreputable people, requiring a strong guard from the Forty-eighth to preserve order. Before cutting the body down, the sheriff desired Assistant Surgeon Morrison to examine whether the man was dead, and on feeling for the pulse at the ankle, and finding none, he pronounced him dead sure enough. Monday, August 3, was election day. By order of General Hartsuff, the doors of the liquor selling establishments were closed, and it was the quietest election the city had ever had, so the citizens said.

Brutus J. Clay, an uncompromising Unionist, was elected a member of Congress from the Ashland District. The day was enlivened somewhat by the arrival of about 150 East Tennessee recruits for loyal Tennessee regiments, en route to Nashville, the rendezvous. Many of these men were barefoot, and but few of them had coats. There were Tennesseans and Kentuckians with whom the Stars and Stripes were safer than with some who wore the blue.

Of course Lexington was under martial law—it had its post-commandant, post-adjutant, provost marshal, etc., with a provost guard to enforce order. The State was infested by desperate gangs of men, who espoused the cause of the rebels, and formed band after band of guerrillas. The rule was to regard every dweller in the county as a rebel, unless some positive, unmistakable evidence of loyalty could be shown. In order to gain correct information, the government established a detective agency, and through the detective force employed by it many a nicely laid rebel scheme was frustrated. The chief of the force in the Department of the Ohio, in the summer of 1863, was Captain Edwards, and his next officer, Lieutenant Stone. One certain day in August, 1863, these two gentlemen reported at the provost marshal's office in Lexington, with authority to search for a couple of noted guerrilla chiefs said to be in the neighborhood. They departed on their mission—

disguised, of course,—without vouchsafing any information as to their movements.

In the afternoon of the same day, the post-commandant, post-adjutant and provost marshal, started out on the Tate's Creek pike for a short ride into the country. It was a lovely afternoon, and the beautiful scenery of the Blue Grass region never showed to better advantage. Our worthy trio were jogging along, enjoying the ride, when they were met and stopped by a farmer. He was a real jolly old gentleman, with an honest, open countenance—much disturbed, however, upon this occasion. He had evidently ridden hard, and had important news to communicate. Seeing that the above officers were in uniform, he inquired if they could direct him to "the military authorities at Lexington." The post-commandant assured him that he was then in the presence of the party he was seeking. The old gentleman then stated that his name was Featherstone, but seemed somewhat incredulous as to the party there being the "military authorities of Lexington." He was convinced finally, and then made the following statement:

"Well, gentlemen, you tell me you are the military authorities of Lexington. Whether you are or not, I want you to arrest a couple of men who've been down to my house to dinner; they're an ugly-looking set of fellows and talk bad. I think they are rebels disguised, and they're here for no good. Any way, I don't like such looking rascals about. They were asking me all about the people around here, and they seem to know a mighty heap about the rebels living about— more 'n a Union man ought to. Well, they want to get to Mt. Sterling, and asked me the nearest and best road. I told 'em to go through Lexington, although the best road takes off this side; but, you see, I wanted these scoundrels captured. My house is on a lane about half a mile in from the pike. When they left I hurried to the stable, jumped on my old horse and cut across the field to head 'em off—they're not far back on the road—you'll meet 'em pretty soon, and I'll get in the fields, as it would never do for them to see me with you."

The old gentleman having delivered himself of this speech, and being assured that these bushwackers should be attended to, stationed himself in a clump of bushes back of the fence to witness the arrest.

Riding on a short distance, a bend in the road brought the two guerillas in view of the officers—but now how to capture them. Not one of the party was armed, not even with a sword; but there were three to two, and this majority of numbers it was determined should, if possible, prevail. The parties slowly approached each other, and, surely, the rebels were a hard-looking party. One was a long, lank

8

fellow in gray, and the other a stouter man in a suit of black, with a high black hat. When close enough to distinguish countenances, the provost marshal put spurs to his horse and soon reached the worthy couple, in whom he recognized Captain Edwards and Lieutenant Stone, of the detective force, and shouting to his companions to advance, that it was all right, explained the mistake made by Mr. Featherstone. However, just around the bend, waited Mr. Featherstone to see if the right parties were captured, and, in order to keep up the secrecy of the men on the detective force, it was agreed that Captain Edwards and Lieutenant Stone should be marched into Lexington, as though under arrest. So Captain Edwards was placed between the post-commandant and post-adjutant, while Lieutenant Stone brought up the rear, guarded by the provost marshal. The procession moved along the pike in a very solemn manner, past the hiding-place of Mr. Featherstone; but the joke was relished hugely when at a safe distance. The solemn air was reassumed and maintained while the procession was passing through the toll-gate and the streets of Lexington, until the prisoners were snugly landed in the provost marshal's office.

The next day Mr. Featherstone came into the provost marshal's office, and he was in high glee over the capture of the two rebels. Imagine his surprise when the provost marshal turned, and, introducing him to Captain Edwards and Lieutenant Stone, remarked that a man as thoroughly loyal as he could be safely intrusted with the secrets of the members of the detective force.

"Well, now," said the old gentleman, "I thought you were either Union scouts or rebels, and played the latter so well that I concluded you ought to be safely housed."

This incident resulted in friendly intercourse between the aforesaid "military authorities" and old Mr. Featherstone, and assured them of a Union man whose services and representations could be relied upon.

On the eighteenth of August General Hartsuff and staff left for the front. The Forty-eighth were now almost the only troops about Lexington. An artillery company from Ohio had relieved Companies B and H, from the duty of garrisoning Fort Clay, and these companies rejoined the regiment. Colonel Sigfried was the ranking officer left. Major Gilmour commanded the regiment. Lieutenant-Colonel Pleasants had gone with General Hartsuff, being provost marshal on his staff. It was evident the regiment would soon be needed at the front. On the eighth of September the marching orders came. On the ninth the Seventh Rhode Island Regiment relieved the Forty-eighth, and preparations for departure the next day were made.

Coming to Lexington over five months before, prepared to meet with coldness and even opposition from citizens of Southern proclivities, how graciously the regiment was treated. And the citizens, having in mind the questionable behavior of some Western troops, who were to be relieved by Eastern, feared from that experience, treatment far worse. Both were agreeably disappointed. How gratifying the following, received by Colonel Sigfried when the regiment was a hundred miles on its way to Knoxville:

LEXINGTON, KY., September 10, 1863.

COLONEL J. K. SIGFRIED.

Dear Sir:—We cannot permit to pass by, your departure from among us and the severance of those relations, personal and official, which have afforded us such satisfaction, without an expression of our respect and friendship to yourself and the other officers and soldiers of the Forty-eighth Pennsylvania Regiment.

Coming among us strangers, you have from first to last treated us as friends; and while you have been compelled to act with firm vigor against the open and secret enemies of the government, your administration of affairs has been tempered with such justice and humanity, and such good order and discipline has been maintained among your troops that all citizens who in good faith have desired to live peaceably and obedient to law, have felt perfect security from all outrage, or even injury or injustice.

From strangers you have become friends, and while we recognize and submit to the propriety of your leaving, in obedience to the requirements of the service, it is with painful regret we bid you farewell.

Be assured that wherever you may go you will carry with you our warmest wishes that success and glory shall attend you, and that through the trials and perils which may beset your path you and your regiment shall return honored and safe to your friends and to your homes.

Respectfully,

George Lancaster,	J. H. Bush,	W. C. Goodloe,
M. P. Lancaster,	W. Vorhees,	John Carty,
James Reidy,	J. M. Elliott,	J. G. Allen & Co.,
D. Burbank,	Joshua P. Shaw,	M. C. Johnson,
John Pew,	Squire Bassett,	Edward Crouly,
George Knight,	Wesley Spencer,	H. Shaw, Jr.,
George W. Brand,	Henry Wolf,	William M. Fishback,
James Hanna,	G. B. Hale,	J. C. Harrison,
George Kraup,	Samuel D. McCullough,	Thomas Norris,
C. R. Fitch,	Robert McElhinny,	J. L. Watson,
D. O. Newbold,	Hiram Shaw,	George A. Bowyer,
P. E. Yeiser,	John P. Tingle,	Richard Higgins,
Frank Fitch,	F. Montinollin,	Fred Fitch,
D. Warner,	P. C. Hollingshead,	Thomas C. Oscar,
T. D. Ballard,	Jacob Smith,	E. K. Stephens,
William Van Pelt, Sr.,	J. P. Miller,	J. M. Bush,
George W. Norton,	A. F. Hawkins,	J. R. Sharpe,

D. A. Sayre,	I. R. Morris,	E. D. Sayre,
William E. Bell,	Charles S. Brodley,	J. W. Berkley,
J. H. Harrison,	C. T. Messick,	John B. Tilford,
C. D. Carr,	W. T. Downey,	Thomas P. Nichols,
Thomas D. Carr,	Charles F. Lowry,	John B. Norton,
S. Swift,	W. B. Emmol,	L. Wheeler,
R. L. Burnet,	R. J. Woodhouse,	E. H. Parrish,
D. S. Goodloe,	John B. Wilgus,	P. C. Harnett,
Charles Y. Bean,	J. Harper,	M. T. Scott, Jr.,
John T. Miller,	G. R. Dunlap,	A. S. Hunt,
H. E. Jones,	John B. Tilford, Jr.,	I. F. Miller,
Joseph Milward,	R. McMichael,	W. P. Nichols,
A. F. Jones,	G. L. Postlethwaite.	

"This was gotten up," said Judge Goodloe, "in an hour; sorry we had not a longer time, for all our people would have esteemed it a great privilege to append their names."

Such a testimonial was equally creditable to the regiment, which merited and received it, and to the inhabitants who thus recognized the orderly deportment and splendid service rendered.

Later on, these noble, patriotic citizens desiring to testify to Colonel Sigfried's ability and fitness to command, united, in a letter to the President of the United States, dated March 15, 1864, strongly recommending his promotion to Brigadier-General. Among other things they said:

"None but those who have suffered from the presence of an undisciplined and incompetently officered army, can form an idea of the blessings to a civil community of an efficient officer and an orderly and well disciplined body of soldiers. The people of Lexington had severely suffered from the former and had never fully experienced the benefits of the latter, until Colonel J. K. Sigfried took command of this post, and the Forty-eighth Regiment Pennsylvania Volunteers constituted the military force of the city."

MAJOR DANIEL NAGLE.

MAJOR JAMES WREN.

MAJOR JOSEPH A. GILMOUR

MAJOR OLIVER C. BOSBYSHELL.

MAJOR JACOB WAGNER.

CHAPTER IX.

EAST TENNESSEE.

The regiment bid adieu to all its good friends in Lexington, on the morning of the tenth of September, 1863. Leaving the quarters so long occupied it passed down Limestone street to Main, and thence to the Kentucky Central Railroad station. The people of the city turned out in great crowds to bid good-bye, and the departure was like leaving home. The little village of Nicholasville was reached about 12 o'clock noon. Leaving the train the command moved along a very dusty turnpike until within three miles of Camp Nelson, where about 2 o'clock tents were pitched off the pike, and the camp named in honor of General John G. Parke, who commanded the Ninth Corps. The next day a regimental inspection was had, and a thorough examination of arms, accoutrements and clothing made. The First Brigade of the Second Division was reformed, consisting of the Forty-eighth Pennsylvania, Second Maryland, Sixth New Hampshire, and Twenty-first Massachusetts. The Eleventh New Hampshire was temporarily attached to the brigade, and remained with it for six days, leaving the command at Pitman's, Ky. Colonel Sigfried, being the senior colonel present, took command of the brigade, appointing the following staff: Captain O. C. Bosbyshell, of the Forty-eighth Pennsylvania, acting assistant adjutant general; First Lieutenant Jacob Wagner, Forty-eighth Pennsylvania, acting assistant quartermaster; First Lieutenant Henry Boyer, Forty-eighth Pennsylvania, acting assistant inspector general; Second Lieutenant John H. Varney, Sixth New Hampshire, acting commissary of subsistence; Surgeon Joseph Beatty, Second Maryland, acting brigade surgeon; First Lieutenant Henry Pennington, Second Maryland, and Second Lieutenant Henry S. Hitchcock, Twenty-first Massachusetts, acting aides-de-camp. These officers constituted the staff of the First Brigade during the entire East Tennessee campaign and the friendships then engendered still remain green and fresh.

Colonel Sigfried's orders were to move the brigade to Knoxville, by the way of Cumberland Gap. Having a march of over two hundred miles to accomplish, he determined to avail himself of the early morning, and later afternoon hours, affording ample time for rest during the heated portion of the day. Orders were promulgated requiring a steady tramp for three-quarters of an hour, and then a halt of fifteen minutes, with three hours' rest during the middle of the day. This systematic march was rigidly adhered to, and resulted in a rapid covering of the distance to be accomplished, with a minimum degree of fatigue on the part of the troops. So punctilious was the Colonel in requiring the brigade bugler to observe the time to blow the "rest" and "forward" exactly on the minute, that a deviation would result in sharp reproof. Indeed, all who carried watches knew to the second when the signal would be sounded, and were ready to obey either with cheerful alacrity.

During the ten miles covered on the twelfth, a terrific rain storm was encountered, and the encampment had at Camp Dick Robinson, was reached by the command in a thoroughly drenched condition. This did not prevent the enjoyment en route, of the grand scenery along the Kentucky River—hilly, rocky and romantic. A fine view was afforded from Heckman's bridge, which spans the river high above the stream.

The rain having effectually settled the dust, the marching on Sunday morning, the thirteenth, was greatly enjoyed. The way led through the small town of Lancaster, a pretty village, the good folks of which were going to service, summoned by the merry ringing of the church bells. The noon rest was had on the estate of Judge Lusk, to whose hospitality Colonel Sigfried and his staff became indebted. It was quite dark when Dick's River was reached, where the command bivouacked, seventeen and a half miles from Camp Dick Robinson.

The next day the forward movement carried the command through the somewhat noted watering place of Crab Orchard, which at the time presented rather a dismal, mean appearance. Some of the springs near at hand were heavily charged with sulphur whilst others were exceedingly briny.

Camp was made nearby under the wide spreading branches of a fine old woods, the delights of which were enjoyed all day of the fifteenth, the weather being clear, cool and invigorating. The sixteenth saw the command in motion—the roads being exceedingly rough, filled with stone and rocks, and very hilly. Eleven miles brought a bivouac within a mile northwest of Mount Vernon.

Camp was broken at 6 o'clock the next morning, and this village, consisting of some twenty odd houses, was passed through. It was curious to the men from the anthracite coal regions of Pennsylvania, to see the people here so easily supplying themselves with coal from the veins cropping out on the surface beside the road. They simply shoveled the black dirt into wagons. The way was up hill and down dale constantly. In many places the road being extremely rough and difficult of passage, especially for the teams. One of the wagons belonging to the Forty-eighth lost a wheel. The command passed over some fairly high mountains and rested the noon hours at Big Rockcastle River. During the morning a brigade of rebel prisoners, a dirty, greasy looking set of fellows, passed on their way to Yankee land, having been captured by Burnside's troops at Cumberland Gap. They were an hour in passing.

The march was resumed at 3 o'clock, and the way led over the Wild Cat Mountain, where the first battle in Kentucky took place, when Nelson's Union forces used up Zollicoffer's command. Bivouac was had at Little Rockcastle River at 5.30, and although but sixteen miles were covered, the rough way made the men weary.

Broke camp at 6.30 a. m. on the eighteenth and marched eight miles—within three miles of London, camping for the night. The place was called "Pitman's." It consisted of a hotel with a proprietor of that name, at the junction of two roads, both leading to Lexington, one via Nicholasville, eighty-two miles, and the other via Richmond, seventy miles. The day's march was short, but the road was rough.

The Eleventh New Hampshire was left at this post.

The march was resumed at an early hour the next day, and the noon halt found that nine miles of ground had been covered. The First Brigade staff dined at the farm-house of Uncle Charlie Colyer, a clever old gentleman who formerly drove teams from East Tennessee to all parts of Kentucky. Off again at 1 o'clock, and after marching but three miles, went into camp for the night by 3 p. m.

Here the paymaster, Major Fell, U. S. A., appeared and the boys' pocketbooks were thoroughly reinforced.

Left at 6.30 a. m. of the twentieth—weather cool and damp, with a dense fog covering field and road. By 9 o'clock old Sol managed to get the better of the fog, and beneath his warm rays the command moved along in good shape, until 1 o'clock, when a halt was had within a mile of Barboursville. Later on this small country village of scattering houses, some stores and a couple of taverns were passed, and a bivouac had on the banks of the Cumberland River—fifteen and a half miles having been traversed since morning. Colonel Simon G. Griffin, of the Sixth New Hampshire, reaching the command at this point, relieved Colonel Sigfried of the brigade, and he resumed the command of the Forty-eighth.

Off at 7 a. m. of the twenty-first—noon rest after marching seven or eight miles. March resumed at 2 p. m. and a camp ground reached by 4 p. m. on the south side of the Cumberland River, directly at Cumberland Ford, having covered thirteen miles. The command were comfortably quartered in an extensive apple orchard. The march so far was enjoyed by all—no complaint reached any ears, straggling was unheard of and no sickness in the command—all seemed hearty and well, not in the least broken down, but fresh and active.

This camp at Cumberland Ford was amidst the most attractive scenery—indeed, as the march followed all day the windings of the river, the charms of the richest autumnal effect impressed the entire command.

Broke camp at 7 a. m. of the twenty-second, the fog quite dense, obscuring the ford. The three Log Mountains were crossed—the road decidedly rough, stony and generally troublesome—noon halt was had on Yellow Creek, after a tramp of nine miles. A couple of hours' rest and off again, over dusty roads and exposed to a hot sun. A long trudge up the Cumberland Mountain brought the command into the Gap by 3.30. How the thirst was slacked at the magnificent spring, which was found flowing out from the side of the mountain on the summit of the Gap! A stone is here erected marking the boundary lines of Virginia, Kentucky and Tennessee. Emulating the example of some earlier writer, the chronicler sat down on Virginia, grasped the stone column, and put his right foot into Kentucky and left into Tennessee. The command halted for the night at the foot of the mountain on the Tennessee side at 4.30, having had a tedious march of fourteen miles.

Off at 7 a. m. of the twenty-third, halted at eleven, beside a cooling brook. Resumed march at 2 p. m., and encamped for the night at 4.30, on the edge of the town of Tazewell. This town impressed all favorably, although a large part of it had been destroyed by fire—the blackened ruins showing its extent. Some fifty-one rebel prisoners, two of whom were Pennsylvanians, were found here, being all that was left of 500, the balance having been released on taking the oath of allegiance. The day's march, thirteen miles, was much interfered with by the wagon trains of the First Division. Left Tazewell at seven the next morning and marched to the Clinch River, about eight miles. The bridge had been destroyed and the stream had to be waded. The ford was a treacherous one, it being necessary midway of the river to follow directly down stream for some distance before striking out for the opposite bank. To give the command an opportunity of washing clothes, a bivouac was had about 11 a. m. immediately south of the river. The tents were pitched beside the road facing the river. The opposite bank, where the command came from, presented high rocky cliffs, jagged and torn, extremely picturesque. The camp was on a plateau shaped like a horse-shoe, the river bending all around it. Some weeks later on, Sutler Isaac Lippman had an experience at this ford which was not pleasant. His wagon stuck in the middle of the river and was in imminent danger of being swamped. The proprietor danced about on the bank, fearful of loss, exclaiming, "Four tousand dollars mit de Clinch, four tousand dollars mit de Clinch!" Quartermaster Wagner came to the rescue with a team of mules and pulled the valuable cargo safely to shore. All wagon trains were ordered back to Tazewell, to get on the Knoxville road, as seven miles from the river Clinch Mountain barred the way, with an almost impassable road over it. Left camp at 6 a. m. of the twenty-fifth and reached the foot of Clinch Mountain by 8.30. The road up the mountain, whilst quite steep in places, was found good. From the summit a superb view breaks upon the sight. 'Tis said four States can be seen: Kentucky, Virginia, Tennessee and North Carolina. A vast extent of country spreads before the vision. The descent was most difficult—the road was like the one to Jordan, a "hard road to trabble." The troops could manage fairly well, but the brigade wagons, which had accompanied the column, had a rough passage. With the aid of long ropes, the men prevented these wagons from slipping over the banks and falling down the yawning precipices.

The task was finally accomplished, with the loss of one wheel and an iron bolt. The noon halt was bad at the foot of the mountain. The column moved again at 2 p. m., and by 4.30 the brigade was snugly quartered on the south bank of the Holston River, after wading through that stream—the entire day's march covering fifteen miles.

Off about 7 a. m. of the twenty-sixth, a mile's march and Beans' Station was passed—where a fine brick hotel was found, used by frequenters of the sulphur springs, which abound at this point. By 9.30 Morristown was reached—a shabby-looking little village, a station on the East Tennessee & Virginia Railroad. Dispatches were received here from General Burnside, directing Colonel Griffin to march the brigade directly to Knoxville. The march was resumed over very dusty roads, and the noon halt was made at Panther Springs. Jutting out of a small hill beside the road flowed an immense stream of water, sufficient to operate a large water-wheel just across the road. The column moved off at 2 p. m. and encamped for the night at Mossy Creek, having traveled some eighteen miles during the day, which, considering the heat and the never ending clouds of dust, was a fair day's work. Camp was broken at 6 a. m. the next day. Noon rest at Beaver Creek from 10 a. m. until 1 p. m., when the march was resumed, and Strawberry Plains reached after four miles' tramp. A railroad bridge spanned the Holston River at this point, but as the plank-walk over it would only accommodate one man in width, the horses had to go three miles down the river to find a ford. Colonel Griffin placed the brigade in charge of the senoir captain, and with the other mounted officers, galloped off to the ford. The command kept on down the railroad tracks, but were eventually headed off by the A. A. A. G., conducted to the wagon road and finally into a good camping ground, well provided with straw, near McMillan's, within thirteen miles of Knoxville. So the Sabbath's march ended, and sinking into piles of straw, beneath the brilliant rays of the moon, the command forgot in sleep its long, long tramp from Lexington!

McMillan's farm was left at 6 a. m. of the twenty-eighth. Over a very dusty road, the last day of the great march over the mountains from Lexington to Knoxville had arrived. Within two miles of Knoxville, the noon halt was had, a tedious delay having been occasioned by a brigade of cavalry heading off Griffin's command at a cross-road. Fresh meat was a part of the day's ration during this halt. Lieutenant Pennington, of Colonel Griffin's staff, brought orders at 3 o'clock to move on, and the column resumed the march, going into camp within a mile of Knoxville, on the top of a small hill to the left of the road, having gone some thirteen miles during the day. Thus ended the 221 miles' march, a march remarkable for its extent and the entire freedom from great fatigue by the men of the command. The regularity of the tramp, with its times for rest nicely adjusted, undoubtedly contributed to so satisfactory a result, and is in every way creditable to General Sigfried's sagacity and good sense.

The command remained quietly in camp during the twenty-ninth, and greatly enjoyed a visit from Generals Burnside and Parke, who rode through the company streets during the afternoon to see how the boys looked after the long tramp. Cheers long and loud greeted their appearance.

On the thirtieth a daily routine of duty was promulgated, amongst other things, requiring a battalion or company drill every afternoon. Colonel Griffin took command of the Second Division, which brought Colonel Sigfried to brigade headquarters in command.

The first of October was a rainy day, and all sought shelter. Still quiet on the second. Lieutenant Wagner, acting brigade quartermaster, under orders, started back to Lexington to bring forward fresh supplies for the command. No movement on the third.

Knoxville, Tenn., as seen during the war, must have presented a far different appearance than the place now presents, still the Union soldier could easily discern the many advantages possessed by its beautiful location.

Built on a hill, or several hills, except the northern portion, which extends over a considerable plain, low and flat. The houses crown the summits of the hills and run down the sides of the same. This formation renders many of the streets hilly. There were a number of fine looking streets—wide, straight and neatly built up. Some handsome residences adorned the town, and the whole place indicated plenty and prosperity.

The venerable Parson Brownlow, wielding a vigorous and trenchant pen through the columns of his *Knoxville Whig*, has made the town famous. Brownlow was a man of strong passion—he could love most ardently and he could hate most vindictively. To show his utter detestation of treason and traitors, he amended the title of his newspaper during the winter of '63 and '64, by adding the words "*and Rebel Ventilator.*" He resided upon the outskirts of the northern side of the town. His residence was a large, double two-story frame dwelling, with a porch in front, from which steps at each end led down to the sidewalks. The appearance of the building was much marred by its coming out flush with the pavement, instead of standing back, with front yard, as most suburban residences do.

The country about Knoxville is very beautiful, and situated, as most of the houses are, on high ground, the views obtained by the dwellers thereof are satisfactory to a degree. The Holston River winds around its southern side, and the scenery up and down this stream is particularly beautiful and engaging. South of the river a broad expanse of excellently wooded country spreads out for miles—broken here and there by cultivated farms of the most productive kind.

The still days in camp were utilized in visiting points of interest in and around the town.

With five days' light rations, without shelter tents or baggage, the command left camp at 9 o'clock on the morning of the fourth, and marched to the railroad station in Knoxville and boarded a train—or rather three long trains—the Forty-eighth and brigade headquarters occupying the first. By 12 o'clock noon the train started, bound toward the Virginia line. The various halting places occupied by the command during its march a week before, from Morristown to Knoxville, were noted. As the train sped on, the most cheering evidences of the loyalty of the men of East Tennessee to the Union cause were apparent. At Strawberry Plains, Mossy Creek, Morristown and other stations, large numbers of the good, loyal men of East Tennessee were congregating, organizing regiments. Many were already armed. It was a motley but earnest crowd—gray-haired, gray-bearded men of sixty jostled striplings of sixteen, all eager to do what they could to uphold the Union cause. The entire trip to Bull's Gap exhibited the same expressions of loyalty on all sides—a demonstration not excelled north of Mason and Dixon's line. A long stop was made at Morristown, awaiting orders, so that 7 o'clock came before the train moved off. Bull's Gap was reached after dark. Colonel Carter was in command at this place. He was reported to by ten, and a half an hour later the command was bivouacked.

Early rising was the rule. The night had been cold and the brigade felt the loss of shelter tents. Off by 8 o'clock of the fifth, marched to Lick Creek, some four miles. Brush huts, supported by fence rails, in line of battle, served for shelter, and thus protected, the command bivouacked. Occupied the same line during the sixth, seventh, eighth and ninth. The brush huts were exchanged for shelter tents on the ninth, the preceding days having been without much incident. The gathering of other brigades and presence of commanding general betokened a forward move. On the eighth, eleven wagons and a number of rebels, who were foraging too close to the Union lines, were captured.

A forward movement began at 9 o'clock a. m. of the tenth, covering some five or seven miles. Colonel Sigfried received an order to push forward his largest regiment, as the commanding general desired to post it. The A. A. A. G. carried the order to the Forty-eighth— up the boys came double quick on ahead of the entire command, and were posted as skirmishers upon a high ridge, the summit of which was covered with trees. The regiment went up the hill in glorious style, occupying the woods, which it was directed to hold. The balance of the brigade moved into the fields on either side of the road to await further developments. The cavalry was skirmishing in front with the enemy, whilst a battery pounded away, feeling the rebels' position. The Twenty-first Massachusetts was next sent in support of the advanced battery. The infantry formed line of battle behind the skirmish line. The advanced forces were placed in two lines: the Second Maryland occupied the left of the front line. General Wilcox, with 4000 new troops, was held in reserve. The infantry pushed the enemy, following them up. The Second Maryland was sent into the woods to hold the crest of a hill. The First Division of the Ninth Corps became engaged in a very lively way just at nightfall, but drove the enemy in good style, receiving the commendation of General Shackleford, who commanded the advance, for the gallant manner in which they went into action. Some prisoners were captured, and a number of both armies were killed and wounded. Night put an end to the fray called the battle of Blue Springs, the victory being achieved by the Union forces.

Early the next morning orders came from General Burnside to inquire of the Forty-eighth and Second Maryland whether any movement of the enemy had been detected in their front during the night. Lieutenant Hitchcock bore this order to the regiments named and soon reported that matters had remained as they were the evening before. About 7 o'clock Adjutant McGinnes, of the Forty-eighth, rode up to brigade headquarters with the information that he had observed two engines, with trains of cars, approach the enemy's lines within two miles of the Union outposts.

The writer carried this information to General Burnside, and whilst at his headquarters, the reconnoitering parties in front reported that the enemy had departed. The troops were pushed forward at 9.30 a. m. at a rapid pace, with but two regular halts for rest the entire day. The enemy, it was discovered, had mostly departed about midnight, so had eight hours' start of Burnside's column. Greenville, the old home of President Andrew Johnson, was hurried through—at many of the houses little knots of ladies were gathered, who showed their sympathy with the Union cause, by vigorously waving their handkerchiefs as the troops passed—on the march went, until Rheatown was reached and two miles beyond. Colonel Foster, with a brigade of cavalry, had been directed to make a detour, get into the enemy's rear and head them off, but like many other plans this failed, although Foster's men had a spirited fight and captured a number of prisoners, which was left at Rheatown. The march covered some twenty-one miles, and the command gladly went into bivouac just after dark.

Remained in camp two miles east of Rheatown all of the twelfth. Daylight showed evidences of the fighting with, and flight of, the enemy—several of their dead were found by the road, and a number of very good army wagons which they had abandoned. An interesting incident of this camp was the receipt of a huge mail for the boys—it was heralded by Quartermaster-Sergeant Schnerr, and eagerly devoured when received.

The command retraced its steps, starting at 7 o'clock in the morning of the thirteenth, passing through Rheatown and Greenville, and going into camp some three miles from the latter place alongside of the railroad. General Wilcox's command was encamped on the hills just east of Greenville—his own headquarters were pitched in a field contiguous to the road. Expecting to take the cars, all teams and horses were sent down the pike to Knoxville—but before retiring orders were received to march to Bull's Gap.

The next morning at 7 o'clock the troops started, not well pleased at having to tramp it, when a railroad ride had been expected. Some of the usually mounted officers succumbed after tramping five miles to Blue Springs, and were obliged to get in ambulances. Rodgersville Junction, Bull's Gap, was reached about 1 o'clock. Here Morrison's Brigade of the First Division, with the general officers and staff passed along on cars—the roadbed and rolling stock so poor, however, that it was with difficulty they could get along. This was so vexatious that General Burnside directed Sigfried's Brigade to march to Morristown before boarding the cars. At 3 o'clock the command pushed on, encamping for the night within nine miles of Morristown, having covered nineteen miles during the day.

The column moved shortly after 7 o'clock on the fifteenth and reached Morristown by 11 o'clock. Here a train was in waiting and with a feeling of intense satisfaction it was soon occupied by the troops. A generous mail was distributed on the cars, as the train sped toward Knoxville. The forty-two miles were made in three hours By 5 o'clock the regiments occupied their old camping grounds, and just got under cover when a tremendous rain storm set in. During the eleven days the brigade rode in cars ninety-seven miles and footed it seventy-two miles.

All were glad to remain close to camp on the sixteenth for rain, rain, rain, made tramping about anything but pleasant. The next day, however, was a glorious, mellow autumn day! The announcement made at dress parade of Curtin's re-election as Governor of Pennsylvania by 20,000 majority, was greeted by tumultuous cheers, making the old woods ring. The Forty-eighth had given the old War Governor a solid vote, 264, all present entitled to vote, and so the boys had a right to yell.

The first Sunday spent quietly in camp since the Forty-eighth left Lexington, was that of the eighteenth of October. On the nineteenth orders to be ready to move were received—all baggage and men not too sick to ride were directed to go along. Intelligence was promulgated of the removal of Rosencrans from the command of the Army of the West, and the appointment of Thomas in his stead, with Major-General Grant in command of all the United States forces west of the Alleghany Mountains. Colonel Sigfried assumed command of the Second Division in the afternoon, and Colonel Thomas B. Allard, of the Second Maryland Volunteers, that of the First Brigade—all owing to the absence of Colonel Hartranft home on leave, and Colonel Griffin in Kentucky. A mail containing over 25,000 letters, the largest to leave the post, was dispatched North this day. Preparations for the contemplated move kept the men of the command busily engaged all day of the twentieth.

Everything and everybody, all prepared to move on the twenty-first, but the command was directed to remain until further orders—these not coming before night tents were pitched in the old camp. The next day was an all day wait with all things ready to move. At 8 p. m. the order came, and the command moved to the railway station in Knoxville. By 10 o'clock the train bearing the troops moved off in the direction of Loudon. This point, about twenty-nine miles southwest from Knoxville, was reached at 1 o'clock a. m. The command bivouacked along the railway tracks—most of the men and officers occupying the ties for a bed, with the rail for a pillow.

A downpour of rain waked all hands good and early on the twenty-third. How it did rain—thoroughly drenching every person exposed to its fury. A camping ground a little better than the railway tracks, was secured in the neighborhood, where the command remained inactive all day, as the storm continued, making the roads almost impassable. Some few of the horses which left Knoxville by the wagon road, the same evening the troops did, arrived during the afternoon, but the most of them and all of the wagons failed to get up before the next morning.

A more comfortable camping ground was secured in the woods during the afternoon of the twenty-fourth. The town of Loudon was on the south side of the Holston River. A number of large chimneys indicated a manufacturing village of some pretensions. Burnside's forces occupied the north side of the river—the railway bridge across which had been destroyed. A pontoon bridge served to accommodate the troops.

The enemy, under Longstreet, was supposed to be in force, some six miles south, at a place called Philadelphia. The presence of Generals Burnside, Potter, Ferrero and White indicated active operations, and the command awaited events with a keen interest. The teamsters had serious work in getting their wagons through the rough and muddy roads from Knoxville—all of which forcibly reminded the men of the Virginia highways—and betokened a rough campaign in East Tennessee. October 25 was a quiet Sunday in camp, with better weather.

Reconnoisances on the twenty-sixth failed to discover the enemy within nine miles, and the belief obtained in some quarters that the rebels were not coming Knoxville way.

Orders were given on the evening of the twenty-seventh to be ready to move at 5 o'clock in the morning, the wagon trains to take the road to Lenoir, and sure enough by 4 o'clock the next morning the men were aroused and in line ready to move by five. The movement was to the river's edge, and then back in rear of a low range of hills, where arms were stacked. By 10 o'clock the troops south of the river had all passed over the pontoon bridge. The command was taken to the river again and the work of demolishing the bridge begun. About three-fourths of the task was accomplished when a squad of rebel cavalry appeared on the south bank of the river, displaying a flag of truce. Captain McKibben, Assistant Adjutant-general, Second Division, crossed the river to ascertain what was wanted. He found a first lieutenant and adjutant of the First Georgia Regiment awaiting him, with a demand from the rebel commander for the surrender of Loudon, or its evacuation within two hours and a half after receiving the dispatch. Loudon had already been left, and the rebels expressed great surprise at finding the Union forces retiring. The bridge was dismantled by 3 o'clock in the afternoon, and snugly placed aboard cars waiting on the railroad track, a half a mile away. At dusk, the command having completed its task, bivouacked in the rear of some high hills, which screened it from observation beyond the river. An incident of the day was the destruction of an engine and four freight cars remaining on the south side, the former being fired up and then started at full speed toward the river. It was a thrilling sight as it swept along to where the bridge had been, and then, amidst the shouts of the soldiers, it shot out into space, plunged into the river and sank out of sight!

Between 9 and 10 o'clock a. m. of the twenty-ninth, the command moved to Lenoir's Mills, reaching there by 12 o'clock noon. This was a small station on the railroad, at the junction of the Knoxville and Kingston wagon roads, some six miles northeast of Loudon. A delightful camping ground was secured, and the men proceeded to make themselves comfortable.

The commanding general's headquarters were pitched the next day immediately on the left of the First Brigade. The headquarters of the corps and division commanders were also quite near. Near by was the Holston River, the encampment occupying the ground on the bluffs overhanging it.

The advent of a large mail from home shared the interest of the thirty-first, with the muster for pay, the latter event foreshadowing the possible approach of the paymaster. Much fixing up to render quarters as comfortable as possible also marked the day. A corduroy bed is not a bad contrivance: four stout posts driven into the ground, with two poles resting upon them, form the skeleton. Upon the poles are placed some dozen or more lighter poles lengthwise and close together. Upon these a quantity of straw, or green pine-needles, are spread, the whole kept in place by a piece of carpet or blanket. It is comfortable and preferable to the ground.

Brigade guard mounting was inaugurated on the morning of November 1, under most favorable circumstances. The proximity of the regiments of the command, and excellent parade ground, coupled with one of the most delightful November days, rendered the ceremony exceptionally fine. Being Sunday, the troops presented a good appearance, having just gotten through the morning's inspection.

It is remarkable the way in which camp rumors start and how they gather importance and strength as they are rolled along from mouth to mouth. On the second, it was stated that the Forty-eighth Regiment was about to be transferred to the Second Brigade. General Potter had a high opinion of Colonel Sigfried's military capacity as a brigade commander. The transfer of the Forty-eighth to the Second Brigade would have made him senior colonel of that brigade, hence commander. The arrangement was: Hartranft at the head of the Second Division, Griffin commanding the first and Sigfried the Second Brigade. The change never took place. Division Commissary of Subsistence, Lieutenant Sam Keys, of New Jersey, was made Superintendent of Railroads in East Tennessee, by order of General Burnside. The First Brigade staff was augmented by the appointment on it of Captain James Cooper, of the Second Maryland, as provost marshal. The son of Pennsylvania's Senator Cooper, "Jim," as an old Pottsvillian, was popular with the boys.

November 3. The living at Lenoir was really decidedly pleasant —provisions could be purchased in the neighborhood at reasonable prices, so officers' messes fared well. General Potter seemed anxious to utilize Colonel Sigfried other than as the commander of a regiment. He asked him on November 3 how he would like to command two regiments of dismounted troops and three regiments of six months' men. Like a good soldier, Sigfried signified his readiness to assume any duty imposed upon him. This was flattering to the colonel of the Forty-eighth. He was highly thought of at both corps and department headquarters, as many expressions of confidence in his ability dropped from Burnside, Potter and Wilcox in the hearing of the writer. Details of carpenters from the regiments were busily engaged in constructing a lot of pontoon boats, and masons in building bake-ovens for the making of bread.

November 4. The halt at Lenoir brought with it applications for leaves of absence. The very able clerk at brigade headquarters, Charles H. Hazzard, of G, contracted chills and fever in Mississippi, and this, combined with the rigors of the East Tennessee campaign, made inroads upon a constitution otherwise strong. An application for a furlough successfully passed division and corps headquarters, and was taken to Knoxville on the fourth by Lieutenant Pennington to get the seal of approval from General Burnside. This was accomplished and Hazzard was assured home and recovery.

One day passes as another in the routine of camp life: so passed the fifth. Word reached the command of guerilla bands infesting the roads north—especially about Cumberland Gap, and fears were entertained for the safety of a wagon train of supplies en route, in charge of Quartermaster Wagner. Part of the First Division left for Greenville at night to reinforce Wilcox's troops, who had been driven out of that place by the enemy. On the sixth came the welcome word that Wagner and his train were through the Gap, having escaped guerillas, although detained at London, Ky., several days to keep out of their way. The sutler of the Second Maryland arrived on the fifth, with terrible reports of the shocking condition of the roads. Sutler Lippman was with Wagner, and the boys awaited his advent with great eagerness.

The seventh, eighth and ninth were routine days—but they were cold ones. A cold snap, bringing ice, rendered big fires comfortable, and made it necessary for the men to hug these fires assiduously.

Surgeon Beatty, Lieutenant Pennington and Clerk Hazzard, from the brigade staff, all left on the tenth in an ambulance train for the trip over the mountains to Lexington, and thence on leave for home: the first to be married, the second to have an operation performed on his eye to prevent blindness, and the latter to regain lost health. In the afternoon, Captain Shuck, Lieutenant Pollock and Adjutant McGinnes reached camp, returning from duties imposed by former details.

The brigade was under arms at 6 a. m. of the eleventh, and marched to the river, just in the rear of the camp, to protect the men who were to lay the pontoon bridge. This bridge was constructed in eight days—it consisted of over thirty boats, and when laid, was 640 feet long. The timber was all cut, sawed and put together in a day over a week. The Twenty-first Massachusetts took boats, crossed the river (Holston) and occupying the opposite bank, pushed forward a picket guard to prevent surprise, should any rebel force be in the neighborhood. By dint of hard work, in a very cold atmosphere, the structure was completed before dark. Picket duty on the opposite shore relieved the guards on the camp side, and the bridge made communication with a section of the country unmolested by either army, well supplied with good forage for the horses.

For the next two days the pontoon bridge was found to be quite useful, and excursions to the opposite side of the river were taken by all who could do so. The thirteenth was made memorable by the safe return of Quartermaster Wagner, from his perilous trip from Lexington, bringing through successfully a train of supplies. He also brought with him the Forty-eighth's popular sutler, Isaac Lippman, and a famous stock of sutler stores. Events proved that the pontoon bridge was only to be used a short time, for on the morning of November 14 camp was broken at Lenoir for active work, and the strong and well built pontoon bridge was totally destroyed in a few hours. The command moved a mile in the direction of Loudon, where a bivouac for the night was had. Early on the morning of the fifteenth, at 2 o'clock, the march toward Loudon was resumed. The recent rains rendered the roads muddy and hard to navigate. Daylight saw the command occupying the banks of the Tennessee River opposite and about a mile below Loudon, so posted as to harass the forward movement of Longstreet's forces, sent to dislodge the Union army in East Tennessee. During the morning part of the Twenty-third Army Corps was engaged in skirmishing with the advance forces of the enemy, and by 10 and 11 o'clock, the First Brigade of the Ninth received orders to hold the enemy in check long enough to give the artillery and wagons plenty of time to get well on the way to Knoxville, so as to prevent capture. The line was held until 4 o'clock in the afternoon, at which time, under orders, the brigade slowly retired. The writer, by direction of Colonel Sigfried, commanding the division, took command of the rear guard, deployed the Second Maryland as skirmishers, and held the advance of Longstreet in check, until relieved by the Second Brigade. Lenoir was reached at dark, about 6 o'clock. Rations were issued and the march immediately resumed toward Knoxville. The brigade was pushed ahead and marched all night, reaching Campbell's Station at daylight, and immediately posted on the Kingston road to hold in check any forces of the enemy appearing from that quarter in an attempt to flank our forces. Twenty-two miles over troublesome roads, with several hours' skirmishing, were made from 2 a. m. of the fifteenth until 6 a. m. of the sixteenth. The cavalry videttes were hurried to the front on the Kingston road, and found the enemy pushing along with the evident intention of doing just what had been anticipated, and just what the First Brigade was stationed there to prevent. During the preceding night, Colonel Hartranft resumed command of the division, and Colonel Sigfried that of the First Brigade. Between 8 and 9 o'clock a. m., matters assumed a serious look—the rebels closed in on both roads, slowly pressing the Union forces toward the junction of these roads, directly at Campbell's Station, and the fighting became the fiercest at this point. It was not Burnside's wish to engage the enemy at close quarters at this point; he was manœuvring for time, intending to retire to Knoxville, where fortifications were being erected. So the battle of Campbell's Station was a fight to hinder the rebels' approach and delay it as long as possible. It became, after the severe little tussle at the junction of the Loudon and Kingston roads, just like a mighty game of chess. The movement of the forces of both armies was clearly discernible, and as the enemy pushed forward a line on the left, the Union commander met it with a counter movement on the right, and so on from left to right. The Army of the Ohio, on the defensive, occupied a wide extent of open, undulating country, perfectly free from woods, or anything to obstruct the view. As the latter retired slowly behind successive lines of battle, formed to the rear, the enemy would approach as successively, each movement being seen by all. The batteries of the contending forces pounded shot and shell into each other's ranks from eligible positions upon the surrounding hills. The manœuvring was perfect. The novel sight, although carrying death into all ranks, was thoroughly enjoyed by the participants. Night closed this great game of chess. The command was put in motion toward Knoxville. Marching rapidly all night, it reached there at daylight on the morning of the seventeenth.

It was subsequently learned that the enemy, whose forces had been observed passing along toward the left flank of the Union lines during the holding of the last position taken by it, had really gotten around that flank and were in force in the rear of the Union army, intending to capture the rear guard, but mistaking that guard for an army corps, found too late that Burnside was safely within the confines of Knoxville.

This place was immediately invested by Longstreet's forces, and Burnside began the preparation for defending it. Shovels, picks and axes were in demand, and hard work fell upon the men, night and day. Formidable entrenchments were erected running from the Holston

River on the southwest side of the town, all around to the same river on the northeast side, with Fort Sanders, an earthwork of strength, occupying the most commanding elevation in the whole line. Indeed, Knoxville was rendered thoroughly defensible, especially on the Ninth Corps' front. Just beneath the bluff occupied by the Forty-eighth Regiment ran the embankment of the East Tennessee and Virginia Railroad—large culverts pierced these embankments to permit the flow of two pretentious creeks. Hartranft saw in this a chance of rendering this front unapproachable. He closed up these culverts, using the railroad embankment for a dam, and so effectually protected the line that it could only have been approached by boats. The pickets were nearly drowned out, but new lines were established on the town side of the dams. In the northern or flat portion of the town, beyond the railroad, firing parties were regularly detailed at nights whose duty it was at a given signal, when an attack was made on the picket line, to ignite a frame dwelling house so as to light up the country, and enable the artillery to use grape and canister on the attacking party. Before this precaution was taken, one night the Union pickets were driven in, and Johnny Reb remained for the rest of the night in possession of the line, scarcely a stone's throw from the main earthworks. Before daylight the Forty-eighth Pennsylvania and the Twenty-first Massachusetts formed line, and just at dawn charged the audacious foe, driving him back to his old lines helter-skelter, and re-established the pickets.

One other time the picket line was driven in, but the Second Brigade of the Ninth Corps swept the "Johnnies" back again re-establishing the Union picket line.

Thursday, the twenty-sixth of November, was the day appointed by President Lincoln as a National Thanksgiving Day. There was no turkey for the troops in the trenches that day—quarter day rations prevailed, and all would have been thankful for much plainer food than turkey, provided there was only plenty of it! " I recall a characteristic scene toward the close of that day when two soldiers were hovering over a fire of twigs they had built in the bottom of the trench, the wind frequently blowing the smoke in their faces, notwithstanding their attempts to ward it off with their hands. They were talking of Thanksgiving at home, and recounting the savory dinners they had thoughtlessly eaten, with thankless hearts, in times past, and were wondering what their people at home were doing, and whether they were remembered. An occasional shot from some misguided 'greyback' passing overhead, attracted less attention than the evolutions of sundry squads of *domestic* 'greybacks' that were endeavoring to gain strategic positions under those soldiers' blouses, and frequent appropriate gestures, that were needed to round off and add grace to some sentence in the conversation, were suddenly arrested and used to intercept some hostile movement." *

Colonel Sigfried commanded the First Brigade during the entire siege, and indeed for the remainder of the Forty-eighth's stay in East Tennessee. He occupied as his headquarters rooms in the house of the leading photographer of Knoxville. He was a delicate looking man, with a fine, healthy, robust wife; both were uncompromising Unionists the latter exceedingly outspoken in her condemnation of rebels—a regular of the Brownlow type.

Much has been said by old soldiers who have experienced it—and where is there a man who served in active field duty, during the war, who has not?—of the bitter tongue of the women with rebel proclivities. Ah! the scorching tirade that has been heaped upon the head of many a Unioner! Indeed, the tongue is "an unruly member"— keener than the sharpest blade! Let any unfortunate individual of Confederate tendencies pass within hearing of Sigfried's hostess, and such a scathing would fall upon his devoted head as to leave him, metaphorically speaking, bald as a new born babe!

The Episcopal clergyman living in Knoxville during the siege was troubled with a severe attack of Rebellionetis. His straight, stiff, starched form loomed up one morning, heading down the street directly by the house of the determined Unionist. She occupied a convenient position at her front gate, and opened up her tongue artillery before he reached her, with: "Here comes this pusillanimous, cowardly stick of a man, who teaches his congregation to pray for the rebels," and so on, with hot words, representing all the grades of ammunition, rapidly pouring in the small shot, with all the ferocity of a Gatling, as he passed close by her, and ending with tremendous big bombs, screeched after him, as he faded in the distance. The effect upon the reverend gentleman was peculiar. The first shot rather took him unawares, but as it was speedily followed up by unmistakable evidences of being meant for himself, he braced up his clerical dignity to ward off the keen, cutting sarcasm. The tirade was, however, too great, or his armor too thin, for he perceptibly wilted at each succeeding step, and almost fairly ran, as the hot words pelted and pounded his retreating back, until he looked all shrunken and wasted away, as limp as the veriest Bunthorne could wish. It was the most withering tongue castigation mortal could be subjected to, and overlapped any thing of the kind from the other side that the writer ever heard.

---

* "Recollections of the East Tennessee Campaign," by Will. H. Brearley, Company E, Seventeenth Michigan Volunteers, p. 34.

On Sunday, the twenty-ninth of November, Longstreet determined on assaulting the Union lines. Before daylight, he hurled a column of sixteen regiments deep against Fort Sanders, with lamentable results to the attacking party. Benjamin, commanding a battery of the Fourth United States Artillery, stationed in this fort, anticipating just such an attack, had taken the precaution to clear away the forest in the front of the fort, leaving the stumps sticking well up. Stretching from stump to stump, he crossed and recrossed telegraph wire. When this column of regimental front, and sixteen regiments deep, moving to the attack in the darkness before dawn, came upon the entangled mass of wire, the troops were thrown into inextricable confusion, their organizations helplessly broken, and the whole command no better than an unorganized mob. So impetuous, however, was the mad rush for the fort, that the flags of the Thirteenth and Seventeenth Mississippi and the Sixteenth Georgia were actually planted on the corner thereof—but only for a moment, as the Union troops captured them. Benjamin was coolly lighting shells, with shortened fuses, and tossing them with his hands over the parapet into the ditch surrounding the earthwork—causing death and confusion to the crowded mass of disorganized troops. "It stilled them down," he said. The strife did not last long, and the enemy fled dismayed. An armistice, lasting from daylight until 7 p. m., marked this Sunday. Four stands of rebel colors were captured, 300 rebel dead laid around Fort Sanders, as many more were wounded, and the same number made prisoners. The corner of Fort Sanders, and the ditch before it, was filled with dead and dying men—the sight was horrible. During the armistice, these dead were buried by the enemy, and the wounded carried away. General Burnside wisely declined to keep the large number of wounded prisoners, the crowded condition of Knoxville precluding the burdening of his army with a helpless lot of men, who would tax the already depleted stock of provisions—so they were conveyed away by the rebels. During this armistice, Yankees and rebels met by the hundreds on the neutral ground between the lines—shook hands and had good long talks with each other. An arrangement was entered into between the men that no more picket firing should be done, and this was kept for some time, the pickets of either side walking their beats in full view of each other. But one day came the following from the enemy: "Git into your holes, Yanks, we've got orders to fire on you." Into the rifle pits dropped the boys and the banging became as lively as ever.

The siege did not worry the Union army much; provisions were not very plenty for the troops, but for the horses and mules, forage was obtainable in the country south of the Holston River for twenty miles, which could be gathered unmolested. Isaac Lippman's stock of sutler's stores lasted well, and the boys took advantage of it. Although woefully short of cash, to Isaac's credit be it said, he willingly trusted them. Good Dr. Cutter, surgeon of the Twenty-first Massachusetts, acting division surgeon, showed his knowledge and skill during the siege in the care he took of the troops. He established a hospital filled with comforts. It was not play, working and watching in the trenches all day—so he instructed his surgeons to note well the men at early roll call, and where one looked fagged out, to send him to his hospital. Here a good bath would be given the unfortunate and a snug and comfortable bed provided, thus enabling him to secure a good rest. Then this good doctor prescribed well-cooked food, with some little delicacy he had procured during the rambles of the troops, and stored for just such purpose. Many a soldier was saved from an attack of sickness by this thoughtful practice of Surgeon Cutter.

Longstreet, finding he could not starve the Army of the Ohio out of Knoxville, that he could not force them out by attacking their lines, and fearing the arrival of Sherman, Howard and Granger's Corps of Thomas' Army, which were approaching, pulled up stakes and departed for Virginia on the fifth of December. The First Brigade left the trenches at 9 o'clock in the morning to reconnoitre, and extended its researches into quite a section of the surrounding country, gathering up some fifty prisoners, found in squads of two or three on the roads traversed.

General Burnside issued the following congratulatory order, to wit:

HEADQUARTERS ARMY OF THE OHIO.
GENERAL FIELD ORDERS, No. 34.
In the Field, December 5, 1863.

The Commanding General congratulates the troops on the raising of the siege. With unsurpassed fortitude and patient watchfulness they have sustained the wearing duties of the defence, and with unyielding courage they have repulsed the most desperate assaults.

The Army of the Ohio has nobly guarded the loyal region it redeemed from its oppressors, and has rendered the heroic defence of Knoxville memorable in the annals of the war. Strengthened by the experiences and the successes of the past, they now, with the powerful support of the gallant Army which has come to their relief, and with undoubting faith in the Divine protection, enter with the brightest prospects upon the closing scenes of a most brilliant campaign.

By command of MAJOR-GENERAL BURNSIDE.
LEWIS RICHMOND,
Assistant Adjutant-General.

From the headquarters of General Grant came the following, to wit:

HEADQUARTERS MILITARY DIVISION OF THE MISSISSIPPI,
GENERAL ORDERS, No. 7.
In the Field, Chattanooga, Tenn., December 8, 1863.

The General commanding takes great pleasure in publishing to the brave armies under his command, the following telegraphic dispatch just received from the President of the United States:

"*Washington, December 8, 1863.*

To Major-General Grant:—Understanding that your lodgment at Chattanooga and at Knoxville is now secure, I wish to tender you, and all under your command, my more than thanks, my profoundest gratitude, for the skill, courage and perseverance with which you and they, over so great difficulties, have effected that important object. God bless you all!   A. LINCOLN."

By order of   MAJOR-GENERAL U. S. GRANT.
T. S. BOWERS,
Assistant Adjutant-General.

On Monday morning, December 7, the brigade left Knoxville, taking the Morristown road, but subsequently leaving it for the Rutledge road, tramped some twelve miles and encamped for the night on the latter road. The next day only six or seven miles of marching was done, and the night was spent near Blain's Cross Roads. On the ninth the march was resumed for twelve miles, and the encampment had within a mile of Rutledge—a small village of wooden houses, save the Court House, which was a large brick building of fine appearance. The town had been completely stripped of provisions—butter, eggs and chickens were not to be had—the rebels having cleared the place out just twenty-four hours previously. The route from Knoxville lay directly between the Holston and Clinch Rivers, and the weather was most delightful for out-door work. Rations were not plentiful—indeed the allowance was extremely small. Whether this had anything to do with the good health of the men of the command is hard to say, but the fact remains that whilst campaigning in East Tennessee, but little sickness prevailed among the troops. The command remained encamped near Rutledge until Tuesday, the fifteenth of December, although orders to be ready to move at 7 o'clock Monday morning were received at 12 o'clock the Sunday night before. Camp was abandoned and line of battle formed, awaiting an expected attack from the enemy, who were said to be returning again toward Knoxville. The line was maintained all day without any demonstration on the part of the rebels, and after dark the command moved to the rear some four miles, and bivouacked beside the road. The retrograde movement was continued the next day for seven or eight miles, when a halt was had, with the idea of here making a stand to battle with the foe. The position occupied by the main body of troops, within two miles of Blain's Cross Roads, was an eligible one.

The Second Division of the Ninth Corps occupied a position two miles in advance of the proposed battle ground, and formed a barricade of fence rails to retard the enemy's approach long enough to enable the troops in the rear to fortify their position. This advanced line was unmolested all day of Wednesday, the sixteenth, and the troops rested well the same night. On the seventeenth a very slight skirmish immediately in the division's front took place—some rebel cavalry appeared on a distant knoll, threw forward a few skirmishers, but soon recalled them—and night closed in without the expected, and by this time really hoped for, advance. The weather became quite cold, making it uncomfortable without tents. The morning of the eighteenth found the enemy invisible. The Twenty-first Massachusetts was thrown forward—it moved some two or three miles to the front, skirmishing with a small force of rebel cavalry, holding its advanced position all day. This was the last the command saw of any rebel troops in East Tennessee.

On the nineteenth the command settled down into camp about three and a half miles in an easterly direction from Blain's Cross Roads, and was employed in picketing the valley. The farthest outpost was possibly two miles away.

A large force of Union troops had reached Knoxville from General Thomas' Army, and the entire safety of East Tennessee from reoccupation by the rebel army was assured.

The weather, whilst clear and bright, became cold, and much time was spent in hugging the wood fires. The First Brigade marched some five miles up the valley on the twenty-third on a reconnoissance, to discover, if possible, the whereabouts of the enemy. The search ended at the junction of the Powder Spring Gap road with the main road in the valley. This expedition is impressed on the mind of the writer from the fact that Lieutenant, afterward Captain, Henry Boyer, serving as quartermaster on the staff of the First Brigade, discovered in the yard of a settler up the Powder Spring Gap road a couple of fine turkeys, and it was not a matter of many moments, with so excellent a forager, before these fowls were swinging over the pommel of his saddle bound for camp—thus ensuring a Christmas dinner of the regular stamp. It is right to say that Boyer paid full value for the birds. Colonel Sigfried was in command this day, and whilst toasting his shins before the fire of a hospitable farmer, his use of a paper of fine-cut tobacco interested the snuff-dipping daughters of his host, and the gallant Colonel won their everlasting gratitude, if not devotion, by presenting them with a fresh paper of the delicacy which he happened to have with him.

Just at this time the exciting business of re-enlistment broke out in all the regiments of the Ninth Corps—particularly in the Second Division, and a spirit of emulation sprang up between the various regiments as to which should secure the necessary three-fourths, in order to be the first to receive the veteran month's furlough. The Forty-eighth Pennsylvania and the Twenty-first Massachusetts were the first regiments in the corps to re-enlist—the latter sent its report in first, hence was the first ordered home, but the Forty-eighth was the first regiment re-mustered—more than three-fourths of the men composing it patriotically determining to see the war ended.

The first of January, 1864, was a remarkable day—the morning was murky and warm, the roads muddy and almost impassable for wagons, many sinking in the mud to the hubs. Before nightfall such a decided change had taken place in the weather, that the same roads were frozen solidly, so much so, that the wagons jolted over the frozen ruts. This cold snap made it necessary to improvise some way for the men to keep warm, but they were equal to the occasion. Before the open end of each little shelter tent a wall of logs was erected, against which a fire of small kindling wood was built, this charring the logs up quite a distance threw the heat back into the tents and rendered the boys comfortable.

The Twenty-first Massachusetts started on veteran furlough on the seventh of January, '64. This event made the 316 men of the Forty-eighth, who had then re-enlisted, most anxious for their turn to come. They were not kept long in suspense. The writer was at corps headquarters on the afternoon of the eleventh of January, and found that orders had just been received directing the Forty-eighth Regiment to proceed to Pennsylvania, there to report through the Governor, to the Superintendent of Recruiting for furlough and reorganization. Before night the welcome news reached the regiment, causing great rejoicing amongst the veterans. The following farewell order to the brigade was issued the next day :

HEADQUARTERS FIRST BRIGADE, SECOND DIVISION, NINTH ARMY CORPS,
NEAR BLAIN'S CROSS ROADS, TENN.

GENERAL ORDER, No. 1. *January 12, 1864.*

I. The following named officers have been relieved from duty with this brigade and are ordered to report to their respective regiments, to-wit:

Captain Oliver C. Bosbyshell, 48th Pa. Vols., as A. A. Genl.

First Lieutenant Chas. Goss, 21st Mass. Vols., as A. A. Q. M.

Second Lieutenant Jno. H. Varney, 6th N. H. Vols., as A. C. S.
First Lieutenant Henry Boyer, 48th Pa. Vols., as A. A. I. G.
Captain Benj. F. Taylor, 2d Md. Vols., as A. A. D. C.
First Lieutenant Henry S. Hitchcock, 21st Mass. Vols., as A. A. D. C.

The Colonel commanding returns his thanks to these officers for their valuable assistance, and expresses his satisfaction with the management of the several departments with which they were connected.

II. In parting with the brigade the Colonel commanding desires to return his sincere thanks to both officers and men for their promptness, fortitude and gallantry. The campaign in which you have been engaged has been one of great severity. It has been attended with long and arduous marches, trying picket duty, severe skirmishing, and hard-fought battles; taxing your powers of endurance to the utmost. A great portion of East Tennessee has been traversed. You routed the enemy at Blue Springs and followed him to the Virginia line, and again you engaged him on the Tennessee River. The trying duties attending the memorable siege of Knoxville you bore with great fortitude, and gallantly drove back the enemy's encroachments on your rifle pits. In addition to all this you have passed through these duties upon an exceedingly limited supply of provisions—an ordeal to test your patriotism, and soldierly qualifications, which you have overcome cheerfully and resolutely. For the many assurances of your good feeling, and promptness in obeying orders the Colonel commanding offers his thanks.

J. K. SIGFRIED, *Colonel*,
Commanding Brigade.

CHAPTER X.

VETERAN FURLOUGH.

On Wednesday morning, 9 o'clock, January 13, the regiment broke camp, and started on the long march back over the mountains to Lexington. The command halted before the headquarters of General Potter, and the men were greatly gratified at the speech that officer made them. With cheers for Potter long and loud the march was resumed, and not concluded until seventeen miles of the way had been covered. The night was spent at a Mr. Walter's, within four miles of Walker's Ford on the Clinch River. The tramp was taken up the next morning at 8 o'clock, and some eighteen miles were accomplished, and the camp pitched within five or six miles of Cumberland Gap. Twelve miles were made on the fifteenth, the halt for the night being had at the foot of the Gap on the north side. Colonel Sigfried, Lieutenant-Colonel Pleasants and Captain Bosbyshell, with an ambulance and two or three orderlies, left the regiment in command of Major Gilmour, after crossing the Clinch River and pushed on ahead, with the intention of procuring needed supplies at Lexington, and of having the same on hand when the regiment arrived. These officers traveled rapidly—some trouble happening to the ambulance, Colonel Pleasants waited for it at Camp Lynn Post Office, whilst the other officers pushed on. Lexington was reached on the nineteenth, and the next day Captain Bosbyshell was sent to Cincinnati to secure 160 infantry jackets for the regiment. The command came along in good shape, and reached Camp Nelson at 2 o'clock in the afternoon of Friday the twenty-second. The next day it arrived in Lexington before 12 o'clock noon, and took up its old quarters out Limestone street. This return to the "old stamping ground" was like a home-coming, and very happy and enjoyable were the two days spent in renewing the friendships engendered by five months' provost duty.

At 12 o'clock noon of the twenty-fifth the Forty-eighth steamed out of Lexington by the Kentucky Central Railroad, and did not reach Covington until 12 o'clock at night, the train being detained by an accident to the regular up p. m. passenger train. During the trip Patrick M. Brown, private, of Company F, was knocked off the top of one of the cars, thrown under the train and killed. This cast quite a gloom over the otherwise enjoyable journey. The regiment was quartered in barracks in West Covington, and remained here until the thirty-first. The muster rolls had not been properly prepared in East Tennessee, so new ones had to be made out, as well as rolls for pay. Sunday, the thirty-first, was a busy day—rolls were signed and the regiment paid. At 6.30 p. m. a train for the East was boarded, and the start for home began in earnest. In the midst of a heavy rain the train sped on. At Columbus a change of cars was made. Breakfast was had at Crestline, and the way resumed at 9 o'clock a. m., February 1. Harrisburg was reached at 5 o'clock p. m. of the second. The next morning at 8 o'clock the State Capitol was left, and Pottsville was reached at 4 o'clock the same afternoon, where a grand reception awaited the command.

Pottsville was in holiday attire for this occasion, its patriotic citizens being determined to give the regiment a hearty welcome home, and thus, by the demonstration emphasize the good work done by the boys, showing how heartily it was appreciated.

Private residences were decorated with large streamers of red, white and blue, whilst flags, large and small, were displayed everywhere throughout the town. Along the route over which the command passed were displayed the names of the battles in which it had participated. At the residence of Mrs. Samuel Sillyman, on Mahantongo street, three medallions were suspended in the centre of the street, bearing the names of Burnside, Nagle and Sigfried, three names the Forty-eighth honored and revered.

General James Nagle was the chief marshal of the procession assembled to do honor to the regiment.

When the train reached Mt. Carbon, the command left the cars amid the rousing shouts of the mass of people gathered to welcome it, and formed line in front of the Mansion House. A beautiful stand of colors prepared by the ladies of Pottsville, was here presented to the regiment. The standard was made of heavy blue silk, with the arms of the State of Pennsylvania, on one side, and the arms of the United States on the reverse, both of which were surrounded by scrolls containing the names of the following battles, in which the regiment had been engaged: Bull Run, August 29, 1862; Chantilly, September 14, 1862; Antietam, September 17, 1862; Fredericksburg, December 13, 1862. The guidons were four in number, a small American flag, and one of red, one white and the other blue, made of stout twilled silk, upon each of which was inscribed: "48th P. V."

Mrs. E. R. Bohannon and Miss Miesse were entrusted with the duty of getting up these flags.

Hon. James H. Campbell made the presentation, most eloquently, as follows:

"*Officers and Soldiers of the Forty-eighth Regiment:*

"I have been honored by the ladies of Pottsville, your sisters, wives, and mothers, with the pleasing duty of presenting this flag, guidons and markers, as their testimonial to and appreciation of your patriotism, bravery and devotion to the cause of the Union.

"You bring with you tattered flags from glorious battlefields— flags rent in conflict, but of stainless honor. The ladies of Pottsville beg leave to place by the side of these, this beautiful flag, the work of their fair hands. Where the white horses romp in the azure field, you see inscribed Chantilly, Antietam, South Mountain and East Tennessee, one and all recalling memories of heroic deeds that will live while time endures.

"The fair donors have watched with sympathetic bosoms, your trials, bravery and suffering—the deadly struggle, the sufferings in hospitals, on the weary march and by the dreamless bivouac, all heroically borne by you. While they have shed tears for the gallant dead, they come to-day, with words of welcome and smiles of gratitude, to greet their returning brothers and husbands.

"Soldiers, you have registered a vow in heaven that the old flag shall fly in all its original splendor over every inch of territory the nation ever possessed, and that too, over free territory. A few years since it was loved and respected everywhere,—for it was everywhere, by glacial pinnacles, and under the suns of the tropics, in the marts of the old world and the wilderness of the new. It must not now be shorn of its glory.

"*Soldiers, you carry peace on the points of your bayonets, and true diplomacy in your cartridge boxes.* We can have no true, lasting or honorable peace until the rebels submit to the laws of the country. We, as good citizens, cheerfully submit to constituted authority. We ask no more of them; we will submit to no less.

"We bid you a hearty, earnest, warm-hearted welcome to this good old county of Schuylkill, a welcome made doubly endearing in that the ladies bid me, in their name, emphasize it with this glorious banner of liberty."

The Forty-eighth responded with three hearty cheers for the ladies, and Colonel Sigfried sincerely thanked them for the great honor conferred upon the command, promising to bring the colors back from the field of battle in honor or not at all. How well the boys ratified this promise is evidenced in that the command never lost a color!

An interesting episode of the occasion was the presentation, by a young lady, to Colonel Sigfried of a beautiful wreath.

The procession then formed and proceeded up Centre street in the following order:

General Nagle and aids.
Colonel Oliphant and staff.
Battalion of Invalid Corps.
Pottsville Band.
Forty-eighth Regiment, under the command of Colonel Sigfried.
Honorably Discharged and Convalescent Soldiers, under command of Major James Wren.
Seventh Pennsylvania Cavalry, under command of Major Jennings.
First New York Artillery, under command of Lieutenant Hall.
Miners' Lodge, No. 20, I. O. of O. F.
Carriages containing Committee of Arrangements.
Citizens on horseback.

As the procession commenced moving a national salute was fired by the New York Battery. The veterans were greeted all along the route by cheers and the waving of handkerchiefs. The streets were filled with thousands of people. A more animated spectacle has been rarely witnessed in Pottsville. The tattered flags of the Forty-eighth were objects of great interest. After passing through the principal streets, the command was halted in front of the Union Hotel. A fervent, patriotic prayer was made by the Rev. Mr. Koons, an address of welcome delivered by John Bannan, Esq., to which Colonel Sigfried replied, thanking the citizens for their kind reception, and telling them of the spirit which animated the men in re-enlisting, expressing a hope that the command would return to the field recruited to its full strength.

A collation prepared by the ladies, followed at the Union Hotel. The boys were dismissed, and each found home in the shortest space of time.

The regiment returned with 340 men. The field and staff officers were: Colonel, J. K. Sigfried; Lieutenant-Colonel, Henry Pleasants; Major, J. A. Gilmour; Adjutant, First Lieutenant D. D. McGinnes; Quartermaster, First Lieutenant Jacob Wagner; Surgeon, W. R. D. Blackwood; Assistant Surgeon, John D. Culver; Sergeant Major, David B. Brown; Quartermaster Sergeant, Charles W. Schuerr;

Commissary Sergeant, Jacob F. Werner; Hospital Steward, William H. Hardell.

The companies were commanded by the following officers: A, Captain Kauffman; B, Captain Bast; C, Captain Gowen; D, First Lieutenant Fisher; E, Captain Winlack; F, Captain Hoskings; G, Captain Bosbyshell; H, Captain Hinkle; I, Captain Schuck, and K, Captain Brannon.

Pottsville became the headquarters of the regiment during its veteran furlough, the boys greatly enjoying the relaxation from their years of hard and dangerous service.

With full ranks, amidst the cheering shouts of friends, the Forty-eighth left Pottsville on the thirteenth of March, 1864, to take its place in the field once more. Harrisburg was reached the same day. The command remained here until the eighteenth, when it left for Annapolis, Md., by the way of Philadelphia, arriving at its destination on the twentieth, where it went into camp on the south side of the city, in company with many of the old regiments of the Ninth Corps.

CHAPTER XI.

WILDERNESS TO PETERSBURG.

The Ninth Army Corps rendezvoused at Annapolis, Md., during March and April, 1864. The various organizations of the corps occupied camps on the outskirts of the city. Camp Parole, the headquarters of prisoners of war awaiting exchange, was also located at Annapolis. The rendezvous of the Ninth Corps was designated "Depot Ninth Army Corps," and was placed in command of Colonel John F. Hartranft. He established headquarters in the United States Naval Academy grounds, occupying one of the buildings belonging thereto. There were over thirty regiments of infantry and cavalry, besides many batteries, reporting daily to Colonel Hartranft's headquarters. Organization into brigades and divisions was not effected until later on. Eight regiments of colored troops were included—these were subsequently formed into the Fourth Division, Ninth Army Corps, composed of two brigades of four regiments each. The drilling of these troops, beside those of the white regiments, was a new experience for the old Ninth Corps, and many doubted whether the colored boys would prove faithful under fire, a doubt set at rest by their excellent work in the subsequent campaign.

In the reorganization, the Forty-eighth was again assigned to the First Brigade, Second Division.

On the twenty-third of April, 1864, the Ninth Corps broke camp at Annapolis and took up its line of march on the road to Washington —General Burnside in command, General Robert B. Potter at the head of the Second Division, and Colonel Z. R. Bliss commanding the First Brigade. The brigade was composed of the Forty-fifth and Forty-eighth Pennsylvania Volunteers, and the Thirty-sixth and Fifty-eighth Massachusetts, Fourth and Seventh Rhode Island Volunteers.

The night of the twenty-fourth the command encamped within six miles of Washington, on the Bladensburg road. At 9 o'clock Monday morning, the twenty-fifth, the head of the corps entered Washington via New York avenue. Halting near Fourteenth street to permit the column to close up, it resumed the march, passing down Fourteenth street. At Willard's Hotel, upon the balcony of which stood President Lincoln and General Burnside, surrounded by many other distinguished men—the compliment of a marching salute was paid to the Chief Magistrate of the Nation. The Forty-eighth passed about noon. All day long tramped the men of the Ninth Corps—their splendid bearing calling forth enthusiastic cheers from the thousands of people gathered to witness the pageant. Over the Long Bridge into Virginia once more, until within a short distance of Alexandria, the tired troops encamped for the night. The regiment left Alexandria on the twenty-seventh, and encamped at Fairfax Court House, some twelve miles away, the same night. Bristoe's Station, fourteen miles further, was made the next day, and camp was regularly pitched here, near the railroad bridge, on the twenty-ninth. On the thirtieth the regiment was mustered for pay. Remained encamped at Bristoe's until the morning of the fateful fourth of May, the commencement of Grant's great campaign. During this campaign the command of the regiment devolved upon Lieutenant-Colonel Pleasants. Colonel Sigfried was placed in command of the First Brigade, Fourth Division (colored) by General Burnside, who personally desired him to take this brigade. In a letter written to General Sigfried from the Senate of the United States, dated April 30, 1881, desiring a copy of the "History of Schuylkill County," General Burnside says: "You, my dear General, will be prominently mentioned if the compilers of the work know as much of your skill, gallantry, and unselfish co-operation as I do. I shall never forget the disinterested patriotism which actuated you when you were asked by me to take command of the First Brigade of the Fourth Division of the Ninth Corps. It was composed of colored troops, and I naturally wanted to give it my best officers for brigade commanders. I well remember the desire you had to remain with your old command, and with what reluctance you yielded to my desire and order. I wanted you with the Fourth Division because you were one of my best officers, and commanded my entire confidence and esteem."

Loath to leave his regiment and the brigade he had commanded, but desirous of gratifying his commanding general, Sigfried reluctantly consented with the proviso that he could select his staff from the officers of the white regiments. This was conceded and the writer was made acting assistant adjutant-general of the brigade. This took him away from the immediate presence of the regiment, and the account of the campaign is chiefly derived from written information sent him by Colonel Pleasants. Other officers and men have furnished some of the material used.

The writer feels, in approaching this, the greatest campaign of the war, his lack of proper knowledge to give the regiment's part in it the prominence deserved, and relies on the memory of the survivors to fill up the incidents connected with it, where he possibly only hints at the work.

The Forty-eighth crossed the Rapidan River at Germania Ford, on the fifth of May, 1864, moving toward the Spotswood Tavern, where a bivouac was had. Very early on the morning of the sixth, the command, with the Second Brigade in front, moved close to the Old Wilderness Tavern and on out the road to Parker's store. A half mile out this road, the Forty-eighth Pennsylvania were deployed as skirmishers to cover the flanks of the column. The enemy's skirmishers were found about a half mile further on, and gave way before the advancing troops. A small stream was crossed, and three regiments of the Second Brigade formed line, advanced until the enemy was found on the opposite side of an open field, drawn up in considerable force, and supplied with a battery, stationed probably a quarter to a half a mile from the junction of the Parker store and Plank roads. A brisk fire was opened by the enemy from the battery as well as from the small arms of the infantry. The line was moved forward to the edge of the woods and the First Brigade formed to cover the left. The action was becoming quite brisk, and General Potter was preparing to charge the enemy, when he received an order to withdraw his command, move it to the left, and attack on the right of General Hancock near the Plank road. This movement was made through a dense wood, almost impenetrable, owing to the tangled underbrush; the new line was formed as quickly as possible on Hancock's right, and the attack made where it was utterly impossible to see anything from the thickness of the woods. The enemy was posted on the opposite side of a swampy ravine behind entrenchments. Sharp firing at very close range ensued, followed by a savage charge, which brought the boys into the enemy's rifle pits in some places. Being unable to maintain the advantage gained, the troops fell back. Twice the charge was renewed—considerable ground was gained, but the enemy retained possession of their lines.

The fighting continued until dark; the brigade remained in the front line and entrenched its position. The Forty-eighth was thrown forward as skirmishers during the night, its line extending over a division front.

The enemy withdrew during the night. The next morning a few prisoners were picked up by an advancing skirmish line; no force of the enemy was found. The Forty-eighth was occupied a part of the seventh in constructing breastworks, whilst exposed to the fire of the enemy's sharpshooters. Some little while past noon the command was withdrawn and went into position between the Wilderness Tavern and the Spotswood House, to be in easy supporting distance of the Sixth Corps. Later on in the night it moved eastwardly toward Chancellorsville, halting on the old battlefield on the morning of the eighth, where the Forty-eighth encamped.

According to General Potter's report the Second Division of the Ninth Corps lost in the Wilderness fight: "Seventy-four (74) killed, three hundred and eighty-nine (389) wounded, forty-one (41) missing. The latter being mostly prisoners taken when we broke the enemy's line."

The command left Chancellorsville on the afternoon of the ninth, going as far as Alsops, where it remained until the afternoon of the next day when it moved toward Spottsylvania Court House. The Ny River was crossed near Gales where an attack or reconnoissance was being made by the First and part of the Second Division on Spottsylvania Court House. Some smart skirmishing took place here, the advance halting within a quarter of a mile of the court house, about 10 o'clock at night. A strong body of pickets was thrown out, and the troops began entrenching the position secured.

The rest of the Ninth Corps having retired to the north side of the Ny River, the Second Division withdrew to the same side about 3 o'clock in the afternoon of the eleventh, halting near the Haines House, but under orders recrossed the Ny at dusk, in the midst of a heavy rain storm. The trenches thrown up by the Third Division were occupied by the Second between 9 and 10 o'clock p. m.

The morning of May 12 was an exceedingly foggy one, and the early movements of that day were greatly obscured by reason thereof.

Two lines of attack were formed by the Second Division, the Second Brigade on the first line, and the First Brigade occupying the second line. The trenches were left at 4 o'clock in the morning, the division advancing to the attack, and in a half an hour the skirmishers were busily engaged—by 5 o'clock the engagement became very hot.

The Seventeenth Vermont Regiment occupied a position on the crest of a hill in front of which was an open field and swamp through which ran a creek—beyond was another hill on which were the rebel rifle pits. On the left was a thick wood extending beyond the swamp to the enemy's line. Whilst the Forty-eighth was waiting to be placed in position Captain McKibben, of General Potter's staff, rode up and directed Lieutenant-Colonel Pleasants to follow him. McKibben, riding a rather sorry looking horse, led the regiment under fire to the hill occupied by the Seventeenth Vermont, and line of battle was formed back of that regiment.

The fog lifting, a party of rebels was discovered occupying the fork formed by the banks of the stream. Colonel John I. Curtin, commanding the brigade, threw the Forty-eighth forward. It advanced around the right of the Seventeenth Vermont, cutting off the retreat of the enemy and captured twenty prisoners before firing a shot. The regiment thus surprised proved to be the Thirteenth Georgia. They were badly situated and fought desperately to resist the attack of the Forty-eighth, but the latter regiment steadily maintained its position under a destructive fire of musketry and artillery. Part of another rebel regiment came to the support of the Thirteenth Georgia.

The engagement was exceedingly lively. Above the din arose the voice of a man of Company C, yelling that the rebels wanted to surrender. "Continue firing," directed Pleasants. The enemy threw down their arms and ran into the Forty-eighth's lines in a body, to the number of 200. It left in its wake one colonel, three line officers and some seventy-five men killed, besides a large number of wounded lying on the field.

The Forty-eighth made another assault in the afternoon, charging forward to the swamp, but being unsupported moved by the flank into the woods, around on to the crest of the hill occupying its former position. This latter charge was made under a most disastrous fire, and resulted in very heavy loss to the regiment. Lieutenant Henry C. Jackson, of Company G, an able and fearless officer, much liked in the regiment, was killed during this engagement. Since starting on this campaign, the Forty-eighth lost 187 in killed and wounded.

During the night of the twelfth heavy entrenchments were constructed by the Forty-eighth on its lines, and indeed the entire position held by the Union forces was entrenched. Amid sharp and unremitting skirmishing, during the thirteenth, fourteenth and fifteenth the trenches and batteries were strengthened and improved in every way possible. A strong demonstration to feel the enemy was made on the sixteenth, resulting in nothing more than the development of a large force on his part. Skirmish firing was incessant, making life at the front most unhappy. On the eighteenth the enemy was attacked with vigor along the whole of the Second Division line.

The Forty-eighth charged on the enemy's works, carrying his first line—it did not reach the second owing to the strength of the position, defended as it was by a heavy abatis. Although the enemy's works were not captured, such important ground had been gained, as to render part of his line untenable.

The Forty-eighth occupied part of the eighteenth in burying eighty-one dead rebels in the swamp where the engagements of the twelfth took place. During the night preparations were made to change position, and before daylight of the nineteenth the command moved off, halting near the Anderson House, where entrenchments were constructed. Two reconnoissances were made by a portion of the division on the twentieth toward Stannard's and Smith's Mills and the Po. General Potter gives the losses of the division in the operations before Spottsylvania as "one hundred and seventy-five (175) killed, seven hundred and sixty-two (762) wounded, two hundred and fifty-six (256) missing; total, eleven hundred and ninety-three."

Every day some skirmishing took place—the boys of the regiment were kept constantly on the alert. General Potter directed Colonel Curtin on the afternoon of the twenty-first of May to push forward with the First Brigade and Jones' Eleventh Massachusetts Battery and possess the crossing of the Po River at Stannard's Mill; he following shortly after with the Second Brigade. Curtin drove the enemy's skirmishers across the river near Stannard's Mill. The rebels were strongly entrenched on the south side of the river and opened a heavy fire of shells on the advance of the First Brigade. The skirmishers became briskly engaged along the bank of the river. Whilst General Potter was examining the ground for position and to find a ford, he received an order to suspend any contemplated attack—to place a brigade with a battery in position to cover the passing column, and to move by way of Smith's Mill to Downer's bridge. The duty of holding this position fell upon the First Brigade and Jones' Eleventh Massachusetts Battery. All night long, until well into the next morning, the men guarded the ford—covering the passing column, consisting of the entire Ninth and Sixth Army Corps. On the twenty-second, being relieved, the First Brigade rejoined the division at Downer's bridge about 1 o'clock in the afternoon. Accompanying the column the regiment moved on to Bethel Church later in the day. The following day the march was resumed to the neighborhood of Oxford, on the North Anna River. On the twenty-fourth this stream was crossed at Chesterfield bridge, under a heavy artillery fire, and position was taken on the right of Mott's Brigade of Birney's Division of the Second Corps. A sharp skirmish ensued, the line moving well up to the enemy. Strong entrenchments were thrown up, an occupation the Forty-eighth became well accustomed to, as Pleasants required the command to protect themselves in this way every night, and by this forethought and prudence saved the lives of many of the men. This enabled the regiment to do very effective work on the enemy, with comparative slight loss to itself. In these operations, the division was under the direction of General Hancock, commanding the Second Corps, as General Potter had been directed to report to him. The twenty-fifth was occupied in picket firing, which, whilst continuous, resulted in trifling loss to the Forty-eighth, protected as it was, with a good line of works. During the afternoon of the twenty-sixth, General Potter attacked the enemy in his front, drove back the whole line of skirmishers and established his line much further in advance. The loss was considerable—particularly to the Sixth New Hampshire, whose lieutenant-colonel, Pierson, was instantly killed. Between 9 and 10 o'clock the Second Division withdrew to the north side of the North Anna, and went into camp near Mt. Carmel Church.

During the afternoon of the twenty-seventh, the command moved from Mt. Carmel Church and marched to Hanovertown, near which place it crossed the Pamunkey River on the night of the twenty-eighth. The next morning the march was resumed—position being taken to the left of Harris' shop, where a line of entrenchments were built. On the thirtieth the forward movement was continued and the Tolopotomy was crossed near Viars. Here the Forty-eighth drove the enemy's skirmishers back upon his main line, having advanced a half a mile from the river. This was a short, sharp skirmish most brilliantly executed.

The position was entrenched, and pickets placed a half mile further to the front. This line was held until the next day, when a further advance of three-quarters of a mile was accomplished over the most difficult ground yet encountered. The regiment displayed conspicuous gallantry in this severe engagement, and lost three valuable officers: Major Joseph A. Gilmour, beloved by all who knew his manly worth, one of the first men to offer his services to the government, and one who had from that hour given his entire time in the defence of the nation—in the fight last mentioned, whilst almost in view of the spires of the rebel capitol, was struck by a minie ball in the left knee, fired from a rebel sharpshooter's rifle. This painful wound necessitated the immediate amputation of his limb. The operation was performed in the field hospital by Surgeon Theodore S. Christ. Gilmour was sent in an ambulance some twenty miles to White House, Va., and bore the painful journey most heroically.

Subsequently he was taken to Seminary Hospital, Georgetown, D. C. where he died on the ninth of June. He was buried in Pottsville with masonic ceremonies, attended with military honors, on Sunday, the twelfth of June, 1864. The occasion was marked by a great outpouring of the people, who loved and honored the dead hero. General Potter, in his report, speaks of the loss of Gilmour as that of an "invaluable officer."

  Lieutenants William H. Hume, of Company B, and Samuel B. Laubenstine, of Company H, were likewise killed on this fateful thirty-first of May—the latter instantly. Lieutenant Hume was shot through the arm, but the trying work of the campaign had so reduced his system that he failed to recover from the shock of the wound and died in a few days. These were good officers—they had proved themselves worthy on many fields of battle.

  Enough of a forward movement was made on the morning of June 1 to discover the doings and whereabouts of the enemy, but care was taken not to bring on any engagement. The line secured by the fight of the thirty-first of May was maintained until late during the night of June 1, when it was abandoned as the Second Corps had withdrawn from the right and the line taken up on the thirtieth of May was returned to. On the afternoon of the second of June the command moved to the vicinity of Bethesda Church. Position was taken on the extreme right. The enemy followed, resulting in some little skirmishing, with quite an attack on the left.

  A heavy rain storm during the night made every one most uncomfortable. Some time was occupied by the men of the Forty-eighth early on the morning of the third in drying their blankets and clothing before wood fires. General Potter directed Colonel Curtin to attack the enemy with the First Brigade. This attack was made with great vigor, and the enemy's skirmishers were driven across the creek, and some prisoners were captured. The advance continued over the creek—the enemy was routed out of houses and outbuildings, as well as some breastworks that were within a few yards of the road running to Shady Grove and Cold Harbor. The rebels occupied this road as their main line. The First Brigade established itself upon the advanced position it had secured. A rebel battery in its front was exceedingly annoying, and the men of the brigade began to pay their respects to it—blowing up two of the caissons, and very effectually silencing the guns. The Forty-eighth formed line of battle about 7 o'clock in the morning facing east, on the right of the road near Shady Grove Church. Company E as skirmishers, deployed to the front, advancing with the main line rapidly following, over a cleared field. The line moved with guide centre. The skirmishers pushed rapidly on through a deep gully, with the regiment in close touch, and as the high ground was reached, the enemy's skirmishers were encountered. Company E's boys went at them with a will, and savagely drove them back on their entrenched lines. Some of the "Johnnies" occupied an old log house, as a superior vantage ground to repel the attack, but almost before they knew it, were made prisoners by the men of Company E. The destructive fire poured into this determined and successful line of skirmishers, caused the men of E to drop rapidly before it. The line retired behind the approaching regiment, when the engagement became general and severe. The Forty-eighth halted within eighty yards of the enemy and at once set about entrenching the position, keeping up a continuous fire of musketry into the ranks of the rebels, who were posted behind breastworks with a battery supporting them.

The howling and shrieking of the grape and canister poured into the regiment made up a regular "inferno," causing the very flesh to creep with horror! During this terrific shower of deadly missiles, the men fought on most gallantly, at the same time gradually covering themselves with the fast growing entrenchments.

"Colonel Curtin's Brigade of General Potter's Division made a daring charge, drove in the enemy's skirmishers, carried some detached rifle pits, forced the enemy—consisting of portions of Longstreet's and Ewell's Corps—back into the inner works, and established itself in close proximity to his entrenchments." *

During this engagement Private Daniel E. Reedy, of Company E, was shockingly wounded. The report reaching the regiment in his case was as follows: "Supposed to have died on board the steamer, bound North from White House, Va. Five minie balls passed through him, two through right leg, one through left leg, one through right arm, and one through right breast; right leg amputated below upper wound." The muster-out roll says "Absent in hospital at muster-out."

General Potter finding the enemy too strong to assail with the First Brigade alone, commenced putting the Second Brigade in position to move across the road, when he received notice to delay his attack until after 1 p. m., to enable General Wilcox to attack simultaneously, the signal for which was to be the opening of the batteries.

However, before the hour to attack came all operations were suspended by order.

---

* Woodbury's "Burnside and the Ninth Army Corps," pp. 397-8.

Quite a furious fusillade was opened on the whole line by the enemy in the afternoon, under cover of which an attempt was made by him by means of prolongs, to haul off his silenced battery. The boys wouldn't have this, however, and by well-directed firing prevented his accomplishing his purpose. The losses of the brigade in the day's work was quite severe. The Forty-eighth lost seventy-five, killed and wounded.

The enemy withdrew during the night, leaving their dead unburied and some wounded on the field. A caisson and ammunition, and several hundred stand of small arms were gathered up.

This same morning, June 4, Colonel Pleasants ordered Companies G and F, of the Forty-eighth to advance. Leaving the breastworks, thrown up amidst the fiery hail of death the day before, these companies deployed as skirmishers, moved up to the enemy's line without molestation, as it was found deserted. A number of new-made graves, eight or ten dead battery horses, and a limber chest marked the abandoned line. The advance was continued for a mile beyond—a straggling Johnny was found in a farm-house and brought back to the regiment a prisoner. The appearance inside of, and around the position occupied by the rebels, indicated a severe drubbing and evidenced great loss.

The road beyond crossed a swamp and the duty of holding this bit of road at all hazards was entrusted to the Forty-eighth. Hastily entrenching the position, with a strong picket line in front, the regiment settled to the work. Potter's Division occupied the ground lying between Woody's and Tucker's, having relieved a brigade of Birney's Division of the Second Corps. The line was changed during the night of the fifth—the right was drawn back and extended and held the hill near Tucker's in the front. On further to the right ran the skirmish line. This skirmish line extended for over two miles.

The Forty-eighth holding that part of the main road running through a swamp, as stated, were subjected to a heavy artillery fire on the afternoon of the sixth. A column of rebel infantry emerged from the woods, drove in the pickets, and assailed the line held by the Forty-eighth with great vigor.

The enemy planted two batteries near the Tucker and Boshen houses, opening fire therefrom with great rapidity. The shells shrieked and yelled, but beyond making a great noise resulted in very little damage.

The Forty-eighth held the road firmly, repulsed the savage attack without loss, and re-established the picket line early the following morning (seventh). Again on the seventh the enemy essayed to drive the

Second Division from the position it held. They drove in the skirmishers on the hill near Tucker's, captured a few prisoners from a working party and opened a furious shelling from a battery. Little damage was done, however, excepting to the horses about General Potter's headquarters. The same night Potter advanced a skirmish line—the enemy fell back and the position was retaken. This line was thoroughly fortified on the eighth, and held by a force sufficient to repel any assault.

These entrenchments and the entire position occupied by the Second Division were maintained without further efforts on the part of the enemy to dislodge it, save the never-ceasing fire kept up on the picket lines, until the twelfth of June. The losses of the division in the operations about Cold Harbor were quite severe. In his report General Potter gives them at 109 killed, 573 wounded and 64 missing, a total of 746.

After dark on the evening of June 12 the division leaving the picket line in position moved out of the entrenchments, and marched to Tunstall's Station, reaching there early the next morning. About noon a further movement was made, toward the Chickahominy, and a bivouac had within less than a mile of that stream. Marching with the rest of the troops of the division the Forty-eighth crossed the Chickahominy River on the morning of the fourteenth of June, moving to within three miles of the pontoon bridge over the James River, remaining over night near Jones'. The Forty-eighth crossed the pontoon bridge over the James River bright and early on the morning of the sixteenth, and directed its march straight for Petersburg. The advanced works on the City Point road, captured a day or two before by Butler's command, were passed about noon, grimly marked by the dead bodies of negro troops, who had fallen in the assault upon them. These were the first dead colored troops the boys of the Forty-eighth had seen and their stiff forms eloquently answered the query as to whether the colored troops would fight or not.

The enemy's works at Petersburg were reached by the regiment about 5 o'clock p. m., in time to witness the assault of Barlow's Division of the Second Corps. This charge was also participated in by the Second Brigade of the Second Division of the Ninth Corps, who were temporarily attached to Barlow's Division by order of General Potter, that officer having been directed to send a brigade to support Barlow's attack.

This charge was unsuccessful, the rebels maintaining their position, obliged Barlow to fall back, which he did, with the loss of some prisoners.

The Forty-eighth were lying in a strip of woods, trying to secure some rest after the hard march from the James River, but this was not to be. The assault having proved unsuccessful, orders came to the Forty-eighth to advance. Line of battle was formed under the frowning ramparts of a small fort, bristling with artillery, directly in the regiment's front. Twilight was rapidly closing in on the scene and all felt that an assault on the rebel works meant serious business for the Forty-eighth, but all were steeled to the task. The advance began; some fifty yards beyond the woods were covered, when the line veered to the right, and filed into a gully through which ran a small creek. The movement continued to the right, following the winding of the creek, and leaving the enemy toward the left, until an abandoned part of the enemy's original line of works was reached. By this time it became too dark to distinguish objects at any distance.

Companies B and G were detailed to reconnoiter the position of the enemy. This was about 10 o'clock at night. Deploying as skirmishers, these companies, with the rest of the regiment supporting, crossed over the little creek and advanced almost up to the enemy's works, who welcomed them with a lively volley of musketry. Under orders the line retired to the position secured in the abandoned works. So determined was Sergeant Wren and a private of B Company to ascertain the exact location of the rebel works that they ran right up against them, and the proverbial hospitality of the South induced the "Johnnies" to gather them into their ranks, and afford them the delights of a Southern prison.

The anxiety of Colonel Pleasants for the safety of the colors, during this midnight foray, is well remembered—he cautioned the greatest care to be observed lest some unforeseen accident should occur and they be lost in the dark.

Very little sleep was permitted the regiment, for at 3 o'clock the next morning (seventeenth) the men were quietly aroused by Colonel Pleasants, who passed along the line, informing each company commander of the assault to be made on the enemy's lines. Caps were removed from the pieces, as reliance was to be had on the bayonet alone. He informed the men of the danger before them, and directed that if any felt disinclined to make the assault, they had permission to remain where they were. There is no record or evidence of any kind that a single man of the regiment took advantage of this offer—not one stayed behind! Tin cups and coffee pots were so secured as to make no rattling sound, and directions were passed along in whispered accents. Bayonets were silently fixed, the pieces, by order, recapped and the regiment moved quietly out of the old rebel works, left in front, with the stealthiness of Indians, over the creek where line of battle was formed, in utter darkness. Moving to the right, for about a hundred yards with panther-like tread, a whispered command "forward!" was given, and the savage rush began. Some firing on the right of the regimental line, resulted in an immediate answer from the enemy, along their entire line, thus marking it vividly by the flashes of their muskets. Directly into this fiery ribbon, belching its leaden hail through the ranks of the charging line, swept the Forty-eighth, emptying its muskets at the instant the rebels' works were reached.

How the heart beat, and the pulse throbbed during that onslaught! If fear or dread marked the supreme moment of the attack, it was banished completely in the glorious rush of the fight! What a harvest of prisoners—they were captured by the score, disarmed, and sent to rear, only to be gathered up by the regiments in reserve and turned in as captives of their own. The Forty-eighth actually secured more prisoners than the regiment had men engaged in the fight. Two flags and two pieces of artillery were likewise part of the regiment's trophies. The colors of the Forty-fourth Tennessee were captured by Sergeant Patrick Monaghan, of Company F, and the colors of the Seventh New York Heavy Artillery were recaptured by Private Robert Reid, of Company G. For this gallant and praiseworthy deed the War Department conferred upon these two soldiers the United States Medal of Honor. The distinction gained by Monaghan and Reid was proudly accorded them by every man in the regiment, as all recognized the achievement as adding additional glory to the command.

The early dawn disclosed the redan further south—which carried two guns that were making sad havoc, by enfilading the attacking line. This work was on the left and front of the Forty-eighth, about a hundred yards distance. The wild rush and wholesale gathering in of prisoners, and generally good time the regiment was having in what had already been accomplished, disturbed the formation of the command considerably, so Pleasants, seeing the necessity of securing this redan, hastily ordered the boys in line, and with the shout of "forward!" made a dash for the fort. Like a savage torrent, the impetuosity of which Pleasants tried to stem, the regiment fairly tore over those hundred yards and swept through the fort irresistibly. The enemy ran in great disorder by squads and singly to their left and rear. The men attempted to fire on the fleeing foe, by reversing the guns, but the rebels foiled this "little game" by having loaded them with sand before leaving. The enemy brought a battery in position and shelled the captured fort, vainly trying to drive the regiment away. The guns were safely hauled to the rear by hand, notwithstanding the heavy fire of shot and shell poured into the captors from the battery referred to.

Whilst on the gun platform, endeavoring with others to fire the guns, Private Robert Reid, of Company G, felt uncomfortably near him flying chips, broken by shot and shell, from the planking used to line the inside of the embrasures. Seeking cover, he dropped into the hole used by the rebel gunners for protection, and lo! a dozen of the "Johnnies," heretofore unobserved, were snugly stowed herein. They surrendered forthwith. Reid, with Sergeant Daniel Donne, of G, marched these captives to the rear, whilst others of the regiment were hauling off the cannon.

The Forty-eighth maintained this line, so gallantly and determinedly wrested from the enemy, fortifying and strengthening it by using the outside of the fortification for the new line, reversing the position from the way the rebels planned it. This was probably, in all its results, the most brilliant engagement for the Forty-eighth of any in which it participated. Praise is due to every officer, from Colonel Pleasants down, and to every man who was in this grand assault, for the splendid record the work here accomplished has given to the Forty-eighth Regiment. This achievement, with the wonderful Mine, are two brilliant and remarkable pages in the regiment's history, the like of which few other commands can boast.

First Lieutenant Curtis C. Pollock, of Company G, and First Lieutenant Joseph Edwards, of Company I, received wounds in this engagement from which they died—the former on the twenty-third of June and the latter on the second of July. They were good officers, rising from the ranks. Pollock was a "First Defender," having served during the three months' service in the "Washington Artillerists." He was literally fearless of danger, and, during the campaign beginning at the Wilderness, was frequently selected by Pleasants where cool judgment and fearlessness were needed.

General Potter, in his report, gives the following formation of Curtin's brigade for the assault: "Curtin formed his brigade with the Forty-fifth and Forty-eighth Pennsylvania and Thirty-sixth Massachusetts in front, supported by the Seventh Rhode Island, Second New York Mounted Rifles and Fifty-eighth Massachusetts Regiments. . . Curtin moved to the left of the house (Shand's) and toward the Redoubt No. —" The following account of this assault is from the pen of Charles Carleton Coffin. It is given because of its accuracy; it thoroughly substantiates every diary kept in the regiment: "About half a mile south of the house of Mr. Dunn was the residence of Mr.

Shand, held by the rebels. . . The house was a large, two-story structure, fronting east, painted white, with great chimneys at either end, shaded by buttonwoods and gum-trees, with a peach orchard in rear. Fifty paces from the front door was a narrow ravine, fifteen or twenty feet deep, with a brook, fed by springs, trickling northward. West of the house, about the same distance, was another brook, the two joining about twenty rods north of the house. A rebel brigade held this tongue of land, with four guns beneath the peach trees. Their main line of breastworks was along the edge of the ravine east of the house. South, and on higher ground, was a redan,—a strong work with two guns, which enfiladed the ravine. Yet General Burnside thought that if he could get his troops into position unperceived, he could take the tongue of land, which would break the rebel line and compel them to evacuate the redan.

"It was past midnight when General Potter led his division of the Ninth down into the ravine. The soldiers threw aside their knapsacks, haversacks, tin plates and cups, and moved stealthily. Not a word was spoken. The watches of the officers in command had been set to a second. They reached the ravine where the pickets were stationed, and moved south, keeping close under the bank. Above them, not fifteen paces distant, were the rebel pickets, lying behind a bank of sand. If their listening ears caught the sound of a movement in the ravine, they gave no alarm, and the troops took their position undisturbed. The moon was full. Light clouds floated in the sky. Not a sound, save the distant rumble of wagons, or an occasional shot from the pickets, broke the silence of the night. The attacking column was composed of Griffin's and Curtin's brigades: Griffin on the right. . . The soldiers were worn with hard marching and constant fighting, and had but just arrived from City Point, yet they took their positions without flinching. The officers gazed at the hands of their watches in the moonlight, and saw them move on to the appointed time,—fifteen minutes past three. Twenty paces,—a spring up the steep bank would carry the men to the rebel pickets; fifty paces to the muzzles of the enemy's guns. 'All ready!' was whispered from man to man. They rose from the ground erect. Not a gun-lock clicked. The bayonet was to do the work. '*Hurrah!*' The lines rise like waves of the sea. There are straggling shots from the rebel pickets, four flashes of light from the rebel cannon by the house, two more from the redan, one volley from the infantry, wildly aimed, doing little damage. On,—up to the breastworks! Over them, seizing the guns! A minute has passed. Four guns, six hundred and fifty prisoners, fifteen hundred muskets and four stands of colors are the trophies. The rebel line is broken. The great point is gained, compelling Lee to abandon the ground which he has held so tenaciously."*

The skirmishing was continued all day of the seventeenth, after the victorious operations of the morning. General Potter put a battery in position near the front of the Second Division at the Shand House, and like batteries were placed in eligible positions in the rear of the line, to cover the attack intended to be made by the First and Third Divisions of the Ninth Corps. The Second was held in readiness to assist. On the morning of the eighteenth the Second advanced in support of the Third Division. The Forty-eighth, with the First Brigade, took part in the attack. The regiment made a vigorous charge, driving the enemy rapidly before them—across the railroad cut and ravine beyond, getting within a short distance of their entrenchments. The position secured was nearer the rebel works than that gained by any other portion of the army. It was strengthened and made secure.

"It was the salient of our own lines during the entire subsequent siege of Petersburg."† This position was held by the Forty-eighth during the greater part of the entire siege, and it was from here that mining operations were carried on. Colonel Curtin, commanding the First Brigade, and his assistant adjutant-general, Captain Mighels, were severely wounded during the operations of the eighteenth, and the losses were especially heavy in all of the organizations participating. The command of the brigade now devolved upon Lieutenant-Colonel Pleasants. Captain Joseph H. Hoskings, of Company F, being the senior officer, took charge of the regiment.

---
* "Four Years of Fighting," pp. 363-4-5.
† "Burnside and Ninth Corps." p. 413.

11

The work of the Second and Third Divisions brought especial mention from General Burnside in his report of these operations. He said: "No better fighting has been done during the war than was done by the divisions of Generals Potter and Wilcox during the attack."

General Robert B. Potter concludes his report of the operations of the Second Division from the Wilderness to and including the investment of Petersburg, as follows:

"From the nineteenth of June to the twenty-ninth of July nothing very marked occurred, each day being a repetition of the preceding. During the fifth epoch (from June 12 to 29) my losses were 173 killed, 744 wounded and 22 missing; total, 939. During the entire period, from the fifth of May to the twenty-ninth of June, 1864, inclusive, embraced in the foregoing report, the losses in action in the division were five hundred and forty-two (542) killed, two thousand five hundred and five (2505) wounded and three hundred and eighty-four (384) missing—making a total of three thousand four hundred and thirty-one (3431) killed, wounded and missing."

The lines were strongly entrenched—traverses, abatis and covered ways were built, as the least exposure of any part of the person was almost sure to result in injury. The nearness of the contending parties, at this particular part of the entrenchments, rendered it extremely important for the soldiers to keep well under cover. The Ninth Corps connected with the Second Corps on the right, and the Fifth Corps on the left, and was constantly under fire from the beginning to the ending of the siege. Life at the front was by no means pleasant or comfortable, yet the merry jest and joke could be heard at all times in the trenches and bomb proofs.

It is extremely difficult to describe the feelings and sensations aroused during the tedious days of the siege. Life was counted of little worth—the familiarity with death almost bred contempt of the grim monster. Still the presence of the great destroyer was daily manifested, sometimes more vividly and closely than at others. On the twenty-fifth of June, whilst doing his full duty on the skirmish line, Captain Benjamin B. Shuck, of Company I, was mortally wounded. He suffered greatly from this wound for over a month, dying in the hospital on the twenty-seventh of July. He was highly esteemed as a thoroughly efficient officer, and a very good man in all respects. These grim reminders of dangers at the front served to keep all constantly alert.

An important work, however, was to fall to the lot of the Forty-eighth, which soon became a never ending source of entertainment, discussed on the picket line, in the trenches, covered ways, and back of bomb proofs—the building of a mine under the rebel works!

CHAPTER XII.

THE PETERSBURG MINE.

Colonel Sigfried having been selected by General Burnside, at the outset of the campaign, as has already been stated, to command the First Brigade of the Fourth (colored) Division of the Ninth Corps, the command of the Forty-eighth devolved upon Lieutenant-Colonel Henry Pleasants. This young and gallant officer was much valued by his regimental, brigade, division and corps commanders. He was a soldier of true grit, possessed of more than ordinary ability as an engineer—ability that he displayed many times during the campaign from the Rappahannock down to Petersburg, in the erection of temporary fortifications which he required the regiment to build every night, and the lives of many of the men were saved through this precaution.

Pleasants was in all respects an American—thoroughly so—a pure type of progressive young America—his career shows remarkable understanding in a young man. He sprang from an old Virginia Quaker family, although his father was born in Philadelphia. Whilst in business in South America, this gentleman married a South American lady, and General Henry Pleasants was the result of this union. His impetuous nature, and quick, fiery temper, but withal generous, good-heartedness, comes of this Americo-Spanish blood. He was born at Buenos Ayres, on the seventeenth of February, 1833, thus being but thirty-one at the time of the completion of this masterly piece of engineering skill. At thirteen years of age he came to Philadelphia—entered the S. W. Grammar School, and graduated from the High School in February, 1851, with the degree of Bachelor of Arts, and in five years thereafter, received the degree of Master of Arts. He began civil engineering in April, 1851, on the western division of the Pennsylvania Railroad—he resigned from that road when it was opened through to Pittsburg, for travel, and was made senior assistant engineer on the Pittsburg & Connellsville Railroad in 1853.

Whilst occupying this position he built that portion of the road lying between the towns of McKeesport and West Newton, on the Youghiogheny River, and began the excavation of the great Sand Patch tunnel through a spur of the Alleghany Mountains, which tunnel was to have been 4200 feet long. Here was a most important work, in charge of young Pleasants in 1854, when he was just twenty-one years of age—a work requiring engineering ability of a high order. During '54 and '55 he sank four perpendicular shafts in the crest of the Alleghanies, whose depths were from 120 to 200 feet, for the purpose of expediting the work and hastening the tunnel to completion. Just at this time, the chief engineer and president of the road, Mr. O. W. Barnes, a warm friend of Pleasants, was, in the latter's judgment, unjustly displaced, so, Pleasants, loyal to his chief, resigned from the road in 1856, and returned to his home in Philadelphia. Having gained considerable knowledge of mining, in the excavations of the tunnels named, and in one on the Connellsville Railroad, and also amongst the mines in the bituminous coal region, he located in January, 1857, in Pottsville, Schuylkill County, in the midst of the anthracite coal region, and devoted his attention to mining engineering with great success, until the breaking out of the rebellion.

Pleasants' career before the war, shows that he took with him into the service, qualities eminently fitting him for the successful carrying through of so grand a project as the Petersburg mine, and should allay the doubts expressed as to his ability as an engineer. Even after the success of the mine was assured, and had been demonstrated, some of the Regular Army engineers still doubted.

It is not surprising that so ardent a lover of his profession as Pleasants, and so earnest a soldier of the war, should employ his active mind in devising ways and means to end the rebellion. When these two salients in the opposing line, so temptingly lying opposite each other came under his notice, his profession came to aid his soldierly qualifications, and his quick eye took in the advantage of the situation, and the idea of undermining the rebel fort was projected.

This was as early in the siege as the twenty-first of June, and the entire practicability of excavating such a mine never for a moment left him. The idea of undermining the enemy's works originated, as I have said, in Pleasants' own mind—the exact location was unconsciously suggested to him by Captain, subsequently Brevet Brigadier-General, McKibben, of General Robert B. Potter's staff, by pointing out the position of the rebel battery. It will be remembered that the Union and rebel lines were so near together on the Ninth Corps' front, that it was perilous to rise above the breastworks. Whilst Pleasants and McKibben were making observations of the point where the battery was supposed to be located, a sharpshooter detected them, and McKibben was terribly wounded in the face. All of Pleasants' subsequent triangulations had to be made under the same danger, and subjected to the same chances.

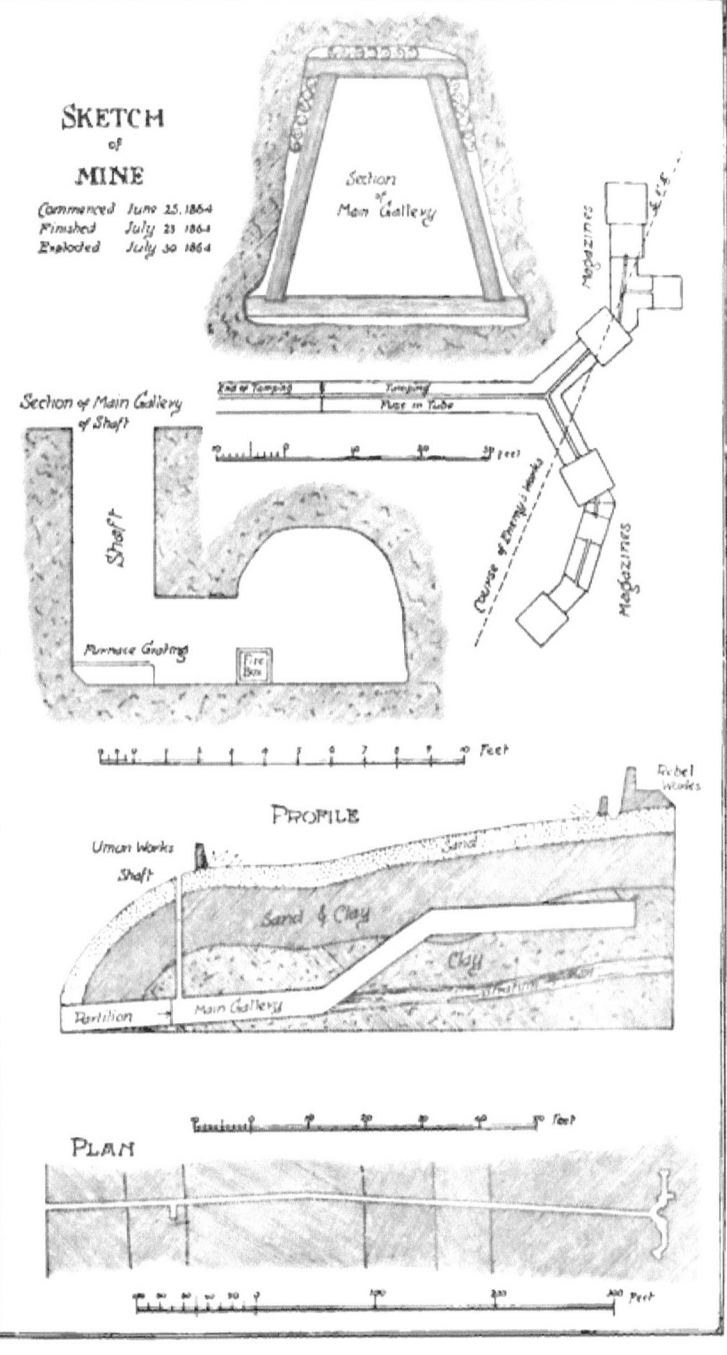

The project being thoroughly conceived, Pleasants first hinted it to Captain George W. Gowen, of Company C. He mentioned it also to Captain Frank Farquhar, of the United States Engineer Corps, at this time chief engineer of the Eighteenth Corps—both of these gentlemen were his former townsmen and friends. General Robert B. Potter, commanding the First Division of the Ninth Corps, was the first person to whom the matter was thoroughly explained. He entered heartily into the scheme aiding it with all the power he could.

The idea of mining the rebel works may have entered the minds of the Regular Army engineers—the matter, it is said, was discussed, but was abandoned as impracticable—the distance to be overcome was thought too great—unheard of in military engineering. The spot selected by Pleasants was some four hundred feet from the front line of the Union works—considered too long a line by many, to hope for success, with the chances of meeting quicksands, underground marshes, and risk of discovery by the enemy. Pleasants, however, never doubted success—he seemed from the initial moment thoroughly convinced of accomplishing it. Before mentioning the matter to Generals Potter and Burnside, division and corps commanders, he required the officers of his regiment to furnish him a list of the practical miners in each company. The men of the Forty-eighth at once devising the object, discussed the feasibility of such a project around the camp fires, and in the trenches, believing with great unanimity in its entire practicability.

This regiment has been called a regiment of miners, probably from the fact of its having been recruited in the mining region, especially marked, however, by these operations in front of Petersburg during the summer of 1864. The designation is by no means a proper one, as the great majority of the members knew little or nothing about the mining business. There were a number of miners in the organization, as there were men of various other trades and occupations. The experiences and abilities of all classes being most successfully tested during its honorable career.

The task, therefore, imposed on them was a very severe one, and they are entitled to great praise for the admirable manner in which they performed the work allotted them.

On the twenty-fourth of June, Colonel Pleasants presented his plan to General Potter, commanding the division, who in turn proposed it to General Burnside. The latter sent for General Potter and Colonel Pleasants and had the matter fully explained to him. General Burnside directed Colonel Pleasants to commence operations the next day, and if General Meade did not approve, the work could be stopped.

General Meade never formally approved of the project, but he did not forbid the work being done. Colonel Pleasants never received any assistance from the headquarters of the Army of the Potomac. The opinion of the engineers connected with those headquarters was adverse to the feasibility of mining at the point selected, owing to the great length of gangway necessary—not understanding how it could be ventilated. When Colonel Pleasants applied for the theodolite at the headquarters to use in making the triangulations, he failed to get it. It was only through General Burnside's influence in securing an old one from Washington City that he was enabled to run his lines successfully.

At 12 o'clock noon on the twenty-fifth of June the mine was commenced. The work was one of great difficulty, attended with imminent danger and arduous labor. There was nothing to do it with except the men,—no tools, no plank, no nails, no wheel-barrows. Army picks were made smaller and straightened for mining purposes. Hickory sticks were fastened to cracker boxes so as to make hand-barrows, to convey the material excavated to a place where it could be piled outside the mine.

In this connection, it is interesting to note what Captain J. C. Duane, Corps of Engineers, United States Army, says on page 208 of his "Manual for Engineer Troops.—Practical Operations in Mining." The "Tools required for Mining operations," he enumerates as follows:

Pickaxe (common),	Plumb-bob,
" (short handled),	Boring rods,
Shovel (common),	Five-foot rod,
" (short handled),	Bellows (miner's),
Push-pick,	Ventilating tube,
Rake,	Flexible joints,
Canvas bucket,	Iron candlestick,
Windlass and rope,	Lamp (miner's),
Rope-ladder,	Lantern,
Wooden wedges and pins,	Oil-can,
" pickets,	Measuring-tape,
Miner's wagon,	Compass,
Wheelbarrow,	Universal level,
Handsaw,	Needles, threads and scissors,
Mallet,	Calico for hose,
Hammer (claw),	Hatchet,
Rough-plane (one-quarter inch),	Tin funnel (for fitting hose),
Chisel,	Rammers (short handled),
Gimlet,	Helves (spare),
Two-foot rule,	Sand bags.

Compare this outfit with Pleasants' meagre supply—this array of articles "required for mining operations," and mining operations, which compared to Pleasants' gigantic task, are insignificant—and then say whether he was far wrong when he afterward told General Barnard he was the superior of any engineer in the United States army. No such mine was ever before excavated in military operations, and the "regulars" said it could not be done. "Such a length of gangway," they said, "could not be ventilated."

The ventilation was accomplished in a very simple way—after a method quite common in the anthracite coal mines. A perpendicular shaft or hole was made from the mine to the surface at a point inside of the Union rifle pits. A small furnace, or fire-place, was built at the bottom of this hole, or shaft, for the purpose of heating the air, and a fire was kept constantly burning, thus creating a draft. A door made of canvas was placed in the gallery, a little outside of this fire-place, thus shutting it in and shielding it from the outside air at the mouth of the mine. Wooden pipes, extending from the outside of this canvas door, along the gallery to the inner end thereof, conducted the fresh air to the point of operations, which, after supplying the miners with pure air, returned along the gallery towards the entrance of the mine, and, being stopped by the canvas door, the vitiated air moved into the furnace and up the shaft to the surface. By this means a constant current of air circulated through the gallery. As the work advanced, the inside end of the wooden pipe was extended so as to carry good air up to the face of the workings. The material loosened by the digging was conveyed outside by the cracker-box hand-barrows, and to avoid the risk of its being observed by the enemy, was kept constantly covered by brush. The exact distance the mine had to go to reach the enemy's fort, and the course of his works, were obtained by five triangulations, made by Colonel Pleasants with a theodolite, secured, as stated, from Washington, under a picket fire which was kept up between the two lines for several months.

The roof of the gallery, where it was wanting in tenacity and likely to fall, was supported by sets of timbers, consisting of four pieces: two props, one cap and one mud sill, notched into one another. Where the material was very soft, boards and planks were placed between the timbers, and the top, bottom and sides so as to form a complete casing. When the gallery approached near the enemy's works, all the timber was notched outside the mine, and put in place without noise or jar of any kind. The plank was obtained from a bridge over the Norfolk & Petersburg Railroad, and the boards from a saw-mill outside the Union lines, some five or six miles distant. To obtain these Colonel Pleasants was obliged to send two companies of his regiment with wagons, to load them. No lumber was furnished from headquarters, and no cavalry escort was proffered to guard against risks. The work in the mine was uninterrupted—it went on night and day—progressing rapidly. The men of the Forty-eighth Pennsylvania Volunteers were the only soldiers employed—they were divided into shifts or details—whose time to work varied as the gallery increased in length. The farther the excavation went the more men it required to carry out the material excavated, until, when it was near completion, almost every one of the 400 effective men of the regiment were pressed into service. Two officers were constantly with each shift to overlook the men. The mine being only four or five feet high, the labor of carrying the material excavated was very hard; so the time of each shift was fixed at two hours and a half, and every man, after doing his work, received a ration of whisky.

On the second of July extremely wet ground was encountered by the miners; the timbers gave way and the roof and the floor nearly met. It was re-timbered, but a stratum of marl of the consistency of putty was encountered, which made the progress exceedingly slow. The men of the regiment made all sorts of oddities: pipes, corps marks, crosses and the like, out of this material, which hardened on exposure to the air and sun. These were sent home in great quantity. To avoid this stratum of marl Pleasants started an inclined plane, rising in a hundred feet about thirteen and one-half feet perpendicularly. The main gallery was finished on the seventeenth of July and was $511\frac{7}{10}$ feet long. Operations were stopped a little while, as information was received that the enemy had heard of the mine and were searching for it.

Pleasants undertook to ferret out this supposed countermining scheme, so about midnight of the seventeenth he routed out Captain Winlack, and another member of the regiment. They cautiously entered the mine, without lights, remaining perfectly silent, and going as far back as the galleries extended, Pleasants remaining at the end of the main gallery, Captain Winlack in the right gallery and the other man in the left gallery. Lying down with every sense alert, in perfect darkness, and supreme quiet for a period of thirty minutes, until a low whistle, the intended signal, came from Pleasants, brought them together at the latter's position. Whispering in Winlack's ear, Pleasants said, "What do you think about any counterboring?" Winlack replied: "The rebels know no more of the tunnel being under them than the inhabitants of Africa." "That's just what I believe," Pleasants said, confirming it with some decided adjectives. Whispering to the other man and not catching his reply, as he spoke very softly, Pleasants broke out at the top of his voice, upbraiding the man for not speaking out so he could hear him. His voice rang from one end of the gallery to the other, putting to flight all his notious cautioning extreme silence!

On the eighteenth, however, operations were resumed and the left lateral gallery began—6 o'clock the same day the right lateral gallery was commenced—the first was stopped at midnight of July 22 and was thirty-seven feet long, the second was stopped at 6 p. m. of July 23, and was thirty-eight feet long—each of these galleries were provided with chambers for placing the magazines containing the powder. The total amount of material excavated was at least 18,000 cubic feet.

The mine was commenced to be charged with powder at 3 p. m. of July 27, and was finished during the night. The charge consisted of 8000 pounds of powder—four tons. This was placed in eight magazines, connected together by wooden tubes half filled with powder. These tubes met from the lateral galleries at the inner end of the main gallery, and were here connected with three lines of fuses running along the main gallery to the face of the tamping. This tamping was about forty feet in length, and consisted of bags of sand placed loosely on one another, with long logs laid diagonally across the gallery, so as to be driven into the sides by the recoil of the explosion. Common blasting fuse was furnished, in pieces, instead of one continuous piece, which Colonel Pleasants was obliged to splice together. These lines were used ninety feet long, and placed in a wooden tube lined with canvas to guard it from the dampness. The tamping was finished and the mine was ready to be fired at 6 p. m. of July 28.

Lieutenant-Colonel Pleasants was ordered to fire the mine at 3.30 o'clock on the morning of July 30, 1864. Who can ever forget that morning, or the stillness of that hour! The covered ways crowded with troops ready to spring into action as soon as the mine was sprung. The ominous silence stirred the hearts of our soldiers, as they never had been stirred, and their countenances were marked with an anxiety never before felt. A moment of profound quiet, to be followed by a tremendous shock. With bated breath the men awaited the decisive moment. Now came the anxious hour—the men of the Forty-eighth were terribly excited—their leader, the man in whose active brain the mine was projected, and whose opinions were about to be verified or proved delusive, stood ready to apply the fatal match—3.30 a. m. arrived and with quick, nervous strides, Pleasants entered the gallery and ignited the fuse. Hastening to the surface he stood with watch in hand mounted on an earthworks awaiting the explosion.

Imagine his anxiety, as he told off, to those beside him, the lapse of seconds, which would soon prove the correctness of his work! The time for the explosion passed. Pleasants became like a maniac —he knew where the defect was—those spliced fuses would defeat his great project!

Lieutenant Jacob Douty, of Company K, and Sergeant Henry Reese, of Company F,—Pleasants' sturdy helpers—immediately volunteered to enter the gallery and ascertain the cause of the trouble. Of course amongst the men all was excitement. The daring couple rapidly ran into the gallery, and finding a knife would be required, Reese hurried out again to borrow one, and returning, the two men tore away the tamping, and came to the extinguished fuse. As Pleasants had surmised, it was where they had been spliced. Cutting the fuse at a point where the dampness had not penetrated they relighted it, and regained the outside as rapidly as possible. All this took time, precious time that could have been saved if army headquarters had furnished proper material, so that it was sixteen minutes before five when the explosion took place. A heavy reverberation shakes the earth—a hollow rumbling sound breaks on the ear. The explosion has come! A vast cloud of earth is borne upward, one hundred feet in air, presenting the appearance of an outspread umbrella, descending in the twinkling of an eye with a heavy thud! Then, from hundreds of cannons' mouths, with a deafening roar, the iron hail poured into the rebel lines.

The mine was proven a perfect success, the effects of the explosion went even beyond Pleasants' expectation. The size of the crater formed by the explosion was at least two hundred (200) feet long, fifty (50) feet wide, and twenty-five (25) feet deep.

The effect upon the enemy was tremendous. He was completely paralyzed. A breach was made in his lines practically four or five hundred feet wide, instead of being bound by the edges of the crater only. He was so completely stunned that after firing a hasty volley, it was nearly, if not quite an hour before he recovered from the shock. The rebel fort, its garrison, together with the line of rifle pits in its front were destroyed. Some three or four hundred rebels were killed by the explosion. The garrisons of the forts to the northwest became panic stricken, and abandoned their guns.

With a shout, sounding above the awful din, the First Division of the Ninth Corps leap the Union works and charge upon the doomed fort, but without a leader! Where is the commanding general of that

First Division. Alas! he never left his safe retreat behind a bombproof on the Union side! His division occupy the crater—the men lying down under cover of the earthworks and the mounds of earth thrown up by the explosion. Fatal halt! The broad gateway opened to Petersburg by Pleasants, is choked and crowded by troops who had been taught all through the campaign to constantly seek cover.

There was absolutely not a thing to prevent the occupation of the hill beyond, and Ledlie's neglect to do so, cannot be excused or atoned. Once secured Lee's troops would have been completely cut in two, and his army then and there destroyed.

Captain W. Gordon McCabe in the "Defence of Petersburg," a paper published in the Southern Historical Societies' papers, writes:

"Pleasants has done his work with terrible completeness, for now the site of the Elliott salient is marked by a horrid chasm, 135 feet in length, 97 feet in breadth, and 30 feet deep, and its brave garrison, all asleep, save the guards, when thus surprised by sudden death, lie buried beneath the jagged blocks of blackened clay—in all, 25 officers and men of the Eighteenth and Twenty-second South Carolina—two officers and twenty men of Pegram's Petersburg Battery (Beauregard's M. S.). The dread upheaval has rent in twain Elliott's brigade, and the men to right and left of the huge abyss recoil in terror and dismay."

One other extract from a newspaper published in the South is pertinent:

"'The explosion of the Burnside mine at a point of the Union defences before Petersburg, has been held by many to have been an entire failure, but it seems that it was otherwise. A recent visitor to the spot had the following information from a gentleman who accompanied him:

"'I was an officer in the Confederate Army, and I was in this fight and all others that occurred in this immediate vicinity. I saw that explosion and know of the effects and let me assure you that it was not a failure. The mine was sprung immediately under a battery supported by 200 men, and of that number only two escaped; and, notwithstanding all our newspapers may have said to the contrary, in those desperate charges which were made on the day of and succeeding the explosion, we lost 3000 men, and no one thing during the whole war produced such a demoralizing influence among our troops, and in my opinion, tended more strongly to terminate the contest. From that day desertions became more frequent, and from the uncertain horrors which that event threw around services "in front" the greatest dissatisfaction began to prevail in all the ranks of the army.'"

The Forty-eighth, by order of General Burnside, did not participate in the attack, he deeming the great service performed by it sufficient work. The regiment acted as provost guard arresting stragglers from the front. Every man in its ranks was under fire. Pleasants wanted to lead the charge with his regiment—had he done so there would have been no failure, or there would have been no Forty-eighth left to hear of it.

He was on General Potter's staff as a volunteer, and made several trips to and from the crater during the engagement. Indeed he was more like a crazy man that day, than one in possession of his senses.

The following acknowledgment of the regiment's service was made by General Meade, commanding the Army of the Potomac:

Acknowledgment of special services of 48th Regiment Pennsylvania Veteran Volunteers.

Head-Quarters, Army of the Potomac,

August 3d, 1864.

General Orders,}
No. 34.   }

The Commanding General takes great pleasure in acknowledging the valuable services rendered by Lieutenant-Colonel *Henry Pleasants*, 48th Regiment Pennsylvania Veteran Volunteers, and the officers and men of his command, in the excavation of the mine which was successfully exploded on the morning of the 30th ultimo under one of the enemy's batteries in front of the Second Division of the Ninth Army Corps.

The skill displayed in the laying out of and construction of the mine reflect great credit upon Lieutenant-Colonel *Pleasants*, the officer in charge, and the willing endurance by the officers and men of the regiment of the extraordinary labor and fatigue involved in the prosecution of the work to completion are worthy of the highest praise.

BY COMMAND OF MAJOR-GENERAL MEADE:

S. WILLIAMS,
Assistant Adjutant General.

OFFICIAL:

Assistant Adjutant General.

It is needless to enter into a discussion of the causes of the failure on the part of the Union forces to achieve one of the grandest successes of the war, after the explosion of the mine. The mine was not a failure—its projector and the men of the Forty-eighth had done their work, so their glory in the event remains imperishable. It is well to record Pleasants' opinion. In a communication to the writer, referring to the mine, he says: "A project, the success of which was perfect, and which, had it not been for the want of harmony between the generals commanding the Ninth Corps and Army of the Potomac, and the bad conduct of the commander of the First Division, would have broken through the thin shell that separated us from the heart of the Confederacy and ended the war then and there."

A Congressional Committee on the Conduct of the War, made a very elaborate and searching inquiry into the causes which led to such an unsatisfactory ending of a project so full of promise. Two extracts are given from the report of this committee, which are conclusive. Here they are:

"Lieutenant-Colonel Pleasants labored under disadvantages in the successful accomplishment of this important work, which would have deterred a man of less energy. It was not merely the evident lack of faith in the success of the enterprise shown by all the officers of high rank, except his division and corps commanders, but that lack of faith was accompanied by an entire failure to furnish the assistance and implements necessary to the success of the undertaking, within a reasonable time. The testimony of Lieutenant-Colonel Pleasants shows that he had to dig and mine with only the men of his own regiment; that the dirt had to be carried out in cracker-boxes, slung between poles, for lack of wheelbarrows; that he was even refused the use of an instrument at headquarters, wherewith to make the necessary triangulations, but that General Burnside had to send to Washington for an old fashioned theodolite. General Meade and Major Duane, chief engineer of the Army of the Potomac, said the thing could not be done; that it was all clap-trap and nonsense; that such a length of mine had never been excavated in military operations and could not be.

"In conclusion, the cause of the disastrous result of the assault of the thirtieth of July last is mainly attributable to the fact, that the plans and suggestions of the general who had devoted his attention for so long a time to the subject, who had carried out to so successful completion the project of mining the enemy's works, and who had carefully selected and drilled his troops, for the purpose of securing whatever advantages might be attainable from the explosion of the mine, should have been so entirely disregarded by a general who had evinced no faith in the successful prosecution of that work, had aided it by no countenance or open approval, and had assumed the entire direction and control only when it was completed, and the time had come for reaping any advantage that might be derived from it." *

---

* Report Conduct of the War, 1865, Vol. 1, Battle of Petersburg.

Speaking of this mine, on page 313 of the second volume of his Memoirs, Grant says: "When it did explode, it was very successful, making a crater twenty feet deep and something like a hundred feet in length."

There, boys of the Forty-eighth, you can rest contented with the truthful summing up of the committee who inquired into the matter. Everyone on duty at the mine can confirm the conclusion reached.

The plan of operations to be pursued upon the completion of the mine had been thoroughly digested. The drilling of the Fourth Division of the Ninth Army Corps was a part and parcel of the plan. It was intended that this division should play an important part in the assault on the rebel works—so the movements in which these troops were daily instructed were just the movements to be executed after the explosion of the mine. The fatal change in the body of attacking troops, made twelve hours before the assault, rendered these weeks of preparations of positively no effect whatever.

Sigfried was to lead the charge with his brigade, and but for the fatal change made in the leading column, would have carried his dusky warriors to the top of Cemetery Hill as certain as Pleasants dug the mine! How grandly his brigade charged over the cleared ground between the lines, raked by minie ball, shot and shell as no single spot had ever been raked before!

The gateway made by Pleasants was choked and closed by troops trained to seek shelter under fire. The order came to Sigfried to charge. Gathering his sword and scabbard up in his arms, he turned to the writer: "Come on, Bosby!" and, leaping the Union parapets, followed by his staff and the black regiments of his brigade, bore down upon the crater, and, finding it crowded with the men of the white regiments, carried his command over the mounds bordering the slaughter-hole, and established his lines to the right. The result is known. No troops could have saved the day after the fatal halt of the First Division. No troops entered the fight under as severe a fire as the colored troops, and no troops marched steadier or behaved with greater coolness. Hundreds of black men's bodies covered the sward that hot July day. Six hundred maimed, rent and disfigured sons of Ham laid suffering at the general field hospital. What does Sigfried say?

"Had it not been for the almost impassable crowd of troops of the leading divisions in the crater and entrenchments, Cemetery Hill would have been ours without a falter on the part of my brigade." Sigfried's Report, July 31, 1864.

"General Grant, himself, in his testimony, expresses his belief that if they (the colored troops) had been placed in advance, as General Burnside desired, the assault would have been successful." Report Conduct of the War.

A participant in the terrible mine fight can never forget its dread horrors. The dead bodies of the rebel soldiers who had garrisoned the fort, lie scattered about, stripped of clothing by the force of the explosion. A Thirty-sixth Massachusetts soldier says: "Sitting on the loose earth in the crater, a soldier felt a movement under him, and, upon removing a few inches of earth, he found a rebel soldier, who was quickly removed from his temporary grave, and after a little time, rallied sufficiently to tell us his experience and opinion of rapid transit. He said he was standing near one of the guns, with one foot on the hub of a wheel; all was quiet, and he was thinking of home, when the earth seemed to give way, a terrific noise, and he lost consciousness. How far skyward he went, he had no means of knowing. His escape from death was most remarkable. We sent him a prisoner back to our lines, and the poor fellow walked as if he expected an explosion at every step. Whether he lived or died we do not know."

The surgeon of the Eighteenth South Carolina Regiment, whose colonel was W. H. Wallace (after the war, Judge Wallace, of South Carolina), gives the following experience of two members of his regiment. This command occupied the ditches on the left of the blown up battery: "In one of the bomb-proofs on the extreme right of the Eighteenth South Carolina Volunteers, and just to the left of the mine, Lieutenant Williard Hill, Company E, and Sergeant Greer, Company A, Eighteenth South Carolina Volunteers, having been relieved from duty an hour before, were sleeping. The first they realized of it was the shock, then a deep darkness, and then a consciousness that the mine had been sprung and that they had been buried, how deep they could not imagine. Their first impulse was a deep, indescribable despair—heart-sickening, heart-rending hopelessness, that left them almost powerless for a time. But what could they do? They had nothing to dig out with but a bayonet that Sergeant Greer had in his belt, and there was but a canteen of water in the cell. . . . Among the missing are Lieutenant Hill and Sergeant Greer. We left them in their almost living grave, Greer digging with his bayonet, while Hill passed back the dirt, with all the desperation of despair. They hear not, heed not the battle that is raging above them, but toil on. Often hope would spring up in their hearts, to give way only to despair.

Hill has often told me how, when he awoke to a consciousness of his condition, the thoughts that flashed through his brain like lightning; how he thought if he could only see one ray of light, or breathe the fresh air once again; that if he could only let his wife know how and where he died, that death would be a relief to him. Almost suffocated for want of fresh air, they worked on; at last it seemed to them that something had crushed them; they had dug through the loose bowlders and the light burst upon them. They both, overcome with the sudden transition from their suffocation and despair to light and hope, fainted. How long they remained there they know not. When they awoke from their swoon, the first sound that broke on their ears was the clash of arms and the quick rolling roar of the battle as it raged around and above. Almost in stupor, trying to realize that they could again see the light of heaven and hear the voice of a living creature, they laid still until they recovered their minds enough to know what was going on. Hill often told me that when he knew and realized that it was a battle, the sound was the sweetest music that ever greeted his ears. At last the cry of victory rose high above everything else. They knew that somebody was vanquished, and that somebody was victor; who, they knew not. They emerged from their awful retreat, weak, worn in body, and with minds almost crazed. They were brought back to me at the field hospital more dead than alive, for, strange as it may seem, they were the most sadly changed men that I ever beheld. Both were fine-looking soldiers before; now they were weak, with sunken cheeks and eyes. Lieutenant Hill, whose hair twenty-four hours before was black, without a single gray hair in it (as he was only thirty years old), was now almost as white as snow."

Shortly after this fight, General Barnard, chief engineer of the Armies of the United States, sent for Pleasants to come and see him.

After a polite salutation, General Barnard said to Pleasants: "What experience have you ever had, sir, as an engineer?" "The old fool!" Pleasants said to the writer, who slept with him the night succeeding this interview, from which he returned with evidences of having been hospitably entertained: "The old fool, he made me mad, so I blurted out, 'I'm a better engineer than you've got in the whole Regular Army.' 'I'm happy to know you! I'm happy to know you,' Barnard replied, bowing low in his sarcasm. 'I am,' returned Pleasants, 'and I'll tell you why—an officer educated at West Point throws aside his theodolite when he leaves the academy, and scarcely has use for it afterwards, whilst I, sir, have to study that instrument daily in order to earn my bread and butter. My existence and those dear to me, depend on my skill with the theodolite, whilst your regular's pay goes on, whether he ever again sees the instrument or not.'"

A long conversation ensued, and wound up by General Barnard requesting Pleasants to walk along the lines of the army and point out suitable places for mining operations, and report to him his suggestions. Pleasants' last words that night were that he'd "see him in h—l first!"

Four months later he left the service a greatly disappointed and disgusted man. The President, on the sixteenth of December, 1864, conferred the rank of Brevet Colonel of Volunteers, which Pleasants declined. On the thirteenth of March, 1865, he received the appointment of Brevet Brigadier-General of Volunteers "For skillful and distinguished services during the war, and particularly in the construction and explosion of the mine before Petersburg." This appointment was subsequently confirmed by the United States Senate. All of which was most richly deserved. Pleasants' name is so intertwined with that of the Forty-eighth—he gave it so glorious a record—that as long as one is remembered, the other will be also.

CHAPTER XIII.

FINAL ASSAULT AND MUSTER-OUT.

The morning of July 31, 1864, was a bright and beautiful one—indeed, the entire day was delightful. The lines about Petersburg were more than usually quiet—how great the contrast compared to the awful scene of carnage twenty-four hours before! The dead and dying still strewed the ground between the contending lines. A flag of truce was sent out in the afternoon, proposing a cessation of hostilities, to permit the removal of the wounded and the burying of the dead, but this was not recognized. General Lee was in Richmond and had to be communicated with. The next morning, however, the white flag was honored for three hours, and under its operation, the wounded were cared for and the dead buried. On the second of August, Captain Bosbyshell, having been commissioned major of the Forty-eighth Regiment by Governor Andrew G. Curtin, upon the recommendation of Lieutenant-Colonel Pleasants and Colonel Sigfried, was relieved from the position of acting assistant adjutant-general of the First Brigade, Fourth Division, Ninth Army Corps, by General Burnside, and reported to his regiment, taking command thereof.

The regiment was on the skirmish line, under the command of Captain Joseph H. Hoskings, of Company F, the senior officer present. At this time the Forty-eighth was temporarily attached to the Second Brigade, with Lieutenant-Colonel Pleasants commanding the brigade.

The tour of skirmish duty terminated on the third of August, but unfortunately for Captain Hoskings, before leaving the front line, he was severely, though not dangerously, wounded by a rebel sharpshooter. The minie ball passed through the fleshy part of his left breast at an angle, taking, in its course, the muscles of his left arm, making four distinct holes.

Matters resumed the regular siege life again—the picket firing constant, and good men lost every day. Whilst sitting beside his tent, on the afternoon of August 5, Lieutenant David B. Brown, of Company H, was mortally wounded, dying as he was being conveyed to the hospital. He was a "First Defender," having served as a private in the Washington Artillerists during the three months' service. He was mustered into the United States' service in the Forty-eighth as seventh corporal of Company H, on the nineteenth of September, 1861, and was promoted sergeant-major of the regiment in September, 1862, serving as such until June 21, 1864, when he was commissioned second lieutenant of Company H. An efficient soldier and officer, Lieutenant Brown was respected and liked by his comrades.

The Forty-eighth, with the Second Maryland, all under the command of Major Bosbyshell, worked lustily on the main line of entrenchments all night of August 5, not being relieved until 5 o'clock on the morning of the sixth.

Resting during the day, the front line was occupied at night—part of the regiment being to the right of the railroad, and the left wing to the left of the same—headquarters being on the railroad. In the trenches all of the seventh, exposed not only to the constant rebel firing, but to a sun of torrid heat. At 8 p. m. the Forty-fifth Pennsylvania and Fourth Rhode Island relieved the command, and camp was gladly re-occupied. The next was a day of rest, but at night the trenches in front were again assigned the regiment. The firing was sharp and rapid all the time along the line. The heat intense. So passed the tenth until 9 o'clock at night, when relief came in the shape of the Second New York Mounted Rifles, then acting as infantry. The monotony of the siege was occasionally relieved by visitation of friends, and in running about to see other organizations—but the transactions of one day could readily describe the transactions of another. A move took place at 2 o'clock a. m. of the fifteenth of August to a portion of the line held by the Fifth Corps. It was quite daylight when the new position was occupied, and the Forty-eighth filed into the place assigned, whilst the troops of the Fifth Corps filed out in full view of the rebels. They, however, remained quiescent, which was really remarkable, the policy thus far having been to fire at the sight of any body of troops. The weather was wet, making life behind the earthworks far from agreeable. The nights of the seventeenth and eighteenth were made especially disagreeable by reason of a heavy cannonading from the enemy. On the afternoon of the nineteenth the regiment moved to the extreme left of the Ninth Corps' lines, assisting in the capture of the Weldon Railroad.

Lieutenant-Colonel Pleasants, having obtained a leave of absence to visit his home, the command of the regiment devolved upon Major Bosbyshell.

The rainy weather continued, and the men of the regiment had an exceedingly rough time. On the twentieth, an advance of half a mile or more was made. Five rebel prisoners were captured, and temporary entrenchments erected. The work on these entrenchments was continued all of the next day, and a very heavy fight took place some distance to the left of the regiment. At noon the skirmishers in front of the command were driven in. Regimental line was formed back of the works and every one in readiness to repel an expected attack. This was occasioned by the enemy attempting to regain possession of the Weldon Railroad. After waiting some little time for the onslaught and no further demonstration being made, the enemy having been repulsed on the left with great loss, Major Bosbyshell desired to re-establish the skirmish line. Lieutenant Jacob Douty volunteered to do this important and risky work. The front of the line of breastworks had been cleared of timber, but on the opposite side of the clearing was a heavy wood, and not a soul knew whether there was any force of the enemy there or not—so it was a brave act to jump our entrenchments, with a spade over his shoulder, as Douty did, and advancing across the clearing until nearly up to the opposite wood, coolly commenced digging a rifle pit in full view of friend and supposed foe alike. Plenty of volunteers followed Douty's plucky act, and in a short time the skirmish line was intact. No opposition was manifested—whether the rebels looked on or not, is not known—still the act of Lieutenant Douty, under the circumstances, exhibited courage of a high order—the kind of courage the medal of honor is intended to approve.

At 4 o'clock in the afternoon the regiment was relieved by troops from the Second Brigade, Fourth (colored) Division, Ninth Army Corps, and camp was had in rear of brigade headquarters.

On the afternoon of the twenty-second the command moved to the front and began the erection of a new line of entrenchments, which were finished the next afternoon. These were quite formidable works, and connected with the works on the right, thus making a continuous line from the Appomattox above City Point to the Yellow Tavern on the Weldon Railroad.

During this tour of duty, there appeared one day a young staff officer, who stated that he had been sent to make an inspection of the regiment. The regiment was ordered into line, but Lieutenant-Colonel Pleasants not being very well, directed Major Bosbyshell to take command. The inspection of arms and accoutrements proceeded quite satisfactorily. At its conclusion, however, the Major was directed to drill the command, as the inspecting officer desired to see how efficient it was in the tactics. A regimental drill to a new field officer is embarrassing enough when there is no one present but the officers and men of the regiment; to be called upon to do so for the first time, under the eye of an inspecting officer, was doubly annoying.

Major Bosbyshell did not appear the least worried or embarrassed in consequence of this demand. He knew the Forty-eighth was a well-drilled body of men—he had no fears on that score; but for the moment he was inwardly endeavoring to determine what movements he should try. Not a single command came to his mind. A lucky thought just then occurred; he looked at the inspecting officer, saw he was young, and at once felt convinced that he was not up in regimental drill himself; so, putting on a nonchalant air, said to the inspector: "What movement would you like to see done?" This question struck home, and with some embarrassed hesitation, the officer replied: "Change front." That was the Major's cue. "Change front, forward on first company, companies right half wheel," came the command, and beautifully it was executed. This over, the Major said pleasantly, "What next, sir." Another movement was suggested, again giving the cue desired, and it was neatly gone through. This kind of tactics on the part of the Major exhausted the inspecting officer's repertoire of commands after the third move, relieved the regiment of further trouble, and the Major from his annoying position.

Matters remained quiet along the lines so far as any movements of magnitude were concerned until the latter part of September, 1864. The never ceasing crack of the rifles of the men in the rifle pits, and occasional shower of mortar shells, with a flurry of shot and shell now and then, served to remind all hands that the war was going on, dangerously near, and ready for death and destruction upon the slightest provocation. An extension of the lines further around the enemy's right flank on the thirtieth of September resulted in a hot fight at Poplar Springs Church. The Fifth Corps felt the force of this engagement severely, and the magnificent manner in which they held their lines served to tighten the coil about Petersburg more securely. The regiments of the Ninth Corps joined on the left of the Fifth, the Forty-eighth being held in reserve at the commencement of the battle in a clearing near the Pegram House. Some of the Massachusetts regiments in the front line, having large numbers of Germans in their ranks, many of whom had not been in the country over six weeks, and were utterly ignorant of the English language, were thrown into great disorder by the savage charge of the rebel regiments. These Germans ran pell-mell through the ranks of the supporting regiments. Pleasants was greatly enraged at these fleeing soldiers as they dashed blindly to the rear, pushing and shoving their way between the ranks of the Forty-eighth, and with drawn sword slashed to the right and left amongst them with the strength of an athlete, staying the flight effectually anywhere near his sweeping sabre. Many a sore head and stinging rib resulted from the blows well laid on by him. The Forty-eighth's line remained intact, but in the forward movement, nearly all of the left wing, with Major Bosbyshell, became separated from the right wing by a heavy undergrowth of trees and bushes, and a swamp. The Major, finding himself and a portion of the regiment on the wrong side of the swamp or ditch, and near enough to the advancing rebel skirmishers to distinguish their features, ordered the men to retire across the swamp as rapidly as possible. This was done without serious loss, although the enemy poured volley after volley into them. Just beyond the swamp, the rest of the regiment was found busily engaged in throwing up entrenchments.

The reunited regiment soon had a well-defined line of works, which was held successfully. The Forty-eighth lost two killed, seven wounded and forty-four prisoners—the second time in the entire service of the command when any prisoners were captured from it. This engagement resulted in the Ninth Corps occupying the works captured from the enemy at Peebles' farm. It connected with the Fifth Corps on the right, with its left refused, covering the Squirrel Level road. These lines were greatly strengthened and permanently held, extending the Union lines some three miles beyond the Weldon Railroad.

Major Bosbyshell, whose presence was necessary at home just at this time, failing to secure a leave of absence, took advantage of the expiration of his original term of service, and applied to be mustered out. This application was granted, and his connection with the regiment ceased on the first of October, 1864. Colonel Sigfried was likewise mustered out on his own application on the eleventh of October. The retirement of these officers promoted Lieutenant-Colonel Pleasants to the colonelcy, to which office he was commissioned but not mustered; Captain Gowen, of Company C, became lieutenant-colonel, and Captain Isaac F. Brannon, of Company K, major.

The Union lines were within a mile and a half of the strong position held by the enemy along the Boynton plank road, threatening not only that line but the South Side Railroad as well; which road was not over three miles away, and the only railroad left the rebels south of the Appomattox. The month of October was occupied in strengthening the positions secured—the entrenchments were remodeled and added to, rendering them defensible at all points.

The Forty-eighth took part in the demonstration made on the Boynton plank road, on the twenty-seventh of October, moving out of the entrenchments early in the morning. Daylight found them rapidly pushing along the Squirrel Level road. The movement was intended as a surprise to the enemy—it was hoped to capture his videttes, and by a rapid march suddenly overwhelm his position on the Boynton road, and wrest it from him. The rebel troops, however, were vigilant—the premature discharge of a musket in the hands of an advancing skirmisher alarmed the outpost and put them on their guard. Strongly constructed works were encountered, protected by abatis and slashed timber along the entire front.

A deployment of the Ninth Corps took place, but to attack so strongly entrenched a position was deemed unwise, so the advance was carried close up to the cleared space, and the work of entrenching began. Some hard fighting took place, resulting in losses to both sides—flags and prisoners were lost and captured by both. The project was abandoned on the twenty-eighth, by the withdrawal of the troops, and re-occupation of their former lines.

In this retrograde movement the Forty-eighth brought up the rear continually skirmishing with the enemy, who followed up closely. To guard against attack the corps, when within a mile of their encampment, formed line of battle in column of divisions, the divisions retiring in line, one through the other.

Another season of quiet fell on the troops of the corps—no change taking place until December. Early in that month, under orders, the Forty-eighth with the Seventh Rhode Island Regiment, and two batteries of artillery occupied Fort Sedgwick, located immediately in front of Petersburg, right over the Jerusalem plank road, a post so near the rebel lines, and so constantly under the heaviest fire, that it was called by the soldiers "Fort Hell." The charge of the post was given to Colonel Pleasants. At this time the Ninth Corps occupied the right line of the army, reaching from the Appomattox to Fort Howard, about seven miles in distance. Immediately in front of Fort Sedgwick the enemy had two batteries of ten-inch and eight-inch mortars, which almost daily opened on the fort, causing the death of several men of the regiment, and making life within that enclosure hazardous in the extreme.

At times this shelling was more severe than usual, which was bad enough. A particularly lively time was the twenty-ninth of December, resulting in the death of Corporal John F. Dentzer, of K, and the wounding of five other soldiers of the Forty-eighth. On the second of

January, 1865, a sixty-four pound mortar shell passed directly through the quarters of Corporal William Levison, of Company C, killing him instantly, as well as wounding Lieutenant James Clark of the same company.

Colonel Pleasants not desiring to remain longer in the service was mustered out, by reason of expiration of his term of service, on the eighteenth of December, 1864. This made Gowen colonel, Brannon lieutenant-colonel and Captain Richard M. Jones, of Company G, major.

Directly opposite Fort Sedgwick on a hill back of their main line of entrenchments, was the rebel fort, Mahone, an earthwork which the Forty-eighth was destined to wrest from the enemy. The weary winter months were spent in garrisoning this dangerous post—a duty requiring the utmost vigilance on the part of the men of the regiment. They were ever alert, however, and performed all required duties with promptness and fidelity.

"Our soldiers were subjected to constant annoyance from the enemy's sharpshooters, and skirmishing took place almost daily. Artillery duels were also frequent. The neighborhood of 'Fort Hell' was especially hot, and appeared to be the object of most spiteful attack."*

So the weary winter months passed amidst daily dangers calculated to deter men from continuing the strife. The Forty-eighth was a regiment of resolute soldiers, however, and this daily dealing with death and destruction only nerved them to greater zeal in the discharge of the important work assigned the command. As the spring came on all felt that decisive action would surely ensue, and all awaited with eager anxiety the time to come for such action. The plans for the final assault were well laid and the time for carrying out the same close at hand, when, unexpectedly, on the twenty-fifth of March, 1865, the enemy swept over the picket line, stormed and captured Fort Stedman, one of the weakest forts on the Union lines. With yells of victory the rebels turned to right and left charging the flanks. General Hartranft with his new Pennsylvania Division went at the rebels with such impetuosity, that he staid their exulting advance, turned back their charging columns, penned them in Fort Stedman, capturing the greater part of the assaulting troops, hurling the rest, mere remnants of disorganized commands, into the rebel lines, and re-established the Union lines.

The Forty-eighth stood to their work of holding Fort Sedgwick during this daring assault—ready and determined to prevent its capture

---

* Woodbury's "Burnside and the Ninth Corps," p. 474

by the enemy. All were proud that Pennsylvanians saved the day. Particularly did the Forty-eighth rejoice in the great honor achieved by one with whom its fortunes had so often been intertwined, the brave and able John F. Hartranft, Major-general by reason of being the "Hero of Fort Stedman!"

On the twenty-seventh of March orders were issued to the Army of the Potomac to be ready to move at a moment's notice. On the twenty-ninth the movement began on the extreme left, and on the thirtieth, the Ninth Corps holding the lines directly in front of Petersburg, was ordered to assault the enemy's works at 4 o'clock the next morning. The exact point of attack was left to the discretion of the corps commander, Major-General John G. Parke. The position of Fort Sedgwick was most commanding, so the most available point to make the attempt was from its front. The troops were put in position for the contemplated movement, but inasmuch as matters had not progressed as far as desirable on the left, the assault was suspended by General Meade and the commands resumed their old positions. Orders were again issued on the first of April to make the assault the next morning, and the troops occupied the position assigned them, the Forty-eighth with Fort Mahone the objective point, formed under the walls of "Fort Hell."

Ten o'clock on the night of the first, under a heavy artillery fire, the Union skirmishers advanced. The enemy's picket line between Forts Hayes and Howard was carried, and some two hundred and fifty prisoners were taken. Four o'clock on the morning of the second a heavy artillery fire was opened all along the rebel lines. The skirmishers were pushed forward, and at half-past four the troops formed for the attack left their place of formation, and advanced with great alacrity and enthusiasm upon the rebel fortifications. Only half rationed, and with scalding coffee hastily swallowed, the Forty-eighth moved toward the rear of Fort "Hell," through the deep cuts made for the protection of wagons in going to and from the front—now filled with a slushy mud—and emerging near the Jerusalem Plank Road, crossed to the left rear of the Fort. The pioneers were cutting away the abatis in front to permit the egress of the troops. The regiment passed through the narrow opening, quickly formed line in front, and moved rapidly forward to the Union picket line. Resting a moment, the order, forward, came, and with a savage rush the rebel picket line was reached and captured without much of a struggle. Eager to achieve greater results away dashed the Forty-eighth in the van of the brigade, General Curtin and Colonel Gowen at the head, the rebel Fort Mahone's guns belching a very "inferno" of shot and shell into the ranks. On, on, pushed the boys determined to capture the dire old tormentor who had troubled them so the winter long. The attack was most impetuous.

Whilst Curtin and Gowen were running ahead the abatis impeded their progress, so with their own hands they tore it apart trampling it under feet, when a cannon shot struck the Forty-eighth's gallant young Colonel, carrying away the half of his face, killing him instantly! So fell one greatly beloved—gloriously at the moment of victory, honored as few have been, mourned sadly by his men; indeed all who knew his splendid worth and promising future were grieved.

Grasping the bloody, lifeless form, the mass, for lines were broken, ran back to the old rebel picket line, having no one near to lead them. General Curtin, apparently unconcerned under the tempest of shot and shell poured into the command, stood leaning on his sword, calling upon the gallant Forty-eighth to "rally once more for the honor of the old Keystone State." He directed Sergeant William J. Wells, of Company F, to have the regimental colors brought to him. This was done. The men rallied around their standard, and led by the brave Curtin, with the ferocity of mad men renewed the assault, pushed through the obstructing abatis, over the moat, scaled the earthwork, securing a lodgment on the walls. Along came the Thirty-ninth New Jersey, the color bearer gallantly springing right into the midst of the rebels, an act of bravery that excited the admiration of all who witnessed it. Captain John L. Williams, of Company F, shouted "Forward, boys, and save the Jersey colors." With one bound the men sprang forward, a hand-to-hand encounter ensued, which lasted but a moment, the rebels were overpowered, the fort was captured, and the enemy driven beyond it for a considerable distance. Being ordered back, the regiment occupied the fortification, using the rear of the entrenchments for protection, and held the works against repeated and furious assaults of the enemy, in attempts to retake it. Lieutenant-Colonel Brannon assumed the command, and directed the further movements of the regiment. In this successful assault the Forty-eighth lost ten killed, fifty-six wounded and twenty-four missing—figures eloquently demonstrating the dangers encountered and emphasizing the victory.*

Petersburg, so long invested, so hotly contested, and so stubbornly defended, was entered by the Union troops on the third; the flag of the First Michigan sharpshooters was raised on the court house and the occupation was complete. It fell to the lot of the Forty-eighth to

---

* For many of the facts of this assault, the writer is indebted to Sergeant William J. Wells and Captain A. C. Huckey.

guard the trains on their way to Farmville. The journey hither was begun on the third. The way showed evidences of the disastrous retreat of Lee's forces, foreshadowing the disintegration of the Confederacy.

Farmville, seventy-nine miles from Petersburg, was reached on the eighth of April, and from guarding trains the Forty-eighth was detailed to look after the prisoners captured by Sheridan's Troopers. Amongst these prisoners were Generals Ewell and Fitz Hugh Lee. This duty was soon ended, as the Army of Northern Virginia surrendered to General Grant on the ninth of April at Appomattox Court House, and the prisoners in charge of the Forty-eighth, being a part of that army, were, like the rest, paroled and let go.

During the stay at Farmville the sad news of the assassination of President Lincoln fell like a pall over the rejoicing army, causing great sorrow amongst the troops. On the day of Mr. Lincoln's funeral in Washington, April 19, the Forty-eighth turned its back on the rebellion, and began its journey toward home. Covering about twenty miles a day, it marched into Petersburg on the twenty-third, and reached City Point on the twenty-fourth. Here it remained for three days, embarking on transports on the twenty-seventh, steamed down the James River, by its old stamping grounds at Newport News and Fortress Monroe, up Chesapeake Bay and the Potomac River, reaching Alexandria on the twenty-eighth, where it went into camp. This became the general rendezvous of the Army of the Potomac, awaiting the final overthrow of the rebellion. The monotony of camp life was broken on the twenty-second and twenty-third of May, by reason of the Grand Review in Washington. With the other veteran regiments of the Army of the Potomac, the Forty-eighth took part in the magnificent pageant which passed down Pennsylvania avenue on the twenty-second of May, a review the like of which will never be seen again. To do this the regiment left Alexandria early on the morning of the twenty-second, returning again to its camp on the twenty-third.

The rebellion was ended—the authority of the government again established all over the country—the blockade of the Southern ports raised on the first of July, hence the disbandment of the army began.

On the seventeenth of July the Forty-eighth was mustered out of service at Alexandria, Va., and the same day, it started for Pennsylvania, reaching Harrisburg on the eighteenth. The command was detained here for four days, the officers perfecting their final reports, and properly winding up the affairs of the regiment. Finally, on the twenty-second, every detail having been completed, the regiment started from Harrisburg for home. Oh how sweet the word to the brave fellows who had been spared through so many and great dangers! Home, blessed name, so soon to be realized! How the hearts of the men on that train throbbed as each mile carried them nearer and nearer to the sacred place! Many could have hugged the trainmen when "Reading" was shouted into the cars! And then the welcome towns of Hamburg, Port Clinton, Auburn and Schuylkill Haven flew by —and then every man on his feet ready to spring to the ground as Pottsville was reached, where great crowds roared, cheered and cried such a hearty welcome, all knew it was HOME!

The following account of the reception is compiled from the columns of the *Miners' Journal* of July 22, 1865:

Great preparations had been made by the people of Pottsville and vicinity for this home-coming of the regiment. On Monday evening, July 17, 1865, a large meeting of the citizens was held at the Union Hotel, on Centre street, Pottsville. This meeting was presided over by Captain John T. Boyle, an honored officer of the Ninety-sixth, while F. B. Wallace, the compiler of the 'Patriotism of Schuylkill County,' was secretary. A committee of three, Generals Nagle, Sigfried and Major Bosbyshell, was appointed to place the citizens in communication with the regiment, by means of a committee to proceed to Harrisburg to make all necessary arrangements at that point. An adjourned meeting of citizens was held the next evening, when Messrs. John M. Clayton, L. F. Womelsdorff, F. B. Kaercher, and William Fox, were selected as the committee to meet the regiment at Harrisburg. A committee was appointed, consisting of Messrs. Adam Shertle, James Focht, Thomas Wren, George Martz, and Thomas Foster, to make all necessary arrangements, and the following gentlemen were named as the Committee of Reception, to wit:

Lin Bartholomew, Esq.; Hon. C. W. Pitman, Judge Charles Frailly, Judge Bernard Reilly, J. T. Werner, Jacob Olewine, Lewis Reeser, John P. Bertram, James J. Connor, J. Franklin Harris, Richard R. Morris, Theodore Garretson, John Drill, James Inness, Henry Auman, Burd Patterson, James Silliman, Jere Reed, F. B. Kaercher, John M. Clayton, L. F. Womelsdorff, George Bright, Benjamin Haywood, William L. Whitney, Nathan Evans, John Shippen, Charlemagne Tower, William Mellen, Jr.; William E. Boyer, Lewis C. Thompson, B. F. Taylor, Marcus Heilner, Henry Gressang, J. G. Cochran, Joseph Derr, Frederick Boedefeld, John P. Hobart, William Fox.

On Thursday morning it was announced that the regiment would reach Pottsville in the afternoon at 2 o'clock. The citizens decorated

Record Flag of the 48th Reg't Pa. Vet. Vol. Inf'ty.

This flag was designed by Capt. Edw. S. Hart, late of the U. S. A., and printed by Wm. Jas. Mudey, of Pottsville

their houses, and all of the flags in the borough were flung to the breeze. About 3 o'clock the special train arrived. A portion of the regiment, the men belonging to Port Clinton, Schuylkill Haven, Cressona and Minersville, stopped at the stations below. With those who arrived on the noon train and those who came in the special, there were about one hundred and twenty-five men. Altogether about three hundred men returned to the county. Most of the men brought their muskets home with them, having purchased them of the government.

The men were escorted up Centre street, amid the firing of cannon, the cheers of the citizens, and the waving of handkerchiefs, and the singing of patriotic songs. At the Union Hotel, an address of welcome was made by Benjamin Haywood, Esq. It elicited the hearty cheers of the war-worn veterans. After Mr. Haywood had concluded, the men partook of a collation at the Union Hotel. There was no formality about the reception. It was a spontaneous expression of thanks on the part of the citizens, and the soldiers appreciated it. In the evening a squad under command of Captain J. Frank Werner reached Pottsville, and were escorted to the Union, where they partook of a collation. They were appropriately welcomed home by Hon. C. W. Pitman. The soldiers toasted the citizens of Schuylkill County, and their former officers, General Nagle, General Sigfried and Colonel Pleasants. These gentlemen returned thanks for the honor, and welcomed the brave men to their homes.

The meetings of the wives and children, with their husbands and fathers, were in many instances touching, in all joyful. When the men reached the corner of Centre and Market, a wife or sweetheart of one of the soldiers in the ranks saw him. His eye caught hers at the same moment. Impulsively they flew with open arms toward each other, and the next moment were locked in a fond embrace. Neither, from emotion, could speak ; but tears of joy trickled down their cheeks. It was a scene the sacredness of which the publicity could not destroy.

Such was the home-coming and here this account must close.

The Forty-eighth, as a regiment now becomes a reminiscence. To its credit and renown, be it said, thirty years after, that its members have been worthy citizens of the great American nation since laying aside the trappings of war.

CHAPTER XIV.

SECOND MARYLAND. SIXTH NEW HAMPSHIRE.

This chronicle of the meanderings of the Forty-eighth would not be complete without a word or two of the two regiments, the Second Maryland and Sixth New Hampshire, with which its life was so closely bound, that the actions of one in the stirring campaigns and battles shared, tells also the history of all.

The naming of these commands calls up Colonel J. Eugene Duryée, of the Second Maryland, whose bravery in the charge on the bridge at Antietam, won him the rank of brevet brigadier-general, and General Simon G. Griffin, of the Sixth New Hampshire, who so frequently and ably commanded the brigade and division with which the Forty-eighth was connected—they seem part and parcel of the latter. Then Captain Malcolm Wilson, killed at Antietam; Captain B. Frank Matthews and his brother Thomas L., Colonel Thomas B. Allard, Chaplain R. S. Hitchcock, Captain B. Frank Taylor, Lieutenant Henry Pennington, who won his shoulder straps for gallantry at Pollocksville, N. C., conferred on the field by order of General Burnside, and hosts of other fine fellows of the Maryland command.

The Forty-eighth's connection with the Sixth began on Hatteras Island, when the Burnside expedition appeared off the coast. It encamped near the Forty-eighth's location—indeed, was the nearest regiment to it. Together the regiments participated in a grand review of the troops on Hatteras on the thirty-first of January, 1862, ordered by General Thomas Williams, commanding the post. With the Second Maryland the Forty-eighth became brigaded at Newbern on the twenty-third of April, 1862.

At Newport News, on the fourteenth of July following, the First Brigade, Second Division, Ninth Army Corps, consisted of the Second Maryland, Sixth New Hampshire and Forty-eighth Pennsylvania—from which time, with only short intervals, these three regiments remained together during the war.

Throughout the pages of this book mention is frequently made of one or the other of these two commands. The roads traversed, the places visited and the battles fought by the Forty-eighth, were traversed, visited and fought by the Second and Sixth, so that what is related of interest to the first should be of equal interest to the two latter.

There was individual work done by each of these commands, conspicuously exhibiting the courage of the men comprising them. No braver charge of the war is recorded than that of the Second and Sixth at Antietam Bridge—mention of which is made on page seventy-nine of this work.

The Forty-eighth, on the bluff immediately over the bridge, witnessed the daring attack. The withering and murderous fire poured into their ranks, at short and easy range, was such that no living person could have reached the bridge, going the entire distance over a road so exposed to the enemy's fire. The failure to reach it in no way reflects upon the commands—the only wonder is that any escaped from the seething storm of shot and shell sweeping the eastern bank of the stream!

It is a pleasure these many years after to call up the memories of the days spent with the men from Maryland and those from New Hampshire. All hail, companions in war—may the survivors be lasting friends to the end of life's journey! This record of the good old Pennsylvania regiment with which you shared the trials and dangers of the Civil War delights in according a full measure of praise to your worthy deeds, and the men who battled in its ranks hold out their hands in warm friendship, thirty years after, to their comrades from the shores of the Chesapeake Bay, and the old Granite Hills.

ROSTER OF OFFICERS.

JAMES NAGLE.—Organized Forty-eighth Pennsylvania in August and September, 1861, authority being granted by Governor Andrew G. Curtin, on August 11, 1861; commissioned Colonel to rank from same date; promoted to Brigadier-General of Volunteers on recommendation of Major-General Reno, to rank from September 10, 1862; resigned May 9, 1863, on account of severe suffering from *angina pectoris*. Colonel Thirty-ninth Regiment Pennsylvania Volunteer Militia, July and August, 1863; Colonel One Hundred-and-ninety-fourth Regiment Pennsylvania Volunteers, July 24, 1864 to November 6, 1864.

JOSHUA K. SIGFRIED.—Major, October 1, 1861; Lieutenant-Colonel, November 30, 1861; Colonel, September 20, 1862; Brevet Brigadier-General of Volunteers, August 1, 1864; mustered out, October 11, 1864, expiration of term.

GEORGE W. GOWEN.—First-Lieutenant Company C, September 11, 1861; Captain, September 28, 1862; Lieutenant-Colonel, December 20, 1864; Colonel, March 1, 1865; killed in the assault on Fort Mahone, April 2, 1865.

HENRY PLEASANTS.—Captain Company C, September 11, 1861; Lieutenant-Colonel, September 20, 1862; Colonel, December, 1864; mustered out December 18, 1864, expiration of term; Brevet Brigadier-General of Volunteers, March 13, 1865; projector and builder of the Petersburg mine.

ISAAC F. BRANNON.—First Lieutenant Company K, October 1, 1861; Captain, August 30, 1862; Major, December 20, 1864; Lieutenant-Colonel, March 1, 1865; Colonel, May 11, 1865; mustered out with regiment, July 17, 1865.

DAVID A. SMITH.—Lieutenant-Colonel, August 20, 1861; not mustered; resigned November, 1861. First Defender.

RICHARD M. JONES.—Sergeant Company G, October 1, 1861; First Sergeant, May, 1861; Second Lieutenant, June 24, 1864; First Lieutenant, July 13, 1864; Captain, September 12, 1864; Major, May 11, 1865; Lieutenant-Colonel, June 3, 1865; mustered out with regiment, July 17, 1865.

DANIEL NAGLE.—Captain Company D, September 23, 1861; Major, November 30, 1861; resigned July 26, 1862; Lieutenant-Colonel, Nineteenth Pennsylvania Volunteer Militia, September, 1862; Colonel One Hundred-and-seventy-third Pennsylvania Volunteers, November 18, 1862 to August 17, 1863.

JAMES WREN.—Captain Company B, September 19, 1861; Major, September 20, 1862; resigned May 20, 1863. First Defender.

JOSEPH A. GILMOUR.—Captain Company H, September 19, 1861; Major, July 28, 1863; died June 9, 1864, of wounds received in action, May 31, 1864. First Defender.

OLIVER C. BOSBYSHELL.—Second Lieutenant Company G, October 1, 1861; First Lieutenant, May 5, 1862; Captain, June 2, 1862; Major, July 23, 1864; mustered out, October 1, 1864, expiration of term. First Defender.

JACOB WAGNER.—Private Company H, September 19, 1861; Quartermaster-Sergeant, October 4, 1861; Quartermaster, December 21, 1862; Major, June 21, 1865; mustered out with regiment, July 17, 1865.

JOHN D. BERTOLETTE.—First Lieutenant and Adjutant, October 1, 1861; Captain and Assistant Adjutant-General of Volunteers, September 25, 1862.

DANIEL D. McGINNES.—First Sergeant Company H, September 19, 1861; First Lieutenant and Adjutant, September 26, 1862; resigned, March 18, 1864.

CHARLES LOESER, JR.—Private Company G, October 1, 1861; Sergeant-Major, October, 1861; Second Lieutenant Company C, September 20, 1862; First Lieutenant, January 1, 1864; First Lieutenant and Adjutant, June 25, 1864; mustered out, October 1, 1864, expiration of term.

HENRY C. HONSBERGER.—Private and Sergeant Company A, September 17, 1861; Sergeant-Major, September, 1862; First Lieutenant and Adjutant, December 17, 1864; mustered out with regiment, July 17, 1865.

JAMES ELLIS.—First Lieutenant and Quartermaster, October 1, 1861; resigned December 20, 1862.

THOMAS BOHANNON.—Second Lieutenant Company E, October 1, 1861; First Lieutenant, September 17, 1862; First Lieutenant and Quartermaster, June 23, 1865; mustered out with regiment, July 17, 1865.

DAVID MINIS, JR.—Major and Surgeon, October 1, 1861; died at Roanoke Island, N. C., February 14, 1862.

CHARLES T. REBER.—First Lieutenant and Assistant Surgeon, October 1, 1861; Major and Surgeon, February 14, 1862; resigned, February 23, 1863.

WILLIAM R. D. BLACKWOOD.—Major and Surgeon, April 28, 1863; mustered out with regiment, July 17, 1865.

ISRAEL BUSHONG.—First Lieutenant and Assistant Surgeon, August 1, 1862; resigned, September 29, 1862.

C. P. HERRINGTON.—First Lieutenant and Assistant Surgeon, September 13, 1862. Promoted to Surgeon One Hundred-and-thirty-eighth Regiment Pennsylvania Volunteers, October 30, 1862.

ALVAH H. MALONEY.—First Lieutenant and Assistant Surgeon, October 22, 1861; resigned, December 5, 1862.

JAMES M. MORRISON.—First Lieutenant and Assistant Surgeon, November 29, 1862; discharged, August 19, 1863.

JOHN M. HUSTON.—First Lieutenant and Assistant Surgeon, March 17, 1863; resigned, June 25, 1863.

JOHN B. CULVER.—First Lieutenant and Assistant Surgeon, June 1, 1864; mustered out with regiment, July 17, 1865.

EUGENE M. SMYSER.—First Lieutenant and Assistant Surgeon, April 8, 1864; mustered out with regiment, July 17, 1865.

REV. SAMUEL A. HOLMAN.—Captain and Chaplain, October 1, 1861; resigned, January 2, 1863.

REV. LEVI B. BECKLEY.—Captain and Chaplain, April 11, 1864; mustered out with regiment, July 17, 1865.

DANIEL B. KAUFFMAN.—Captain Company A, September 17, 1861; dismissed August 1, 1864.

HENRY BOYER.—Second Lieutenant Company A, September 17, 1861; First Lieutenant, September 29, 1862; Captain, August 27, 1864; mustered out, October 1, 1864, expiration of term.

ALBERT C. HUCKEY.—Sergeant and First Sergeant Company A, September 17, 1861; Second Lieutenant, September 3, 1864; Captain, October 30, 1864; mustered out with regiment, July 17, 1865.

ABIEL H. JACKSON.—First Lieutenant Company A, September 17, 1861; resigned, September 29, 1862.

LEWIS B. EVELAND.—First Sergeant Company A, September 17, 1861; Second Lieutenant, September 29, 1862; First Lieutenant, August 27, 1864; mustered out, October 1, 1864, expiration of term.

WILLIAM TAYLOR.—Sergeant Company A, September 17, 1861; First Sergeant; First Lieutenant, October 30, 1864; mustered out with regiment, July 17, 1865.

HENRY H. PRICE.—Private Company A, September 17, 1861; Sergeant; Second Lieutenant, October 30, 1864; mustered out with regiment, July 17, 1865.

ULYSSES A. BAST.—First Lieutenant Company B, September 19, 1861; Captain, September 20, 1862; mustered out, September 30, 1864, expiration of term.

THOMAS P. WILLIAMS.—Corporal Company B, September 19, 1861; First Sergeant; First Lieutenant, September 12, 1864; Captain, December 11, 1864; mustered out with regiment, July 17, 1865.

JOHN L. WOOD.—Second Lieutenant Company B, September 19, 1861; First Lieutenant, September 20, 1862; resigned, December 30, 1862.

WILLIAM H. HUME.—First Sergeant Company B, September 19, 1861; Second Lieutenant, September 20, 1862; First Lieutenant, September 1, 1863. Died, June 30, 1864, of wounds received in action May 31, 1864.

THOMAS JOHNSON.—Sergeant Company B, September 19, 1861; Second Lieutenant, September 1, 1863; First Lieutenant, July 24, 1864; discharged on surgeon's certificate, August 7, 1864. First Defender.

JOHN WATKINS.—Private Company B, September 19, 1861; Sergeant; Second Lieutenant, May 22, 1865; mustered out with regiment, July 17, 1865.

WILLIAM CLARK.—Sergeant Company B, September 11, 1861; Second Lieutenant, November 26, 1862; First Lieutenant, June 26, 1864; Captain, March 1, 1865; mustered out with regiment, July 17, 1865.

THOMAS J. FITZSIMMONS.—Second Lieutenant, September 11, 1861; First Lieutenant, September 28, 1862; resigned, November 22, 1862.

JAMES CLARK.—Corporal Company C, September 11, 1861; First Sergeant; First Lieutenant, March 1, 1865; mustered out with regiment, July 17, 1865.

HENRY WEISER.—Private September 11, 1861; Sergeant; Second Lieutenant, May 21, 1865; mustered out with regiment, July 17, 1865.

WILLIAM W. POTTS.—First Lieutenant Company D, September 23, 1861; Captain, November 30, 1861; discharged for disability, January 8, 1863.

PETER FISHER.—Corporal Company D, September 23, 1861; First Lieutenant, December 10, 1862; Captain, September 1, 1863; discharged, July 21, 1864. First Defender.

Jacob F. Werner.—Private Company D, September 23, 1861; Commissary Sergeant Regiment, September 23, 1861; Second Lieutenant Company D, September 12, 1864; Captain, November 28, 1864; mustered out with regiment, July 17, 1865.

Charles Kleckner.—Second Lieutenant Company D, September 23, 1861; First Lieutenant, January 1, 1862; Colonel, One Hundred-and-seventy-second Regiment Pennsylvania Volunteers, December 1, 1862.

James K. Helms.—Sergeant Company D, September 23, 1861; Second Lieutenant, December 10, 1862; First Lieutenant, September 1, 1863; commissioned Captain, July 22, 1864, and not mustered; discharged by S. O., October 19, 1864.

Henry E. Stichter.—Corporal Company D, September 23, 1861; Second Lieutenant, September 1, 1863; First Lieutenant, September 22, 1864; mustered out, October 6, 1864, expiration of term.

Henry Rothenberger.—Private Company D, September 23, 1861; Sergeant; First Lieutenant, June 16, 1864; mustered out with regiment, July 17, 1865.

Alexander H. Fox.—Sergeant Company D, September 23, 1861; Second Lieutenant, November 30, 1861; died, December 25, 1861.

Henry P. Owens.—First Sergeant Company D, September 23, 1861; Second Lieutenant, February 5, 1862; resigned, November 27, 1862.

Henry C. Burkhalter.—Private Company D, September 23, 1861; Sergeant; Second Lieutenant, May 22, 1865; mustered out with regiment, July 17, 1865.

William Winlack.—Captain Company E, October 1, 1861; mustered out, September 30, 1864, expiration of term.

Charles W. Schneer.—Commissary Sergeant of Regiment, September 21, 1861; Second Lieutenant Company E, March 16, 1864; Captain, October 30, 1864; mustered out with regiment, July 17, 1865.

William Cullen.—First Lieutenant Company E, October 1, 1861; killed at Antietam, September 17, 1862.

Joseph H. Fisher.—First Sergeant Company E, September 21, 1861; Second Lieutenant, September 17, 1862; discharged, February 23, 1864.

James May.—Corporal Company E, September 21, 1861; Sergeant; Second Lieutenant, October 30, 1864; mustered out with regiment, July 17, 1865.

Joseph H. Hoskings.—Captain Company F, October 1, 1861; mustered out, September 30, 1864, expiration of term.

John L. Williams.—Second Lieutenant Company F, October 1, 1861; First Lieutenant, July 13, 1864; Captain, October 30, 1864; mustered out with regiment, July 17, 1865.

Henry James.—First Lieutenant, October 1, 1861; discharged on surgeon's certificate, June 26, 1864.

James A. Easton.—Sergeant Company F, October 1, 1861; First Sergeant, Second Lieutenant, July 13, 1864; First Lieutenant, November 15, 1864; mustered out with regiment, July 17, 1865.

Henry Reese.—Sergeant Company F, October 1, 1861; Second Lieutenant, October 30, 1864; mustered out with regiment, July 17, 1865.

PHILIP NAGLE.—Captain Company G, October 1, 1861; resigned on account of disability, June 2, 1862. First Defender.

WILLIAM AUMAN.—Corporal Company G, October 1, 1862; Sergeant; Second Lieutenant, July 24, 1864; First Lieutenant, September 12, 1864; Brevet Captain, March 3, 1865; Captain, June 4, 1865; mustered out with regiment, July 17, 1865. First Defender.

CYRUS SCHEETZ.—First Lieutenant, Company G, October 1, 1861; resigned, May 3, 1862. Captain, Co. A, One Hundred-and-seventy-third Pennsylvania Volunteers, November 13, 1862 to August 17, 1863. First Defender.

CURTIS C. POLLOCK.—Corporal Company G, October 1, 1861; Second Lieutenant, May 5, 1862; First Lieutenant, June 2, 1862; died, June 23, 1864, of wounds received June 17, 1864. First Defender.

WILLIAM H. HARDELL.—Hospital Steward of Regiment, September 29, 1861; Second Lieutenant Company G, September 15, 1864; First Lieutenant, June 4, 1865; mustered out with regiment, July 17, 1865. First Defender.

HENRY C. JACKSON.—First Sergeant Company G, October 1, 1861; Second Lieutenant, June 2, 1862; killed at Spottsylvania, Va., May 12, 1864; buried in National Cemetery, Fredericksburg, Va.

GEORGE FARNE.—Corporal Company G, October 1, 1861; Sergeant Major of Regiment, December 22, 1864; Second Lieutenant Company G, June 11, 1865; mustered out with regiment, July 17, 1865.

WILLIAM J. HINKLE.—First Lieutenant Company H, September 19, 1864; Captain, August 28, 1863; commissioned Major, January 2, 1865; not mustered; mustered out, March 11, 1865, expiration of term.

ALBA C. THOMPSON.—Corporal Company H, September 19, 1861; Sergeant and First Sergeant; Second Lieutenant, September 12, 1864; First Lieutenant, October 30, 1864; Captain, March 3, 1865; mustered out with regiment, July 17, 1865. First Defender.

ALEXANDER S. BOWEN.—Sergeant Company H, September 19, 1861; Second Lieutenant, October 11, 1861; First Lieutenant, August 28, 1863; mustered out, September 30, 1864, expiration of term. First Defender.

THOMAS H. SILLYMAN.—Private Company H, September 19, 1861; Sergeant; Second Lieutenant, October 30, 1864; First Lieutenant, March 3, 1865; Brevet Captain, April 2, 1865; mustered out with regiment, July 17, 1865.

EDWARD C. BAIRD.—Second Lieutenant Company H, September 19, 1861; promoted Captain and Assistant Adjutant-General United States Volunteers, September 19, 1861.

CHARLES H. MILLER.—Sergeant Company C, September 11, 1862; Second Lieutenant Company H, January 16, 1862; resigned, May 7, 1862; re-enlisted in Sixteenth Pennsylvania Cavalry, September 9, 1862; Sergeant I Company; Sergeant-Major, November 20, 1862; Lieutenant and Adjutant, April 30, 1863; Captain and Assistant Adjutant-General Volunteers, May 1, 1864; mustered out, September 19, 1865; Brevet Major, March 31, 1865, "for long, faithful and meritorious conduct during the war."

SAMUEL B. LAUBENSTEIN.—Corporal Company H, September 19, 1861; Sergeant; Second Lieutenant, September 1, 1863; killed near Shady Grove, Va., May 31, 1864.

DAVID B. BROWN.—Corporal Company H, September 19, 1861; Sergeant; Sergeant-Major, September, 1862; Second Lieutenant Company H, June 21, 1864; killed front of Petersburg, Va., August 5, 1864. First Defender.

JOHN R. PORTER.—Captain Company I, August 23, 1861; resigned, December 30, 1862.

BENJAMIN B. SCHUCK.—First Sergeant Company I, August 23, 1861; Second Lieutenant, August 12, 1862; Captain, August 28, 1863; died, July 27, 1864, of wounds received in action, June 25, 1864.

FRANCIS D. KOCH.—Sergeant Company I, August 23, 1861; First Sergeant; Second Lieutenant, March 16, 1864; Captain, September 12, 1864; mustered out with regiment, July 17, 1865.

GEORGE H. GRESSANG.—First Lieutenant August 23, 1861; drowned by the sinking of the "West Point," month of Potomac River, August 12, 1862. First Defender.

MICHAEL M. KISTLER.—Second Lieutenant, Company I, August 23, 1861; First Lieutenant, October 20, 1862; transferred to Veteran Reserve Corps, October 21, 1863.

JOSEPH EDWARDS.—Corporal Company I, August 23, 1861; Second Lieutenant, September 1, 1863; First Lieutenant, March 16, 1864; died July 2, 1864, of wounds received in action, June 17, 1864.

OLIVER A. J. DAVIS.—Corporal Company I, August 23, 1861; Sergeant; First Sergeant; First Lieutenant, September 12, 1864; mustered out with regiment, July 17, 1865.

FRANCIS ALLEBACH.—Private Company I, August 23, 1861; Corporal; Sergeant; Second Lieutenant, October 30, 1864; Brevet First Lieutenant, April 2, 1865; mustered out with regiment, July 17, 1865.

HENRY A. M. FILBERT.—Captain Company K, October 1, 1861; killed at Second Bull Run, Va., August 29, 1862.

FRANCIS A. STITZER.—First Sergeant Company K, October 1, 1861; Second Lieutenant, August 29, 1862; Captain, November 28, 1864; Brevet Major, April 2, 1865; mustered out with regiment, July 17, 1865. First Defender.

JACOB DOUTY.—Second Lieutenant, Company K, October 1, 1861; First Lieutenant, August 29, 1862; mustered out, September 30, 1864, expiration of term.

THOMAS IRWIN.—Sergeant Company K, October 1, 1861; First Sergeant; Second Lieutenant, October 4, 1864; First Lieutenant, December 1, 1864; mustered out with regiment, July 17, 1865. First Defender.

JOHN C. HINCHCLIFF.—Sergeant Company K, October 1, 1861; Second Lieutenant, December 4, 1864; mustered out with regiment, July 17, 1865.

INDEX.

A, Company, 18, 38, 61, 97, 106.
Acquia Creek, 56, 102.
Alexandria, 70, 71, 147, 187.
"Alice Price," 44, 50.
Allard, Colonel Thomas B., 127, 190.
Allebach, Lieutenant Francis, 198.
Alsops, 149.
Altoona, 104.
Amissville, 91.
Anderson House, 151.
Annapolis, 145, 146.
Anthony, Major Joseph, 95.
Antietam, 78, 191.
Antietam Iron Works, 83.
Appomattox Court House, 187.
Army balloons, 83.
Army of the Potomac, 52, 55, 73, 102, 185, 187.
Atkinson, William P., 109.
Auman, Henry, 188.
Auman, Captain William, 197.

B, Company, 18, 22, 38, 42, 45, 59, 61, 75, 79, 106, 114, 157.
Baird, Captain Edward C., 18, 63, 197.
Band mustered out, 60.
Baltimore, 104.
Barbara Fritchie, 74.
Barboursville, 119.
Barlow's Division, 156.
Barnard, General, United States Army, 167, 176, 177.
Barnes, O. W., 164.
Bartholomew, Linn, 188.
Bast, Captain Ulysses A., 18, 99, 145, 195.
Bathing order, 48.
Bealton Station, 59, 92.
Beans' Station, 121.
Beatty, Surgeon Joseph, 117, 130.
Beaver Creek, 122.
Beckley, Chaplain Levi B., 194.
Benjamin, Lieutenant, United States Army, 135.
Bennett, Captain, 41.
Bertolette, Captain John D., 18, 43, 67, 87, 194.
Bertram, John P., 188.
Bethel Church, 151.
Bethesda Church, 153.

Big Rock, Castle River, 118.
Birney's Division, 155.
Blackwood, Surgeon W. R. D., 106, 144, 194.
Blain's Cross Roads, 137, 138.
Blake, Lieutenant Clarence H., 57, 67.
Bliss, Colonel Z. R., 146.
Bloomfield, 88.
Boedefeld, Frederick, 188.
Blue Springs, 125, 126.
Bohannon, Lieutenant Thomas, 18, 48, 99, 197.
Bohannon, Mrs. Thomas, 143.
Bolivar Heights, 86.
Bosbyshell, Major O. C., 18, 38, 99, 105, 107, 111, 117, 139, 141, 145, 178, 179, 180, 181, 182, 188, 193.
Boshen, 155.
Bowen, Captain Alexander S., 18, 45, 99, 197.
Bowen, Joseph W., 87.
Boyer, Captain Henry, 18, 99, 117, 137, 140, 195.
Boyer, William E., 188.
Boyle, Captain John T., 188.
Boynton Plank Road, 182, 183.
Brannon, Colonel Isaac F., 18, 99, 145, 182, 184, 186, 193.
Breckenridge, Rev. Robert J., D D., 108.
Brown, Lieutenant David B., 144, 178, 179, 198.
Brown, Patrick M., 141.
Brownlow, Parson, 123.
Bright, George, 188.
Bristoe's Station, 147.
Buford, General, 62.
Bull Run, Second, 65.
Bull's Gap, 124, 125.
Burial party, 100, 151.
Burkhalter, Lieutenant Henry C., 196.
Burnside, General A. E., 38, 39, 40, 41, 44, 47, 48, 72, 73, 77, 78, 83, 84, 85, 89, 90, 91, 92, 94, 99, 101, 102, 105, 107, 121, 122, 125, 126, 127, 129, 130, 132, 135, 136, 146, 147, 160, 162, 163, 165, 166, 172, 173, 175, 178, 190.
Bushong, Assistant Surgeon Israel, 194.
Butler, General B. F., 23.

(199)

C, Company, 18, 38, 45, 61, 106, 150.
Caddy's Junction, 104.
Campbell, James H., 143.
Campbell's Station, 131, 132.
Camp Curtin, 17-19.
Camp Dick Robinson, 118.
Camp Hamilton, 19.
Camp Lyon P. O., 141.
Camp Nagle, 45.
Camp Nelson, 117, 141.
Camp Winfield, 38.
Cape Hatteras, 34.
Carter, Colonel, 124.
Catletts' Station, 64.
Cedar Mountain, 60.
Centreville, 69.
Chadwick, Jim., 32, 33.
Chancellorsville, 149.
Chantilly, 69, 70.
Chickahominy, 156.
Christ, Surgeon Theodore S., 152.
Cincinnati, 104.
City Point, 160, 180, 187.
Clark, Lieutenant James, 184, 195.
Clark, Captain William, 105.
Clark, Lieutenant-Colonel W. S., 70, 98.
Clay, Brustus, Jr., 112.
Clayton, John M., 188.
Clinch Mountain, 121.
Clinch River, 120, 131, 137, 141.
Cochran, J. G., 188.
Coffin, Charles Carleton, 78, 80, 159.
Coho, M. V. B., 71.
Cold Harbor, 153, 156.
Colored troops, 146, 147, 156.
Colors, 18, 142.
Columbus, 104.
Colyer, Uncle Charlie, 119.
Committee, Conduct of War, 173.
Company officers, 18.
Completing circuit, 92.
Condon, Michael, 188.
Congratulatory order, 172.
Connor, James J., 188.
Contrabands, 46, 53.
Cooper, Captain James, 129.
Corduroy bed, 129.
"Cossack," 41, 49, 50, 52, 55.
Crab Orchard, 118.
Cram, Colonel T. J., United States Army, 20.
Crater, Size of, 170.
Cressona, 189.
Crosland, Lew, 59.
"C. S. A.," 77.
Cullen, Lieutenant William, 18, 81, 196.
Culpeper Court House, 50.
Culver, Assistant Surgeon John B, 144, 194.

Cumberland Ford, 120.
Cumberland Gap, 120, 130, 141.
Cumberland Mountain, 120.
Cumberland River, 119, 120.
Curtin, Governor Andrew G., 17, 19, 126, 178.
Curtin, General John I., 150, 151, 153, 154, 159, 160, 161, 185, 186.
Cutter, Surgeon, 136.

D, Company, 18, 38, 45, 56, 61, 106.
Davis, Lieutenant Oliver A. J., 198.
Declaration against Confederate Government, 27.
DeKay, Drake, 20.
Dengler, George M., 53.
Dentzer, John F., 183.
Derr, Joseph, 60, 188.
Devine of "F," 37.
Dicks' River, 118.
Diehl, Philip, 26.
Dix, General John A., 102, 103.
Donne, Daniel, 159.
Douty, Jacob, 18, 79, 81, 99, 105, 170, 180, 198.
Downer's Bridge, 151.
Drill, John, 188.
Duane, Major J. C., United States Army, 166, 173.
Dunn House, 159.
Durell's Battery, 75, 92, 93.
Duryée, General J. Eugene, 190.

E, Company, 18, 20, 38, 46, 49, 61, 79, 106, 153, 154.
Easton, Lieutenant James A., 196.
East Tennessee, 107, 117.
Edwards, Captain, Secret Service, 112, 114.
Edwards, Lieutenant Joseph, 73, 150, 198.
Eighth Corporal of "G," 30.
Eighteenth May, 1864, 150.
Eighteenth Michigan, 103.
Eighteenth South Carolina, 171, 175.
Election Day in Lexington, 112.
Eleventh Massachusetts Battery, 151.
Eleventh New Hampshire, 98, 117, 119.
Eleventh Pennsylvania Cavalry, 53.
Elliott Salient, 171.
Ellis, Quartermaster James, 18, 38, 50, 194.
Enfield Rifles, 45, 103.
Engine, 48; Destruction of, 128.
Epitaph, 26.
Evans, Clem, 80.
Evans, Nathan, 188.
Eveland, Lieutenant Lewis B., 99, 195.
Ewell, General, 154, 187.

F, Company, 18, 20, 38, 46, 61, 106, 155, 158, 186.
Fairfax Court House, 147.
Fairfax Station, 71.
Falmouth, 56, 93.
Farquhar, Captain Frank U., United States Army, 165.
Farmville, 187.
Farne, Lieutenant George, 197.
Featherstone, Mr., 113, 114.
Ferrero, General Edward, 90, 105, 127.
Field officers, 18.
Fell, Major, United States Army, 119.
Fifth Army Corps, 162, 179, 181, 182.
Fifth Pennsylvania Reserves, 63.
Fiftieth Pennsylvania, 53.
Fifty-first New York, 79, 80, 98.
Fifty-first Pennsylvania, 39, 46, 79, 80, 81, 82, 84, 93, 98.
Fifty-eighth Massachusetts, 146, 159.
Fifty-sixth Pennsylvania, 56, 57.
Filbert, Captain Henry A. M., 17, 18, 57, 198.
Final assault and muster out, 178.
First Defenders, 18, 46.
First Georgia, 128.
First Michigan Sharpshooters, 186.
First shell, 63.
First Tennessee, 107.
Fisher, Lieutenant Joseph H., 99, 105, 145, 196.
Fisher, Lieutenant Peter, 195.
Fitzsimmons, Lieutenant Thomas J., 18, 45, 195.
Flags captured, 158.
Focht, James, 188.
Fort Clarke, 22, 23, 28.
Fort Hatteras, 22, 23, 28.
Fort Hayes, 185.
Fort "Hell," 183, 185.
Fort Howard, 183, 185.
Fort Mahone, 184, 185.
Fort Sanders, 133, 135.
Fort Sedgwick, 183, 184, 185.
Fort Stedman, 184, 185.
Fort Totten, 45.
Forty-fifth Pennsylvania, 146, 159, 179.
Forty-fourth Tennessee, 158.
Fortress Monroe, 19, 21, 52, 55, 102, 103, 104.
Foster, Colonel, 125.
Foster, General John G., 40, 41, 42, 44, 46, 47.
Foster, Thomas, 188.
Fourteenth Brooklyn, 68.
Fourth Division, Ninth Army Corps Charge, 174, 180.
Fourth of July, 50, 111.
Fourth Rhode Island, 40, 41, 93, 146, 179.

Fourth United States Artillery, 83, 84.
Fox, Lieutenant Alexander H., 196.
Fox's Pass, 75, 77.
Fox, William, 188.
Frailly, Charles, 188.
Frederick City, 74.
Fredericksburg, 56, 57, 58, 61, 93, 94, 96, 97, 98, 99, 100.
French, General, 99.
Frick, Colonel Jacob G., 95.

G, Company, 18, 20, 26, 33, 38, 46, 49, 59, 61, 64, 79, 82, 88, 92, 106, 155, 157, 158, 159.
Galloway, 39.
Garretson, Theodore, 188.
"George Peabody," 38, 39, 42, 45.
"Georgia," 19.
Germania Ford, 148.
Gibson House, 105.
"Gilbert Green," 55.
Gilmore, General O. A., 106.
Gilmour, Major Joseph A., 17, 18, 43, 53, 61, 66, 88, 97, 99, 107, 111, 114, 140, 144, 152, 153, 193.
Glen Mills, 91.
General Order, No. 38, 108, 109.
Goodloe, W. C., 116.
Goss, Charles, 139.
Gowen, Colonel George W., 18, 46, 73, 99, 145, 165, 182, 184, 185, 186, 193.
Grand ball, 110.
Grand review, 187.
Granger, George, 136.
Grant, General U. S., 82, 126, 137, 187.
Graveyard, 25, 26.
Green, Adjutant David B., 3, 71.
Greenville, 125, 126, 130.
Greer, Sergeant, 175.
Gressang, Lieutenant George H., 18, 198.
Gressang, Henry, 188.
Griffin, General Simon G., 119, 121, 122, 127, 129, 160, 190.

H, Company, 18, 38, 61, 92, 106, 114, 179.
Haeseler, Dr. Charles H., 52.
Haines' House, 149.
Hampton Roads, 20, 21, 50, 52.
Hancock, General W. S., 99, 148, 152.
Hanging murderer, 112.
Hanovertown, 152.
Hardell, Lieutenant Wm. H., 18, 45, 145, 197.
Harper's Ferry, 83, 86.
Harris, J. Franklin, 188.
Harrisburg, 17, 105, 142, 145, 187, 188.

Harris' Shop, 152.
Hartranft, General John F., 46, 79, 81, 127, 129, 132, 133, 146, 184, 185.
Hartsuff, General, 110, 112, 114.
Hartz, Captain Wils T., United States Army, 64.
Hawkin's Zouaves, 80.
Hatteras, 22.
Hatteras Inlet, 21, 50.
Haymarket, 64.
Haywood, Benjamin, 188, 189.
Hazzard, Charles H., 130.
Helms, Captain James K., 196.
Heilner, Marcus, 188.
Hendley, Adam, 74.
"Henry W. Johnson," 39.
Herrington, Assistant Surgeon C. P., 194.
Hetherington, Jim, 57.
Hester, Aunt, 24.
"Highland Light," 49, 50.
Hill, Lieutenant Williard, 175, 176.
Hinchcliff, Lieutenant John C., 198.
Hinkle, Major William J., 18, 47, 67, 145, 197.
Hitchcock, Lieutenant Henry S., 117, 125, 140.
Hitchcock, Chaplain R. S., 190.
Hobart, John P., 188.
Hobson, General, 110, 111.
Hodgson, Frank, 59.
Holman, Chaplain Samuel A., 18, 20, 85, 91, 194.
Holston River, 121, 122, 123, 127, 120, 131, 136, 137.
Home, 142, 188.
Honsberger, Adjutant Henry C., 194.
Hoopskirts, 27.
Hoskings, Captain Joseph H., 17, 18, 99, 145, 161, 196.
"Hotel d'Afrique," 39.
Howard, General O. O., 99, 136.
Howell, Johnny, 72.
Huckey, Captain A. C., 186, 195.
Hulburd, Captain Edward, 105, 106, 107.
Hume, Lieutenant William H., 99, 153, 195.
Humphrey, General, 99.
Huston, Assistant Surgeon John M., 106, 194.

I, Company, 18, 38, 61, 106.
Inness, James, 188.
Inspection, 180.
Irwin, Lieutenant Thomas, 198.

Jackson, Lieutenant Abiel H., 18, 195.
Jackson, Lieutenant Henry C., 31, 32, 35, 97, 99, 100, 106, 150, 197.

Jackson, General T. J., 61, 64.
James, Lieutenant Henry, 18, 99, 196.
James River, 156, 187.
Jerusalem Plank Road, 183, 185.
"John A. Warner," 103, 104.
Johnson, John, 63.
Johnson's President, Home, 125.
Johnson, Lieutenant Thomas, 195.
Johnson, Stafford, 20.
Jones, Lieutenant-Colonel Richard M., 34, 184, 193.

K, Company, 18, 20, 33, 38, 46, 49, 61, 79, 106.
Kaercher, Francis B., 60, 188.
Kauffman, Captain Daniel B., 17, 18, 30, 45, 47, 145, 197.
Kearney, General Phil, 64, 66, 70.
Kelly's Ford, 61, 62, 63.
Kentucky Loyalist, 109.
Kentucky River, 118.
Keys, Quartermaster Sam, 102, 129.
Kistler, Lieutenant Michael M., 18, 198.
Kleckner, Colonel Charles, 18, 48, 53, 196.
Knoxville, 122, 123, 126, 127, 131, 132, 133, 134.

Lacy House, 93, 94, 95.
Lancaster, Ky., 118.
Laubenstein, Lieutenant Samuel B., 153, 197.
Ledlie, General, 171.
Lee, General Fitz Hugh, 187.
Lee, General Robert E., 82, 83, 178.
Lenoir, 128, 129, 130, 131.
Levison, Corporal William, 184.
Lexington, 104, 140.
Lick Creek, 124.
Lightning's work, 62.
Lighthouse, Hatteras, 34.
Lincoln, President, 60, 84, 133, 137, 147, 187.
Lippman, Isaac, 20, 31, 37, 93, 102, 121, 130, 131, 136.
Little Rockcastle River, 119.
Living on country, 59, 60.
Loeser, Adjutant Charles, Jr., 18, 53, 99, 194.
Log huts, 93, 94.
Log Mountains, 120.
London, 119, 120.
Longstreet, General James, 61, 127, 131, 132, 135, 136, 154.
Loudon, 127, 128, 131.
Loudon Heights, 86.
Lovettsville, 87.
Loyalty, 107, 109.

Macalester, Mrs. Eliza, 110, 111.
Maloney, Assistant Surgeon Alvah H., 194.
Manasses Junction, 64.
Mansfield, General, 19, 20.
Martz, George, 188.
Maryland Heights, 86.
Matthews, Captain B. Frank, 190.
Matthews, Adjutant Thomas L., 190.
May, Lieutenant James, 196.
McCabe, Captain W. Gordon, 171.
McClellan, General George B., 50, 55, 70, 71, 82, 84, 85, 89, 90.
McDowell, General Irwin, 60, 61, 68.
McGinnes, Adjutant Daniel D., 87, 95, 99, 125, 130, 144, 194.
McIlvaine, Lieutenant, 92.
McKibben, General, 128, 149, 150, 164.
McMillans', 122.
Meade, General George G., 63, 165, 172, 173, 185.
Meagher, General Thomas F., 96.
Mellen, William, Jr., 188.
Methodist Meeting House, 25.
Middletown, 74, 75.
Miesse, Miss, 143.
Mifflin, 104.
Mighels, Captain, 161.
Miller, Major Charles H., 197.
Mine, 163.
Mine, charge in, 169.
Mine, firing, 170.
Mine, Grant's opinion, 174, 175.
Mine, not a failure, 171.
Mine, Pleasant's opinion, 172.
Minersville, 189.
Minis, Surgeon David, Jr., 18, 194.
Molasses boiling party, 32.
Monaghan, Patrick, 158.
Morgan, John, 111.
Morris, Richard R., 188.
Morrison, Assistant Surgeon James M., 106, 112, 194.
Morristown, 121, 123, 124, 126.
Mossy Creek, 121, 124.
Mt. Carmel Church, 152.
Mt. Vernon, 118.
Mud March, 101, 102.
Muscle vs. Steam, 49.

Nagle, Abraham, 18.
Nagle, Colonel Daniel, 17, 18, 38, 193.
Nagle, General James, 17, 18, 19, 20, 38, 43, 45, 46, 48, 50, 53, 67, 73, 83, 88, 91, 93, 97, 101, 104, 105, 110, 142, 144, 188, 189, 193.
Nagle, Captain Philip, 17, 18, 29, 197.
Neis, James C., 97.
Newark, 104.
Newbern, 37, 38, 39, 43, 50, 190.

Newport News, 52, 102, 190.
Neuse River, 39, 42.
Nicholasville, 117.
Night march, 61.
Niles, Lieutenant, 57.
Ninety-fifth New York, 56.
Ninety-sixth Pennsylvania, 52, 69, 83, 101, 188.
Ninth Army Corps, 99, 101, 102, 104, 107, 133, 139, 146, 147, 149, 151, 156, 160, 161, 162, 164, 181, 182, 183, 185, 190.
Ninth New Hampshire, 81, 98.
Ninth New Jersey, 44, 46.
Ninth New York, 80.
Non-Commissioned Staff, 18.
"North America," 102.
North Anna River, 151, 152.
Ny River, 149.

Officers' mess, 73.
Olewine, Jacob, 188.
One Hundred and Third New York, 46, 47.
One Hundredth Pennsylvania, 53, 70.
One Hundred and Twenty-ninth Pennsylvania, 71, 83, 95, 101.
Orange and Alexandria Railroad, 92.
Organization, 17.
Owens, Lieutenant Henry P., 196.
Oxford, 151.

Pamlico Sound, 39, 50.
Pamunkey River, 152.
Panther Springs, 121.
Pardee, Major, 59.
Parke, General John G., 40, 41, 46, 104, 117, 122, 185.
Parker's Store, 148.
Patterson, Burd, 188.
Patterson, William S., 71.
Peebles Farm, 182.
Pegram House, 181.
Pegram's Petersburg Battery, 171.
Pennington, Major Henry, 117, 122, 130, 190.
Petersburg, 156, 157, 181, 186, 187.
Philadelphia, 145.
Phillips' House, 94, 99.
Phœnix Hotel, 105.
Piedmont, 89.
Pierson, Lieutenant-Colonel, 152.
Pitman, C. W., 188, 189.
Pitman's, 117, 119.
Pittsburg, 104, 105.
Pleasants, General Henry, 17, 18, 45, 87, 95, 96, 98, 99, 100, 106, 111, 114, 141, 144, 147, 150, 152, 155, 157, 158, 159, 161, 162, 164, 165, 166,

167, 168, 169, 170, 171, 172, 173, 174, 176, 177, 179, 181, 183, 184, 189, 193.
Pleasant Valley, 85, 86, 87.
Pollock, Lieutenant C. C., 70, 99, 130, 159, 197.
Pontoon bridge, 94, 95.
Pope's Army, 58, 61.
Pope, General John G., 60, 61, 62, 64, 65, 68, 70, 71.
Poplar Spring Church, 181.
Po River, 151.
Port Clinton, 189.
Porter, General Fitz John, 71.
Porter, Captain John R., 17, 18, 99, 198.
Pott, " Doc.," 59.
Potter, General Robert B., 127, 129, 130, 141, 146, 148, 149, 151, 152, 153, 154, 156, 159, 160, 161, 162, 164, 165, 172.
Pott, Frank, 60.
Potts, Captain William W., 18, 43, 45, 195.
Pottsville, 142, 188.
Price, Lieutenant Henry H., 195.
Prince, Sergeant, 82.
Pringle, Old, 53.
Prisoners, 112.
Prisoners returned, 85.
Purcellville, 88.

Rank determined, 55.
Rapidan, 60.
Rapidan River, 148.
Rappahannock River, 56, 58, 62.
Rappahannock Station, 62.
Rebel sword, 80.
Reber, Surgeon Charles T., 18, 45, 194.
Reed, Jere, 188.
Reedy, Private Daniel F., 154.
Reese, Lieutenant Henry, 170, 196.
Reeser, Lewis, 188.
Reilly, Bernard, 188.
Reid, Robert A., 158, 159.
Reno, Captain, 90.
Reno, General Jesse L., 40, 41, 44, 45, 46, 47, 50, 55, 60, 62, 65, 72, 73, 75.
Review on Hatteras, 30, 190.
Rheatown, 125.
Roanoke Island, 37, 39.
Rothenberger, Lieutenant Henry, 196.
Rosecrans, General, 126.
Rossiter, Pres., 57.
Roster of officers, 193.
Rowan, Commodore, 44.
Rutledge, 137.

Schackelford, General, 125.
Scheetz, Captain Cyrus, 18, 29, 34, 197.

Schnerr, Captain Charles W., 125, 144, 196.
Schuck, Captain B. B., 99, 130, 145, 162, 198.
Schuylkill Haven, 189.
Second Corps, 96, 151, 152, 153, 155, 156, 162.
Second Maryland, 46, 47, 65, 67, 77, 79, 80, 102, 117, 124, 125, 126, 129, 130, 131, 179, 190, 191.
Second New York Mounted Rifles, 159, 179.
Secret Mails, 108.
Secret Service, 112.
Seventeenth June, 1864, 157, 158, 159, 161.
Seventeenth Mississippi, 135.
Seventeenth Vermont, 149, 150.
Seventh Michigan, 95.
Seventh New York Heavy Artillery, 158.
Seventh Rhode Island, 98, 114, 146, 149, 183.
Seventy-second New York Highlanders, 53.
Seward, Sergeant, 81.
Shady Grove Church, 153, 154.
Shand House, 159, 160.
Sheafer, Mattis, 56.
Sherman, General, 136.
Shertle, Adam, 188.
Shippen, John, 188.
Sickels, General Daniel E., 64.
Sigfried, General Joshua K., 18, 43, 45, 48, 61, 66, 67, 73, 81, 87, 88, 94, 101, 104, 105, 106, 107, 114, 115, 116, 117, 118, 122, 124, 126, 129, 131, 132, 134, 138, 140, 141, 143, 144, 147, 163, 174, 178, 182, 188, 189, 193.
Silliman, E. H., 85, 107.
Silliman, Captain James, 59.
Silliman, James, 188.
Sillyman, Thomas H., 197.
Sillyman, Mrs. Samuel, 142.
Sixteenth Georgia, 135.
Sixth Corps, 149, 151.
Sixth New Hampshire, 59, 65, 66, 67, 79, 80, 98, 102, 104, 117, 154, 190, 191
Sixty-fifth Illinois, 109.
Smith, Lieutenant-Colonel David A., 18, 193.
Smith, Robert, 77, 88.
Smith's Mills, 151.
Smyser, Assistant Surgeon Eugene, 194.
Snow, 89, 93.
South Mountain, 75, 77, 85.
Southern hatred, 100.
South Side Railroad, 182.
Special muster, 60.
Spotswood Tavern, 148, 149.

Spottsylvania Court House, 149, 151.
Springfield Rifles, 103.
Squirrel Level Road, 182, 183.
"S. R. Spaulding," 21.
Staff officers, 18.
Stannard's Mills, 151.
Stevensburg, 61.
Stevens, General Isaac I., 62, 70.
Stichter, Lieutenant Henry E., 196.
Stitzer, Captain Frank A., 99, 198.
Stone, Lieutenant, 112, 114.
Stowe, Caleb, 31.
Strawberry Plains, 122, 124.
Stringham, Admiral S. H., 23.
Strothers, General, 65, 68.
Stuart's Cavalry, 91.
Sturgis, General Samuel G., 73, 76, 91, 104.
Summit, 89.
Sumner, General E. V., 95, 99, 101.
"Swash," 22, 38, 39, 50.

Taylor, Benjamin F., 140, 188.
Taylor, Captain B. Frank, 190.
Taylor, Rev. Marble Nash, 27.
Taylor, Lieutenant William, 195.
Tazewell, 120, 121.
Testimonial, Lexington, 115.
Thanksgiving Day, 133.
Thirteenth Georgia, 150.
Thirteenth Mississippi, 135.
Thirty-fifth Massachusetts, 98.
Thirty-ninth New Jersey, 186.
Thirty-sixth Massachusetts, 146, 159, 175.
Thomas, General, 126, 138.
Thompson, Captain Alba C., 197.
Thompson, Lewis C., 188.
Tolopotomy, 152.
Tolston, Benjamin, 36.
Tower, Captain Charlemagne, 188.
Trainer, Sergeant, 81.
Trent, 32.
Trent River, 41, 43, 45.
Tuckers, 155, 156.
Tunstall's Station, 156.
Twelfth Rhode Island, 98.
Twentieth Indiana, 19, 21, 22.
Twenty-fifth Massachusetts, 47.
Twenty-eighth Pennsylvania, 59.
Twenty-first Massachusetts, 40, 98, 117, 124, 131, 133, 136, 138, 139.
Twenty-fourth May, 1864, 151.
Twenty-fourth Massachusetts, 39.
Twenty-third Army Corps, 110, 111.

Union Hotel, 188, 189.
Union woman's tongue, 134.
Unwritten history, 49.
Upperville, 89.

Vallandigham, C. L., 108.
Varney, Lieutenant John H., 117, 140.
Ventilation Mine, 167.
Veteran furlough, 141.
Viars, 152.

Wagner, Major Jacob, 18, 43, 45, 82, 117, 121, 122, 130, 131, 144, 194.
Wallace, F. B., 188.
Wallace, Colonel W. H., 175.
Warrenton, 63, 64.
Warrenton Junction, 63, 64, 92.
Warrenton White Sulphur Springs, 63, 92.
Warwick Court House, 54.
Washburn, Lieutenant Jay, 64.
Washington City, 71, 72, 146.
Waterloo, 90.
Watkins, Lieutenant John, 195.
Weber, General Max, 20.
Weiser, Lieutenant Henry, 195.
Weldon Railroad, 179, 180, 182.
Wells, William J., 186.
Werner, Captain J. Frank, 18, 145, 189, 196.
Werner, John T., 18, 188.
Whitby, Jackson, 24.
Whitby, Widow, 24.
White, General, 127.
Whitney, William L., 188.
Wilcox, General O. B., 91, 98, 101, 106, 109, 110, 124, 126, 130, 154, 162.
Wild Cat Mountain, 119.
Wilderness, 148, 149.
Williams, Captain John L., 18, 99, 186, 196.
Williams, General Thomas, United States Army, 28, 30, 31, 37, 190.
Williams, Lieutenant Thomas P., 195.
Wilson, Captain Malcolm, 190.
Wind, 28.
Winlack, Captain William, 17, 18, 38, 81, 99, 145, 168, 196.
Womelsdorff, L. F., 188.
Wood, Lieutenant John L., 18, 48, 99, 195.
Woody's, 155.
Wool, General, United States Army, 20, 23.
Woolford's Cavalry, 111.
Wren, Andrew, 157.
Wren, Major James, 17, 18, 79, 87, 99, 110, 144, 193.
Wren, Thomas, 188.
Wren, Captain William, 71.

Yellow Creek, 104.
Yellow Tavern, 180.
York, 104.

www.ingramcontent.com/pod-product-compliance
Lightning Source LLC
Chambersburg PA
CBHW020858230426
43666CB00008B/1225